Safari

Safari

⬦⬦⬦

A MEMOIR OF
A WORLDWIDE
TRAVEL PIONEER

GEOFFREY KENT

WITH KRISTINE GASBARRE

HARPER

NEW YORK · LONDON · TORONTO · SYDNEY

HARPER

FIRST HARPER PAPERBACK PUBLISHED 2016.

Designed by Leah Carlson-Stanisic

Library of Congress Cataloging-in-Publication Data has been applied for.

ISBN 978-0-06-229921-5

16 17 18 19 20   OV/RRD   10 9 8 7 6 5 4 3 2 1

This book is dedicated to my parents, Colonel John and Valerie Kent, who shared my vision for how photographic safaris could help protect African wildlife and gave me an amazing childhood in the wilderness of Africa. To my sister, Anne, who has been with me throughout this great journey and has always been at my side and supported me in all my endeavors. And to my son, Joss, who loves the thrill of a great expedition as much as I do.

And to my extended family at Abercrombie & Kent, men and women who are passionate about their countries and share my commitment to travel that both enhances and changes lives. To Jorie Butler Kent, who worked with me to expand A&K beyond Africa.

And above all to my wife, Otavia, who has shared many great adventures with me around the world and who urged me to share these stories about my life and some of the remarkable people I've been privileged to meet along the way.

Abercrombie & Kent's famous "Iron Snake" safari in Kenya. This steam loco-motive hauled us from Nairobi to Mombasa in the mid-1970s.

Contents

✧✧✧✧✧

FOREWORD

✦✦✦✦✦

BY JEFFREY KATZENBERG,
CEO OF DREAMWORKS ANIMATION

I am one of the lucky few who has had the privilege of personally journeying with Geoffrey Kent. Now, thanks to this book, any reader can experience what it's like to tag along with him to some of the world's most exotic destinations. The spirit of discovery is deeply embedded in Geoffrey's DNA, and it rubs off on his clients. In my case, traveling with him to Africa, Egypt, and China directly inspired such films as *The Lion King, Madagascar, The Prince of Egypt*, and *Kung Fu Panda*. In this book's pages, there's an amazing "you are there" feel to Geoffrey's travel tales. And, in one chapter, I actually *was* there, as he describes the extraordinary South American trip my wife and I participated in that included snorkeling in the Galápagos, boating down the Amazon, crossing Indiana Jones–like suspension bridges in the rainforest, exploring the heights of Machu Picchu, and hiking past the peaks of Patagonia … all in eight incredible days. There's simply no adventure Geoffrey has met that he hasn't fallen in love with. This is a must-read for anyone who is captivated by the magic, mystery, and majesty of travel, which Geoffrey understands better than anyone else on the planet.

Lone bull elephant in the wildflowers on the floor of the Ngorongoro Crater.

FOLLOWING PAGE: *It's time for a four-wheel-drive safari.*

PREFACE

SAN FRANCISCO, 1976

"Meet me at Trader Vic's."
Richard Burton's voice on the other end of my hotel phone is like tires on gravel—strained, as usual, from smoking, and tonight, it seems, from stress. He's in conflict, as he is any time he asks me to meet him for mai tais at San Francisco's most famous tiki restaurant.

On the line, I try to work out what could be the matter; he's just gotten engaged to Suzy Hunt, the English model, following his second divorce from Elizabeth Taylor earlier this year. "I'll be there," I tell him. "See you at eight o'clock."

When I arrive, there's a fresh cigarette wagging between his lips. "Lucky you were in town," he says, hardly raising his gaze.

This is a modern tent, just like the one that Richard Burton would have stayed in on safari.

"Only just." I take my place across from him in the leather cushioned booth lit by an overhead wicker lamp. "I leave for safari tomorrow."

"I ought to come with you, Geoff." He lights his smoke, tosses the book of matches onto the table, and wrings his forehead. "I need to get away."

"It's Suzy?"

"No, it's not Suzy. Suzy is wonderful; in fact, Suzy is the one thing keeping me sane right now." He looks up at me with tired eyes. "But work's been mad, and frankly, this divorce from Elizabeth has been a nightmare."

"I've heard that, actually."

"I don't know how much longer I can dodge the reporters, Geoff. Meanwhile, her lawyer won't stop calling me, not to mention the children and still trying to sort out our properties." Finally, his eyes meet mine. "You know why I called you, don't you?"

"You need a safari."

He exhales, a long stream of smoke diffusing into the lamplight above us. "I need a safari."

On my way over, I'd done all the calculations about the one location that I'd been saving for Richard Burton, just in case he wanted to escape. If we leave first thing tomorrow, we'll be in the bush in no more than forty-eight hours.

The Masai Mara in Kenya is a world away—and that's precisely why I've brought him here. The ride from the Nairobi airport to my camp is smooth until the very end, when the road becomes so rough it makes our jaws rattle. Inside the Land Rover, Richard turns to me and grins. I hit the gas a little harder.

Africa never fails.

With its broad acacia trees and giraffes moseying among the grasslands, the Mara River is the ultimate escape: so

Cheetahs prefer a high spot for a view of the surrounding plains.

wildly beautiful and beautifully wild, so incredibly much to take in that he has no choice but to lose himself in his surroundings and forget his troubles. They say only time heals a broken heart, but any man with a purpose knows that the far faster cure is adventure—and there's no greater adventure than a safari.

Though on this, our first night out, as dusk sets in over our tents on the edge of the river, Richard Burton revisits his pain. "Elizabeth," he says with a sigh. "This sunset reminds me of the day we got married."

"Which time?"

"The second time," he says, flicking flame under a Marlboro Light and taking a long drag. "In Botswana. Oh, rubbish," he says, searching the sky for some solace. "Forget her. Thank heaven for Suzy, Geoff . . . that's all I can say."

In front of our dinner table roars a great fire, built by my best guide. He carries out two cold martinis and sets them on the table in front of Richard and me before discreetly turning back inside. "How that woman loved to fight," Richard says, in a way that makes it seem as though it's just dawned on him.

"Elizabeth?"

"Oh! You can't imagine. Knock-down, drag-outs, and insults one could never dream of forgetting. And she thinks that's love! Geoff, anyone who knows me knows that I'm all for passion . . . but a film set is the only place for her brand of drama—"

Just then my attention shifts to a sudden commotion. A buffalo is charging into camp with three lionesses at its heels, and for a moment it looks as though they will end up in our laps. Richard freezes in terror and dives to the ground. "Geoff!" he hollers. "God, Geoff! I can't look!"

I upend the dinner table, our martini glasses splashing and shattering to the ground in the chaos. The lionesses team up to wrestle the wailing buffalo to the ground, finally ripping him apart at the foot of our fire.

Richard stays ducked behind the table until the hisses and snarling have quieted. Slowly, he rises and joins me to look out over our makeshift shield at the pride of lionesses slinking away in satisfaction and the buffalo carcass crackling over the fire. He turns to me. "Geoff . . ."

"What is it?" I keep my eyes fixed ahead.

"If I bring Suzy here, will you do that again?"

"Do what again?"

"Would you set up that scene again?" He turns again to marvel at the lions making their way far off into the bush. "Suzy would just love it."

◇◇◇◇

Without a doubt, Richard Burton was on to something: a safari wins anyone's heart. Since those days, the only things that have changed about the thrill of East Africa are how greatly its appeal has grown and how we at Abercrombie & Kent have worked to refine this most rugged experience.

My typical morning on a modern safari usually starts when the rest of the world is still sleeping. In the hush of dark, the tent attendant hums one of his native Kenyan songs as he walks along the path to my tent—this, and the quiet step of his shoes through the canvas tent, his manner of announcing his polite arrival. "Bwana Commander?" His voice is gentle and low and I know I am home: "Bwana Commander" is my Kenyan nickname. "It's five thirty. Your breakfast is ready. Here is your early morning coffee and orange juice."

There is a delicate clinking—teaspoon inside sugar bowl—as I call out my thanks. I push aside the thickness of my comforter and set my feet on the woven bedside rug. Of all the things we've done over the years to evolve and refine the safari experience, these sensations remain the same. Nothing can keep me from the carafe of hot coffee and a few meditative moments on the deck as the land prepares for sunrise.

When I step outside, there's the yawn of the hippos just below, already resting in the cool Mara River to protect their skin from the first morning light. The stars sparkle over the river, which moves placidly around the rocks, and on the opposite riverbank are found only the shadows of the savanna—the tops of the trees, the bushes in cozy clusters. Here, each element of nature rests together. The person observing it is also a part of it all.

The sun will peek its face within the next half hour—a gracious golden glow across the savanna, so beautiful that even after witnessing it for the past seven decades, I still feel my heart go tender at the sight. After more than fifty years in this industry,

My parents, John and Valerie Kent, canoeing down the Tana River.

I read clients' faces easily on a morning like this as I make my way to the dining room for a breakfast meeting. This is the moment of thrilled uncertainty. Anticipation. As their guide ushers them inside their Land Rover, they're aware that life doesn't get more daring than this. *Are we pushing our luck?* they wonder. They are pushing it—right over the boundaries of the wild. The Swahili word *safari* combines the ideas of "a long journey" and "adventure." By nature, the only thing that's predictable about a game drive is that it will be unforgettable. One day on safari *is* the great adventure that will change the rest of an individual's life.

Throughout my career, whenever I've asked my clients why they travel, nearly all of them have given me some version of this response: they travel to learn about the world beyond their own experience. Travel teaches us as much about ourselves as it does about the world—it shifts our focus away from the meager challenges of every day and recalibrates our life's vision to something broader and much more significant. One of my

An early safari on the shores of Lake Baringo.

prevailing philosophies is that if any individual were to find out that he or she had only six days to live, all people's final thoughts would revolve around life's most important things: the people they've loved and the places they've explored. Nothing shapes an individual as much as these two influences.

My parents and I started Abercrombie & Kent out of necessity when the land in Kenya that we'd spent our lives developing was taken away from us. Many entrepreneurs agree that it's our worst vulnerabilities that inspire us to find our greater purpose. When the most precious part of yourself is taken away, you will do whatever it takes to get your power back.

You'll even travel to the ends of the earth.

This book is more than a collection of the best moments that I've experienced along the path; this book is my love story. By bringing the same sense of adventure found on safari to other places around the world, I defined luxury experiential travel . . . but my own greatest adventure has been this business itself.

Safari

Life in the Aberdares, South Kinangop

✧✧✧✧✧

KENYA, 1936–1948

O n her first and only visit to a fortune-teller, my mother was told she would marry a tall, dark, handsome man and travel extensively in faraway places. Turning to her friends, she giggled and dismissed it: anyone who knew Valerie Worke knew she was as committed to the idea of finding a husband with an aristocratic upbringing as she was to her studies at Benenden School, the upper-crust all-girls boarding school outside London.

However, it was just a short while later at a debutante dance in central London in 1936 when, surrounded on the ballroom floor by dozens of elegant young women and their suitors, she laid eyes on him: he was bronzed and brooding, achingly handsome in his regimental dress, laid-back and laughing inside an alluring huddle of friends. As if suddenly under a spell, my mother excused herself from the music and glided to an area of the room where she could delicately position herself for this young soldier to see her. When he crossed her

---

Taking a bath on my way to Ethiopia—my first safari.

path, he too was taken immediately—and by the time the band was breaking down, the young Valerie had fallen in love and decided that perhaps there'd been some truth to that absurd fortune. Indeed, she resolved that this man would be her husband.

John Kent's affinity for adventure is what made him equal parts intriguing and impossible to pin down, and the fact that the world was about to go to war didn't do much to support her mission. After she had dashed all her desires for an elitist engagement and renounced the postgraduate debutante scene, there was no choice but to go all-in; in order to marry a soldier of the King's African Rifles who spoke fluent Swahili and had been trained as an administrator for the British Empire, a woman had to commit herself completely. Over the next three years, my mother trained in London for the wartime nursing reserve and asked for an assignment in Kenya, where her beloved John was stationed. When the nursing reserve refused her request, she promptly signed up to join the First Aid Nursing Yeomanry. "Are you out of your mind?" her mother asked her, in a moment that became famous within our family. "The nurses in the FANY are sent to the front lines of the war!"

"I can manage," my mother retorted.

"You can manage? Your father owns one of the world's most important exporting businesses between England and India; he raised you with a driver and a Jaguar . . . and now you're going to learn to drive wounded soldiers inside an *ambulance*?"

At that point, my grandfather boomed in. "You're a girl from Mayfair, for God's sake—one of the best neighborhoods in London. You could be killed out there, all for this ridiculous romantic fantasy of yours!"

In response, the next day Mummie boarded a military convoy in Scotland that was scheduled to zigzag across the Atlantic and leave her in Kenya. When they docked in Mombasa, she encountered my father—sunburned and solemn—for the first time since he'd left England.

"It's been three years, darling," he told her. "Do you think you still love me?"

Mummie's eyes welled up and she wrapped her arms around his neck, overwhelmed with joy. "Of course I do!"

"Well, I'm not sure you'll like me very much when I tell you this."

Mummie stepped back calmly, composed herself, and braced for the worst. "By God, John, if you've brought me all this way to tell me there's been someone else—"

"There's no one else, darling," he said. "But in our letters, we made a pact to wait at least a month before the wedding."

"Go on . . ."

"But I learned this morning that in six days they'll send me off to Abyssinia. I put in for three days' leave immediately—we're getting married this Saturday."

"But John—"

"Darling, I've made all the arrangements—"

"Then who will present me?"

"Sir Charles Markham has agreed." Nothing like being given away by the second baronet of one of the most lauded noble families in Britain. "Have you got a dress?"

Mummie looked at her leather suitcase and back up at him. "Of course I have."

"Good. Then this is the way forward."

On December 12, 1940, Mummie walked down the aisle of Nairobi's Anglican Cathedral of the Highlands surrounded by Dad's fellow officers and a host of other unknown faces. "You'll be fast friends with all of them," Dad promised in a whisper, and after the exchange of vows, Dad's brother officers made a row of swords arched above their heads while the other guests roared in applause. Then they all headed to a reception at the legendary Muthaiga Country Club, where Mummie and Dad posed for their wedding portrait under a lush stand of bamboo bestowing a sweet blessing.

Two days later when Dad caught up with his battalion in Abyssinia—known today as Ethiopia—Mummie was sent to stay with the other wartime nurses in Kenya in the last place a young wife in a strange land would dream of spending her first days as a newlywed: a convent.

Quickly she won over her colleagues and proved her proficiency at nursing. When Dad returned from Abyssinia on leave, he found a house to rent for two dollars a month, located on an abandoned sisal plantation about thirty minutes southeast of Nairobi. After her first look at the place, Mummie stepped outside cheerfully. "It'll do," she said. "But where's the loo?"

"There," Dad said, pointing to a dusty hole outside the front door.

Mummie nodded.

"I know it's not what you're used to, darling," Dad said, "but soon we'll have our own land."

By the end of that year Mummie found herself expecting, and on July 14, 1942, while on safari in Northern Rhodesia (later to become the independent country of Zambia), she delivered me. My birthday on the anniversary of the fall of the Bastille and during prime safari season, when the rain is non-existent and the animals parade out in search of water, suggested to my parents that, like my father, I too might possess a natural brave streak. It took no time for them to witness the degree to which this was true: I wasn't just fearless, I was born a survivor.

Within a few days of my birth, I fell desperately ill. Immediately Mummie observed that I'd become dehydrated if I continued to refuse to nurse, and when I started to have forceful vomiting attacks, she knew the diagnosis: pyloric stenosis, then a life-threatening stomach illness that sometimes afflicted newborns. "He'll die if we don't find a doctor right now," Mummie told Dad. "We've got to get him out of here."

My mother chartered a plane and flew with me to the children's hospital in Nairobi which later came to be known as Gertrude's Garden Children's Hospital—named after Colonel Grogan's wife. There, one of the best doctors in Kenya, Dr. William Boyle, performed a miracle surgery. My mother watched me through a window, knowing that her freewheeling days as a soldier's wife were over. From now on, she would need to keep her little boy very close to her.

Life back on the plantation in Kenya proved this to be truer by the day. Hyenas barked just outside our windows through the night; snakes crossed the front garden so frequently that one had to look before stepping out onto the stoop. Once a rhinoceros nearly destroyed us when it barreled into our house with such force that the impact shook us awake. One day while my mother was pushing me in my pram, a leopard crossed her path, but she remembered what Dad had advised her: stay calm, stay still, and hope that it will be more surprised to see you than you are by it. Fortunately, that's precisely what happened, and when the leopard ducked into the bush, Mummie turned the wheels of my pram to push me at a flat run directly back home.

One night when I was in bed and my father was out on duty, Mummie was sitting up with a nurse friend when they heard crying from my room. With the intent to nurture my independence, Mummie and her friend let me wail on until the cries turned to screeches more violent than she'd ever heard from me. "What on earth could be wrong?" she asked, and when her friend followed her into my bedroom, they found a legion of insects invading my crib.

"Valerie! *Safari ants*!" her friend exclaimed, and, growing ever more resourceful, my mother ran off to grab a can of kerosene. When she returned, she drowned the ants as best she could and spent the rest of the evening picking them from my body. Some clung to me with bits of my flesh in their jaws, so reluctant to let go of me that they preferred to lose the lower halves of their bodies rather than to loosen their grips. When we arrived at the hospital, the doctor told Mummie that another baby in the area had been left alone in the house for a couple of hours and had been attacked by a column of the same type of ant. When the child's parents returned, they had been terrorized to discover their child's skeleton picked almost completely bare.

Mummie lay awake when Dad returned from duty that night. As he climbed under the covers, she turned to him. "It's clear we won't be returning to England anytime soon, John," she said. "But for goodness' sake, isn't it getting time we find someplace where we can build our own home?"

After my father's several years as an officer in the King's African Rifles, no one knew every corner of the continent better than he did. "There's some land northwest of here that I've had my eye on," he said. "It would be ideal for running a farm when I retire, and lots of fresh mountain air to strengthen Geoff's lungs."

"Little by little, we've been saving," my mother said. "How big is the property?"

"At least a few dozen acres." His excitement grew. "It's an earthly paradise, Valerie. Gorgeous, wide-open views, trout streams, our own little quarry near the Sasumua River. Plenty of space for the family to grow . . . and you could have your own garden! When Geoff grows up, the place would be his. This land will be our legacy. Darling, people back home spend their whole lives dreaming of something like this. We could make it ours."

Seeing how happy my father was just at the idea of it, my mother was sold. Together they went and purchased fifty acres of land fifty miles northwest of Nairobi.

Our new farm on the South Kinangop (pronounced *keen-en-gop*; Mummie's helpers laughed as they guided her pronunciation) was an area of outstanding beauty, situated at over eight thousand feet in the foothills of one of the Aberdare Mountains' three magnificent peaks. The mountain, nicknamed "Elephant's Head" for the shape of its contours, rose to nearly thirteen thousand feet behind the farming area. Its slopes were covered with thick forests boasting a never-ending abundance of cedar, evergreen, and African olive trees, and white ribbons of waterfalls crashed into the valley where clumps of bamboo shoots grew. The earth, green as emerald, was dappled with sunlight and carpeted with wild blue salvia (similar to English bluebells) and fiery pink drum lilies that bloomed almost a foot wide. Taking a break from leading her workers to erect a temporary cottage of mud and wattle while she pondered the blueprints of the permanent main house, Mummie loved to remind me that "Daddy worked his whole life for us to have a place like this, Geoff . . . but now we live in the loveliest land in the world."

Exactly what to do with it was a separate question altogether. Mummie hired nearly three hundred people—mostly Kikuyu tribesmen who took keenly to her direction—to help her clear the land to start a farm that she'd begun affectionately referring to as "Kiamweri," named after a mountain peak in the area. It also meant "running water" in Kikuyu, which she was learning to speak. With Dad back in Abyssinia as hopeful murmurs of the war's end increased, Mummie— the former first class–raised debutante from the haughtiest section of London—got her hands dirty clearing the undergrowth and plowing the soil to plant fruits, vegetables, and pyrethrum, little white daisies that served impressively as a natural pesticide when they were burned. She knew that if the workers continued to respond to her enthusiastically, she'd be able to set things up right and make the pyrethrum her main cash crop. She grew ten acres of it, and once a week she put me in the back of her car with her dried flowers and bushels of produce to drive into Nairobi and sell it all.

In my father's absence and while Mummie was busy working, one of the young Kenyan men she'd brought in to run the house so impressed her that she asked him to consider leaving his post as our cook to look after me every day. Nelson Omolo Osewe, whose name I affectionately pronounced *o-MO-lo*, was only a teenager but possessed such gentleness, good humor, and sense of responsibility that my mother trusted him every bit as much as she did Isawa, the family's butler, who was six foot three, stone-faced, and efficient, and Angawa, my father's loyal personal assistant who'd sponged his brow when he contracted malaria and had done his personal laundry since Dad arrived in Africa eight years earlier. Indeed, Omolo accepted my mother's offer to watch me, and he quickly became more than my teacher and my nanny: he became my guardian.

Omolo eased any fears Mummie might have had of my suffering loneliness or boredom. With Omolo in the family, I was never alone—and certainly never bored. Every day he woke me up and ushered me to the kitchen, where he'd serve me my morning tea and his delectable scrambled eggs on toast with the crust sliced off on all four sides. "Omolo," I'd tell him with a mouthful of toast, "did you know that I was born when Daddy was on safari?"

"No, GJ," Mummie would interrupt, using her favorite term of endearment for me, my initials, "you were born when your *mother* was on safari."

"*Toto wangu!*" Omolo would laugh. *My child.*

My sister, Anne, and a friend sit with me on the roof of an army truck looking for lions as we drive into camp.

In these early years, he regarded me as just that. On the bank of the river, on the dirt road, and in the forest, he taught me everything a little boy growing up in Africa should know: how to ride a bicycle, where to catch trout, and how to speak Swahili, which for years I spoke better than English. On special occasions he indulged my plea for him to bake me his famous chocolate cake, and every night he tucked me into Mummie's bed while she looked over her blueprints or tied up loose ends with bookkeeping.

Having company to sleep with made Mummie and me both feel more secure. When the war ended, I pouted when she stood in the doorway as Omolo tucked me into bed in a different room. Over Omolo's shoulder, I asked her, "Mummie, who is that strange man sleeping in our bed?"

"That's your father, darling!" she said, beaming. "The war is over and he's going to be here with us now. Once we finish the main house, he'll run the farm with me. Do you think you'd like that?"

I rolled my eyes and slowly slunk down beneath the covers that Omolo had just creased neatly over my chest. From my mother's expression, it was clear that I didn't have much choice.

Months later, when I was finally getting used to this crowded new arrangement, Mummie dropped another bomb: she was going to have a baby. While she and my father worked fast to finish building the main house, plant potatoes, and stock the farm with pigs, turkeys, ducks, and hens, Omolo kept me occupied. My parents agreed that life in the wild was making a strong boy out of a baby who'd been born so spindly and sick, so when my sister, Anne, was born in 1947, Mummie and Dad further approved of the effect of Omolo's charge over me, now a healthy, active near-five-year-old.

In those days, Omolo supervised me while our syce,

With my father and sister, Anne, on the South Kinangop, 1954.

Kimani, taught me to ride a horse with skill and confidence. Every morning while Mummie fed Anne, Omolo or Kimani trailed behind me as I galloped five miles to fetch the newspaper and the mail from the South Kinangop stores. Omolo taught me how to track wild animals in the forest and looked on as I practiced shooting an air gun to hit a target square-on. Mummie nearly had a heart attack when she saw me at the wheel for the first time, six years old and propped up on cushions inside her Land Rover as Omolo coached me to stretch my

Driving our Series 1 Land Rover with my father and sister, Anne, at Lake Baringo, 1955.

leg for the clutch. "You're not even wearing shoes!" my mother shouted through the car window.

"Mummie, don't be silly!" I hollered. "I never wear shoes!"

When I started school, she sat me down at the radio. "You speak Swahili as well as your father, dear," she said, switching on the BBC, "but from now on, you'll spend two hours each day listening to the reporters' words. You've got to learn a proper accent, darling—the King's English."

Dreadful this was, as the sun shone outside and the children of our closest neighbors, the Nightingales, rode up the mountain on their horses to invite me out to play. "Mummie, I've practiced my English for the day," I'd yell through the window to where she worked in the garden, overemphasizing the length of my vowels and the precision of my words.

"Go on, then," she'd say with a sigh, "but don't get on a horse without Kimani next to you."

My mother worked day and night, continuing to develop the property, usually aided on the weekends by my father. By the time Anne and I were old enough to sleep on our own, we had our own wing in the permanent house—which was shaped like the letter "E" but with the center stroke missing—while my parents' room was in the other wing. The living areas occupied the middle section. The walls were made of rough-hewn gray stone pulled out of our quarry near the river, and the shingles were made of cedar. Having found that there was no window glass available at any of the glaziers' shops in Nairobi, my parents designed the house's windows with small panels to fit the glass from picture frames.

The inspiration for this down-to-earth design was born from my parents' desire for us to exist in the grace of our wild surroundings and in perfect harmony with the land.

And, at Kiamweri, we did.

Chapter 1

The Masai Mara

✧✧✧✧✧

KENYA, 1957

When I turned fifteen, my parents make arrangements to honor a customary African ritual to mark my passage out of boyhood, when a young man demonstrates his capability to protect and ensure the safety of his loved ones. To do this, they send me off on an elephant hunting safari with none other than Major Lynn Temple-Boreham.

Lynn is the suntanned, hard, active game warden of the Masai Mara—the greatest big game hunting district in Kenya—and a close friend of my father's from their days in the King's African Rifles. Lynn is also well pleased that my birthday falls smack in the middle of summer—ideal time for hunting. "You'll get to see the great wildebeest migration, Geoff. More than a million wildebeest move across the Mara between July and August," Lynn tells me. "This is the best time all year for a safari in East Africa."

Years ago, Lynn and his wife established their own camp with a lovely dwelling at Siana Springs, a bubbling source of

With a Samburu warrior in northern Kenya, 1981.

The Masai Mara, or "dotted plain," was protected as a wildlife sanctuary in 1961.

fresh groundwater in a rarely travelled pocket of the reserve. Lynn keeps the oasis hidden for himself as one of the best-kept secrets of the Mara. A dozen foot-high vervet monkeys dance on the hollow roof of Lynn's dining pavilion as we finish breakfast and discuss the day ahead. "Any boy in Kenya knows the most difficult animal to shoot," Lynn says, tossing his napkin onto the table and leaning back in his seat for a final examination of my hunting prowess. "Doesn't he, Geoff?"

"Sure," I tell him. "It's the buffalo."

"The buffalo. That's right. Take the time it took you to spot him, and divide that figure by two, you follow? That's how long it took that buffalo to see you first."

I nod.

The Masai are a semi-nomadic people who live in southern Kenya and northern Tanzania along the Great Rift Valley. Here, a young Masai warrior is starting a fire.

"Then, by the time you've got a good grip on your rifle, the buffalo is charging at you, and while your instinct might be to shoot him straight-on at the broad space of his forehead, right between the eyes, you're all wrong. Aim there, and what will happen?"

"Bullet meets bone."

"That's right, you'll barely make a dent. You ever hear the

word 'hardheaded'? That was coined after him. The buffalo is the epitome of a thick skull."

He goes on, reinforcing what I've already studied: If you make this mistake, you will certainly wound the buffalo, but it will cost you your life. When you follow his blood trail, he'll turn off his line into a thicket and wait for you to pass, suddenly charging you from behind with an unimaginable speed and fury. You'll be gored through your back before you ever think of getting a second shot. "The experienced hunter knows to stalk the buffalo with utmost cunning and wait until he lifts his head," Lynn says. "Aim above his brisket and shoot at the throat, or take him from the side, and hit him right behind the shoulder with a heart shot."

I know why we're covering this in such detail: it's to prepare me for the day ahead. The buffalo is the toughest beast in Africa to hunt, but the elephant, which we're after today, is nearly as tricky. I remember the line from one of my favorite books, *West with the Night* by Beryl Markham: "Find your elephant, then vanish, so that you may live to find another."

As our gunbearer and two trackers load up Lynn Temple-Boreham's Land Rover, his coaching keeps my nerves steady. "That Mauser .256 of yours is fine for crocodiles and antelopes around Lake Baringo," he says, reaching into the back of the truck. "But we're not in your mum's back garden anymore, Geoff. Here, go on. Take my .458 Magnum Winchester." I take the double-barreled elephant rifle from his grip and look it over—the massive cartridge, the barrel longer than my arm. "You're lean, but you're strong, Geoff. You'll manage."

"Do you think I should fire a couple rounds at a target before we go, then?"

"No use," Lynn says over his shoulder as he hoists into the truck. He doesn't take to fools gladly. "You need adrenaline, Geoff—a moving animal. Otherwise the rifle will kick back so hard it will crush your shoulder. Go on then, give it to the guys so they can load it in." Lynn wipes his forehead on his forearm. "Crikey," he says. "Today's meant to be a hot one indeed." As I climb into the passenger seat, he looks in his rearview mirror to be sure his staff have hopped into the back of the vehicle. He starts up the truck.

On the ride out, I silently review everything I know about the elephant from having grown up in Kenya. You never shoot a female elephant—she's the matriarch, needed to look after her calves. It's the male that the hunter with hungry eyes wants. His weight is a hundred times the average man's weight, and his tusks, Lynn says, are worth a fortune.

The elephant isn't reactive like the buffalo—he's very shortsighted—but he can think, fast. In the thick bush where he usually hides, his color is the most deceiving camouflage in the wild. The trick after you've spotted him is to move in close; he's so heavily armored that the hunter needs a heavy bullet, a *really* heavy bullet, which has accuracy only at a very short distance.

"When we stalk one," Lynn says, "he's likely to sniff the wind. We have to get that bit exactly right. If an elephant lifts its trunk and detects you, you'll hear a trumpeting that will downright chill your spine. Then you'll be stampeded, and it will be all over."

He's not referring to my first-ever big game safari. He's referring to my life.

"The most promising shot is the brain shot," Lynn says. "Just see whether you can nail the thing head-on."

After hours of stalking in the scorching July sun, Lynn's trackers spot an elephant through the tall grass drinking from a river. "Those tusks have to weigh about seventy pounds each," Lynn whispers. He crouches down and moves in, and I edge in front of him to do the same. "Remember what I've told you, Geoff. If he sees you and you have to get down, just *sit*. Do not lie on the ground: that gun will recoil against you so hard you'll never shoot again."

A breeze rises up and sways against us. I take the lead and watch the trunk rise like a snorkel.

Our scent has carried across the wind.

"Closer," Lynn says.

We inch forward. I know that at this distance, there will never be time for a second shot. "That's it," I whisper, subtly pointing toward the elephant's left shoulder. "That's my shot." Lynn nods, his eyes fixed on the elephant. I bite down and steady the gun against the crook of my armpit, aiming not for the center of the forehead but for the gutsier shot: a heart shot, from the side.

I fire.

"Yes!" Lynn hisses.

No, I think. *No . . . no.*

I pulled the trigger too fast. I've hit him before I wanted to.

I watch, my fingers still choked around the trigger. The elephant absorbs the bullet above his shoulder and stumbles. He gains a second of footing and takes off toward us, just past the left of me, so close that he nearly knocks me down. He loses all of his tracks—and then, suddenly, crashes down like a boulder.

I'm in horror—not because a few yards more and I'd have been trampled, but because I've just killed the most beauteous and magnificent beast I've ever seen.

I lower the gun, heartsick.

Lynn takes off toward the kill and calls over his shoulder, "Well done, Geoff!" Right then I make a vow to myself and to Africa:

If I ever shoot an elephant again, it will be with a camera—not a gun.

◇◇◇◇

Despite the heat and fatigue, Lynn and his staff are in high spirits when we return to camp. To celebrate my official passage into manhood, they craft for me a ritual gift: a bracelet made of the bristly hairs from the elephant's tail. My attention to the bracelet softens the emotion that's sitting in the pit of my stomach like a rock. "You like it?" says one of the trackers.

"Very much." I turn it in my fingers, studying the assembly.

"Is a charm for good fortune. I teach you to make one, is not so difficult."

As Lynn prepares dinner, I follow the men's instructions, making a fine bracelet out of two long hairs . . . and in the tent before bed, I make twenty more. Not difficult indeed, and the best souvenir I've ever seen.

When I return to Nairobi, I walk into the curio shop owned by Mr. Kanji, a cheerful but discerning Indian trader who often sells his wares to my mother as hostess gifts for her

Africans have an old proverb, "When two bull elephants fight, the only thing that gets damaged is the grass."

Guiding actor James Brolin on a camel safari for the television show To the Ends of the Earth.

friends. "Look at all those bracelets you're wearing," says Mr. Kanji. "Where did you get those?"

"They were a birthday gift, in a way," I explain. "I got them as a souvenir after I got my first elephant. Would you like to have a look?"

"Indeed," he says. "You make these?"

I nod.

He studies one in his palm and asks me, "How much would you charge me for these?"

"Seven shillings each," I tell him, rounding it out to the equivalent of a dollar. "More if I use more hairs. I only used two for this one, but I can put in as many as eight."

Mr. Kanji holds his hand out for a handshake. "We're in business, my friend," he says. "I'll take as many as you'll sell to me."

I shake his hand firmly and dash out, his doorbell jingling behind me. I race straight to the Kenya National Parks headquarters, where I seek out Lynn Temple-Boreham's office. "Lynn," I say, breathless. "Could I possibly have all your elephant tails?"

"What would you want with dead elephant tails?"

"I'm starting a project."

He dips his chin, doubt in his eyes. "All right . . . you want them all?"

"Yes please. The ones from this year that died from natural causes, and the ones the game department killed in the annual culling."

Again, the look.

"No sense in letting them go to waste," I say with a shrug.

"How much were you thinking to pay?"

"Well, I've heard they're quite wretched actually, crawling with maggots and rather unpleasant in general. I was wondering whether you'd be interested in paying *me* to take them off your hands."

He studies me. "How much?"

"Five shillings a sack."

"Ha!" he says, rising from his seat. "I ought to pay you ten."

I run out for my father's truck, and Lynn helps me load up a few dozen sacks.

Back at the farm, Mummie's eyes raise from her newspaper when I run past her in the lounge. "What have you got there?"

"Elephant tails!"

"And where do you think you'll store those?" She's risen and is sailing on my heels.

"Outside, in the old workshop next to the truck!"

"Geoff!" my father calls.

"What?" I reverse and follow Mummie toward where Dad is seated in the drawing room.

"It's the rainy season," my father says, his eyes down on the newspaper.

"They'll be all right," I tell him. "They're waterproof!"

As the final weeks pass before school resumes, I sit in the shade under Mummie's kitchen window making bracelets. Then, at one of Mummie's Sunday curry luncheons, the chief executive of Ethiopian Airlines makes an appearance. Mummie's friends take the bait, asking me to show them the bracelets I'm wearing. "You know what you should do?" I direct the question to the head of the airline.

My mother's friends go dead silent.

"Why don't you give one of these bracelets each to your first-class passengers?"

Gently, Mummie sets down her fork.

"Is that what you think I should do?" he says.

Silence—then after a moment: "It *would* be a lovely souvenir," says his wife.

"I sell them in town for a dollar or two each, but I'll cut you a deal," I told him.

"You know," he says, "that is actually a great idea." He puts in an order so big that the Kenyan women who work on our farm join me to turn out the product. They're delighted for the additional income: I pay them each twenty-five cents per bracelet.

After a couple of months, my business is growing rapidly, and it only improves when I discern that my bracelets made from white elephant hairs—which are considerably rarer to find—should be priced higher than the typical black brace-

PRECEDING PAGE: *Waterhole in the Masai Mara.*

lets. Wares and money trade hands so often between Mr. Kanji and me that by the time school has begun in September, I've saved enough to purchase a motorbike so gorgeous and shiny, it practically sings. "Mind yourself," Dad says. "You go to the best boarding school in Kenya, and the headmaster won't be pleased with all that flash."

In fact, to have a motorcycle is completely against the rules at the Duke of York School, so I keep mine hidden in the *bundu*— Swahili for "bush"—just outside the perimeter of the school grounds. "You and Leakey must be in love with wildlife!" my schoolmates tease, referring to our chum Richard Leakey— but in fact it's another form of life that I'm interested in. About twenty miles from Nairobi is the girls' school that my sister, Anne, attends, and I visit it often to see a particularly attractive young lady whose company I quite fancy.

One afternoon, while my girlfriend and I are rendezvousing in one of the nearby coffee fields, I hear a car approaching slowly along the adjacent road. I dash off on my bike, recognizing the woman inside the vehicle: the headmistress of the girls' school. I lose her only by veering off the road and disappearing into a thick area of the bundu.

Unfortunately, she'd already noted the contents of my license plate. At school the next morning, the headmaster of the Duke of York School, Mr. R. H. James, sends a messenger to my early class to request that I report to the administrator's office immediately. "Your parents are friends of mine, Geoffrey," Mr. James says, "and as such, out of consideration for their feelings, we shall not be expelling you immediately."

"Thank you, sir."

"However, you will be leaving the school at the end of the term—and you will not be invited back. Is that clear?"

"Yes, sir."

"Good. I'll leave it to you to share the news with them."

When school ends for the holidays I know I can't keep

On a game drive surrounded by a herd of wildebeest.

it from my parents for long. My father goes out of his mind. "Your mother and I work hard on our farm and in our community to ensure the best education for you, Geoff!" he says. "What have you got to say for yourself?"

I lean back in my chair, silent.

"You're among the top three in your class, and you are just two A-level exams away from a scholarship to Brasenose College at Oxford University!"

"You're the one who says my tastes are too lofty," I tell him, "and you want to send me to *Oxford University*?"

"I know several of the top management at the Royal Dutch Shell—do you know how many young boys in Africa can only dream of a career in oil?"

"My working in oil is *your* dream! I'm through with studying Arabic—"

"Clearly!" he shouts.

"I can't discuss this with you any further." I push out from the table and thunder to my bedroom. The next morning after breakfast, I start up my bike and take the dirt roads toward town, straight to the dealer who sold the motorbike to me. I look at bigger ones, louder ones, and I quickly settle on a sleek Austrian-German model: a brand-new 250cc two-stroke, split-twin Steyr-Daimler-Puch. It costs me three hundred pounds, but it can do one hundred miles per hour.

My father is waiting for me at the entrance to our farm when I return home. "Where the devil do you think you'll go on that thing?"

"I know exactly where I'll go," I tell him, brushing past him and into the house. "To Cape Town."

"You think you'll be the first to make the trip from Nairobi to Cape Town on a motorbike?" he shouts behind me. "It's over three thousand miles—you *really* think you've got what it takes?"

I turn on my heels and defy him with my stare.

"Rubbish," he says. "You'll never make it."

Chapter 2

Nairobi to Cape Town

✧✧✧✧✧

1958

K nowing there's no talking me out of my motorcycle ride to Cape Town, my mother steps in to lend support. "It's the beginning of the rainy season, GJ," she says. "Are you sure you want to do this?"

"Without a doubt."

"Right then, love," she says, sighing. "We'll try and make the best of it." She gives me two hundred pounds sterling and a brown paper bag filled to the brim. "Raisins and your biltong," she says, referring to my home-made dried meat made from the fillet steak of buffalo or eland, which is seasoned with crushed pepper and salt. "You have some hard days ahead," she says. "The sugar in the raisins and the protein in the biltong will keep you feeling strong."

"Thanks, Mummie."

"It's all right, darling. Listen, I've mailed letters to my friends along the way. Hang on to the list of addresses I tucked in the side pocket of your bag, and look up those contacts as you go. It could save your life."

The motorbike I rode from Nairobi to Cape Town, a Daimler Puch 250cc, on Nairobi's Delamere Avenue.

"I will do that."

I head into the center of Nairobi, where I buy a Shell Oil road map, and then I stop at the Salvation Army to get a poncho and a tarpaulin sheet. Then I visit the motorbike shop to have containers for spare water and fuel fitted onto my bike. Then, on the back of it, I fasten a hand-painted sign:

NAIROBI TO CAPE TOWN
3,000 MILES

I stuff as many elephant hair bracelets into my bags as I can—my equivalent of trading beads—and sling my saddlebags across the bike. The gear that I fasten to either side of the bike contains my food and supplies; I've fixed the bags to bear equal weight and to protect my food from the beating sun. Then I rev up and roar off, speeding straight down the Mombasa Road before turning south at Athi River to take me via Kajiado into Tanganyika (now Tanzania).

The acacia bushland is primitive and wild, the acacia trees rooted sparsely—romantically—across the savanna. Elephants eat the baby acacias and keep the land clear for the antelope; the trees that remain standing on the savanna are the often-solitary survivors.

I take note of leopard tracks on my trail, the harems of zebras that fix their strange striped stares on me, the giraffes nodding among the bush. Day by day, as I continue on the road, the giraffes I see have smaller and smaller spots— Mummie once told me that the more intense the sun is in a given location, the larger the giraffe's spots will be as they absorb the heat of the sun to release it away from the giraffe's body. The animals seem to whisper the promise of thrills to come—should I make it.

Yes, I resolve. *I'll make it.*

Later, in the distance on my left, comes Mount Kilimanjaro—nearly four miles high and capped with gleaming white snow. *You're my next challenge*, I pledge silently, *just as soon as I return to Kenya.* Something about the long road opens my mind to a much wider vision for my life. Suddenly I'm realizing that possibilities exist far beyond producing the next bunch of elephant hair bracelets. *In this whole great world, who is Geoffrey Kent? What do I think is worthwhile?* The only way I can sum up the answer is what I'm living, right here, right now. Being one with the wild. The wide, open road.

As I near the Tanganyika border, the wind flies harder against me as I twist the accelerator a little harder and cruise. The freedom is magical; the scenery, stunning. My father travelled every nook and cranny of Africa during his time in the army, and even he shied away from this journey—maybe I've got more nerve than he does after all. (Of course, I admit, he never rode a motorcycle.)

Then, within minutes of crossing into Tanganyika, the road surface changes instantly from hard clay to soft sand. I skid across the road and come off ass over end, pinned under my bike, half stunned, the hot exhaust pipe sizzling my arm. For a moment I look around, trying to place what's just happened. When I extricate myself and get to my feet, only one thought keeps me from turning tail and heading back home: my father's words. *You'll never make it.*

I could never let that happen. I get back on my bike—with my burnt and wounded right hand—and limp toward Arusha, still several miles away.

Within a few miles, I see a coffee plantation on my right. I drive in and knock on the door of the large house out front, and a kindly woman answers. "I'm riding from Nairobi to Cape Town and I've just wrecked my bike," I tell her, exposing my injured arm.

"Oh dear," she says. "That's quite a burn."

"Could you possibly use some help on your farm for a few weeks?"

"Please, come inside."

For the month it takes my burn to heal, I drive a tractor and help this woman and her husband, Mr. and Mrs. Knieb, in the coffee crops in return for room and board.

Then I start out again.

My route takes me down across the Masai Steppe, to Dodoma, then to Iringa, where I bear to the southwest alongside the Iringa mountains covered in lush greenery. I ride along the northern tip of Lake Nyasa into Nyasaland (changed to Malawi in 1964).

The roads outside the towns are pitted and rough. Each day I rise with the sun and ride all morning, then stop at midday to catch shade from the broiling heat. I spend these hours resting and reading at the base of baobab trees' mammoth trunks. I relish living on my own schedule, doing everything I want. Each time I get back on the bike, my destination—and my destiny—are in my hands exclusively.

The savanna is a field of gold in the afternoon light. On the bike I can smell the clean African soil; I can feel the thud of rain pounding into the ground. Around dinnertime, I find a sidetrack off the main road and seek out an acacia tree, under which I lay out my tarpaulin sheet and my sleeping bag. The nightjar birds have started their call to signal the end of the day as I begin to pray for a night of no rain.

When morning comes, I locate the marketplace—the center of any African village or town—to try to sell a bracelet or

FACING PAGE: *Cape Point, the southernmost tip of Africa, where the Atlantic and Indian Oceans meet.*

two to raise a little cash. I might spend my money on supplies, food, or a clean, dry map to show me the way to my next stop. Traversing nearly the whole length of Nyasaland north to south, about seven hundred miles, I arrive at the capital, Zomba. This is my first planned stopping point.

Here I'll visit the governor of Nyasaland, Sir Robert Armitage, a friend of my parents'. As I pull up to the residence, Lady Armitage is gardening on the lawn. "Geoffrey Kent, I presume?"

"Hello, Lady Armitage!"

"Where have you been? Your mother's letter arrived ages ago; you're five weeks late! We've been terribly worried. Whatever happened?"

I hesitate to tell her the truth: I've taken the scenic route.

That night at dinner, the Armitages applaud my effort to make the trip to Cape Town, but for the sake of my welfare they urge me to turn back and head home. Sir Robert explains that he's preparing to lock up Dr. Hastings Banda, the self-titled president for life of Nyasaland. He describes the progress of the freedom movement in southern Africa. "At any moment things could erupt in bloodshed, Geoff. This is a serious risk you're taking."

Lady Armitage adds her plea. "It's particularly dangerous in the districts you intend to travel through. I know you and your father had a row, Geoffrey, but this could mean life or death."

When they see how adamant I am about persevering, the Armitages finally resolve to help me conquer the route. "That face of yours was the color of mahogany when you pulled up today, young man," Lady Armitage lectures me with a softness to her voice. "Please do stay here at Government House for a week. You'll have a lovely time, and our doctor will give you an ointment that will do wonders for those blisters."

Indeed I stay, and the Armitages work with their staff to arrange several trips for me. First is a coffee estate, whose operations interest me, considering the month I spent with the

Kniebs in Arusha. They also take me to tour some of the capital's public buildings, but my favorite trips are the outdoor excursions to Lake Nyasa (now Lake Malawi), which is one of the Great Lakes of Africa. I ride down through the mountains toward Lake Nyasa—so clear I can see to the bottom—and I pull my mask and snorkel out of my travel bag for a swim. Under the water, I watch in wonder: Lake Nyasa is the only home in the world to several hundred species of colorful freshwater fish known as cichlids, which I've always wanted to see up close. Here their metallic colors flash before my eyes, a magical moving prism.

A haze of fog hovers above the patches of wildflowers and palm trees that cover the Mulanje Plateau, which famously houses the tea plantations that produce the tea that some of Mummie's friends from England insist is better than anything they've ever tasted from China and India. As I tour a plantation, I think longingly of Mummie, who hosts a proper tea every afternoon: how she'd enjoy learning that the tea grows slower but sweeter up here on the mountains, how she'd love watching the workers pluck the bushes by hand, careful only to take the top leaves and the bud—these have the most flavor. Following the dirt path that winds down through the tea garden, the pluckers work away with wicker baskets on their backs, creating a beautiful rustle as they toss the fresh leaves for keeping.

The night before I leave Nyasaland, Sir Robert invites me into his study, where he lays out several maps and helps me chart a route to avoid the areas of political turmoil. He also gives me a letter of introduction to Mr. Costas Perfitas, the owner of the Ambassador Hotel in Salisbury, Southern Rhodesia (now Harare in Zimbabwe). "The Ambassador is one of the grandest hotels in Africa," he explains. "Eighteen massive stories high and *the* mecca for travellers who like to be as comfortable as money can make them."

From Zomba I enter Portuguese East Africa (now Mozambique). Here the roads are horrific, which is not surprising since this is one of Africa's poorest countries. As usual I barter some of my elephant bracelets for supplies of gasoline, for more dried meat and raisins, and for accommodation in village rest houses. If it's not raining, I sleep outside under the endless sky—though this becomes increasingly rare as I reach the height of the rainy season.

I make steady progress, optimistic by the time I approach the Zambezi River. My map suggests that the village of Tete must be near, and there I'll find a bridge to get my motorbike across the river. When I reach Tete, however, the river is nothing like I'd imagined. It's ochre-colored and so swollen that with another day's rain it could flood. I find a huddle of villagers and ask them where I can find the bridge. "The bridge?" they say with a laugh, speaking to me in their local language with a few Swahili words which I can understand. "A storm washed our bridge away long ago!"

In its place, they've contrived an alarming sort of ferry—a flat craft pulled across the river by ropes attached to either bank. To board the ferry, a motorist has to drive up two planks, one for his passenger's side wheel, and the other for his driver's side wheel. The ferry, meanwhile, zigzags in the river between the ropes, the planks swerving this way and that while the vehicle tries to drive up them. Even in a car it would be a challenge, but I have to make it along just one swaying plank!

The only strategy is to get enough speed to obtain some balance, roar up the plank, slam on the brakes, and hope I can stop before I land in the Zambezi. I rev up, get a running start—and I make it. Only when I reach the other side of the

The harbor in Cape Town, once one of the world's busiest trading routes, with Table Mountain visible in the background.

river do I realize that I must negotiate another plank to get my bike and me onto dry land.

"*Go!*" shout the locals from the side I've just conquered. "*Go hard!*"

With no chance to work up speed to launch my bike down the plank, I give it my best go . . . but halfway down the slippery, narrow plank I wobble—and the next minute, I'm in the raging current of the Zambezi. Around me are crocodiles and more crocodiles and six-foot monitor lizards suddenly woken from their sprawling naps on the riverbank. It takes fifteen frantic villagers to haul me and my bike out of the water. They take me to their village and feed me a dinner of bananas and fish. "If you get hungry," one of them tells me, "the catfish makes a good dinner—easy to catch because they swim so slowly. It cooks quickly over a small fire, as well."

I stay there for days working on my bike; my carburetor needs cleaning, my oil is low, and the bike's chain has turned to pure rust. Then one day, a military vehicle pulls up alongside me. A white soldier leans out through the front window. "Hey, man!" he calls. "What are you doing here? This is a war zone! Get in with us!"

He and his brother officer jump out to load my bike into the bed of their truck. They drive me all the way to Southern Rhodesia, where I find a shop just inside the border. "Have you got any oil?" I ask the salesman. He reaches behind himself and hands me sardine oil. I shake my head. "Never mind." I clench my teeth and head back to the military truck.

"Any luck?" one of the soldiers calls through the window.

I shake my head.

"Well you'll never get all the way to Salisbury with your engine in that condition. Get in. We'll take you there."

"I can't ask you to take me all the way to Salisbury."

"Well, we can't let you try to make it on your own."

I'm embarrassed at the whole thing, but I can think only of going on. When I finally reach the city, I locate a garage to take a look at the bike. One of the shop's workers gives me walking directions to the Ambassador Hotel. A few blocks before I find it, the heavens open up and nearly drown me in a rain shower. After I climb the hotel's grand front steps, the doorman declines to let me in.

I can hardly blame him. I'm a grisly sight, an apparition—a scraggly beard, greasy hair, and unkempt, mud-stained clothes. I dig out my letter from Sir Robert Armitage to Mr. Perfitas, and instantly the effect is dramatic.

The doorman accompanies me to the reception desk, where the manager greets me with great deference. "Mr. Kent, I'm afraid Mr. Perfitas is not here today, but he's given us instructions for your arrival. We'll set you up in your room and he'll meet you tomorrow, will that do?"

"Certainly it will."

The elegantly dressed guests sitting in the lobby stare at me incredulously, and I note a large sign that reads: *All gentlemen will please wear long trousers and jackets while in the lounge.* The manager directs a bellman to accompany me in the elevator, followed by a porter carrying my dripping-wet baggage.

"You've got one of the best suites in the hotel," says the friendly bellman, and he unlocks my room and gestures me inside. The place is adorned with velvet and brass, a giant bed in the middle and a bathroom with floor-to-ceiling marble. It's pure opulence, the kind of place my mother would love. As soon as the bellman and porter leave the room, I have a bath and order an excellent meal. Then, joyously, I crawl into my bed and bask between the smooth sheets.

This is the first time I've ever stayed in a hotel, and I've started at the top. *This is really the life*, I muse. *Riding my bike across Africa by day, sleeping in the Ambassador Hotel by night. Unpaved roads by day, fresh sheets and a spring mattress at night. Adventure by day, security and luxury at night. I could live this way forever.*

The following day I meet Mr. Perfitas, who is affability itself. After three glorious days as his guest while the chain on my bike is replaced, I set out almost due south. Travelling through the Union of South Africa—a dominion of the British government that unified four British colonies—I make excellent time along the tarmac roads, across the veldt, through Pietersburg, and across the Springbok Flats. I reach Pretoria in two days.

There I find a telephone box and ring up an old friend— several times—but there's no answer, and therefore no chance I'll have any place to sleep tonight. I look around, lost and clueless in this big, strange city. "You look lonely, young fellow." A stranger speaking Afrikaans—to me. "Come join me for a drink." I muster my best Afrikaans and gratefully accept. Over Castle Lagers I tell him about my journey. Impressed, he offers to put me up for the night.

The next day, I push on to Johannesburg, but it's still only morning when my exhaust pipe falls off. I ride on making the noise of a jet plane until I discover a friendly little town. A group of locals surrounds me, and a few of the men crouch down to help me work on the bike.

Beyond Johannesburg the weather turns filthy with fog, but the tarmac roads keep me moving at a decent pace. When the haze lifts slightly, the countryside through the Drakensberg Mountains bears the enchantment of a storybook.

Finally nearing the suburbs of Durban, I'm haunted again by the fact that I have very little money. Just as I roll out my sleeping bag on the lawn of a tiny park, a policeman rides along on his bike. "You can't sleep there," he says.

"Sir, I've just arrived in Durban and have nowhere else to sleep."

"Either you move off," he says, "or you'll spend the night in jail."

I gather my things and push off into the night.

As dusk sets in, I come to Forest Hills—one of the most stylish suburbs. I drive slowly, considering my options, when I pass a large and handsome house standing back on well-kept grounds: 35 Valley Drive.

An idea.

I take out a pencil and a greasy piece of paper from my pocket, and write, *Llewellyn, 35 Valley Drive.*

I smudge the writing, crumple the paper, and put it in my pocket. Then I approach the main gate, taking a deep breath before I ring the bell. A compact man—clearly the butler—answers.

"May I see the Llewellyns, please?" I ask him.

"Sorry, the Llewellyns?"

"Yes sir, they are friends of my parents, who live in Nairobi."

"You are mistaken, sir. This is the Butchers' residence."

"Oh, I'm sorry. I thought this is where the Llewellyns lived—see? This is the address my parents gave me." I fish out the grimy paper and hand it to him. "I've come a long way," I explain, "and I think I must be terribly lost." Nodding toward the spacious lawns that stretch to the main house, I ask him, "Your garden looks quite safe—do you think I could stay there with my sleeping bag?"

"Ehm . . ." He looks me over. "Would you wait for a moment, please?"

"Of course."

He retires into the house. When he returns, he says, "Please come with me, sir. The lady of the house would like to have a word with you."

With my heart pounding in my ears, I follow him into the

lounge. A woman rises from her sofa: she's exquisite, just like the room around her. "Mrs. Butcher, our guest," says the butler.

The minute he exits into the corridor, I confess. "Mrs. Butcher, please accept my apology. I'm travelling from Nairobi to Cape Town on my motorbike, the son of Colonel John Kent and Valerie," I tell her. Knowing these names must mean nothing to her, I rattle on. "I was desperate to find a place where I could sleep without being hauled to jail."

She examines my face, and then bursts out giggling. "I'm sorry, it's not that I find your troubles amusing," she says. "Listen, why don't you dine with us, and you're welcome to spend the night. Let me call to the butler to show you to your room, and then you can have a bath before dinner. Though you may have to sing for your supper," she says. "My husband and son may be grown men, but they're like children when it comes to stories of a good adventure."

"Adventure." It strikes me that there's something authoritative about the word, something grown-up and extremely alive. Over dinner, the family chuckle at my accounts and take warmly to me, and at one point I note a silent exchange between Mr. and Mrs. Butcher. "Geoff, my wife and I want you to know that you're welcome to stay for as long as you like," Mr. Butcher says. "You've spent time in villages and valleys, but no traveller should come to Durban and not spend some time at the coast."

With surprise I accept their offer. "Do you think a week is enough time to see everything?"

"Not if you want to fit in some squash-playing," Mr. Butcher says.

"And a young man from the highlands of Nairobi must be missing riding terribly," Mrs. Butcher chimes in. "Here you can find some of the finest horse stables in all of Africa. Why don't you plan to stay on for ten days?"

The next morning I venture out to the beach, smiling at

the visitors transported by rickshaws that are painted in brilliant colors and driven by men wearing suits made of monkey skins. I visit the aquarium, nothing but a plate glass window separating me from thousands of fish, turtles, stingrays, devilfish, and sharks. I take Mrs. Butcher's advice and go out on a gorgeous gelding, riding so hard that I limp sorely home. The Butchers' son takes me to see the Valley of 1,000 Hills, curvaceous and dimpled and blanketed with trees, as well as the Kloof itself—a massive gorge with rock walls that drop straight down. He laughs at my reaction when he takes me to see *Passport to Shame*, a spicy film about prostitutes in London starring Diana Dors. When the day arrives for me to depart, I almost long for something to delay me.

I get my wish when I enter an argument with the garage that had serviced my bike. "This bill is exorbitant!" I tell them. "It needed minor tuning and some air in the tires!" By the time we settle, I'm officially ready for my exit from Durban. I set off southwest toward East London, staying close to the coast. The miles on my odometer fly by—the trip is effortless.

In the afternoon, the sky looms gray, and all at once I'm in the middle of a hurricane that seems to blow up from nowhere. The wind shoves me relentlessly from the side and nearly takes me down. When it's clear enough to see through the rain, I spot a pub with an inn attached and careen into its parking lot to get a room. In the morning, the hurricane is just a memory—the grass is high and wild, and the entire countryside sparkles like emeralds.

For the next leg of my trip, I head almost due west to Port Elizabeth—the most southerly city on the Eastern Cape. There I find a phone and call my mother's friends, who drive me to a spot on the coast where hundreds of porpoises surf the waves and skim just underneath the water's surface. They move in pairs, faster than I thought any sea mammals could. "What do you think?" asks Mummie's friend.

"It's one of the most remarkable sights I've ever seen."

From there, they take me to the Snake Park, where the warden plays with snakes as though they're harmless lengths of rope, coiling them around his limbs and even onto his head.

Before I leave, I visit the General Motors factory . . . and I am sadly not impressed by their technique. They simply clip the chrome on, and if the trunk doesn't fit on closing, they give it a blow with a sledgehammer. I decide to think twice before I ever buy one of their vehicles.

With less than three hundred miles before I reach Cape Town, I visit the Cango Caves. The best part comes at the end of the tour when the guide asks whether anyone in our group—seventy in all—would like to go spelunking. Four of us raise our hands.

I climb the ladders, swing on chains down cliffs, belly-crawl through tunnels, and wriggle up a chimney less than two feet wide.

The next morning marks the last leg of my journey—just a mere few hours before I reach Cape Town. I rise early and hit the road at eight o'clock, the bike humming and speeding like a horse that knows he's approaching the stable.

I take the well-known Garden Route, famous for its beauty, but it's early March and it dawns on me that the wildflowers won't return until the South African spring arrives in August. There's drizzle and bitter cold for the first two hundred miles, and the road is harrowingly slick.

When I pull in for gas at Riversdale, I'm one rand short of the bill. "I'm headed from Nairobi to Cape Town," I tell the man behind the counter. "It's been five months and I'm nearly there . . ." It's clear he's not budging on the bill. I consider my options. "Will you accept a check?" I feel a tap on my shoulder, and behind me an Afrikaner smiles and offers me the final rand.

I arrive at my destination, the attractive suburb of Rondebosch, at three o'clock in the afternoon—exactly seven hours after I started out that morning. I feel a profound sense of achievement . . . and then my thoughts turn immediately to my next challenge: *How will I get home?*

I pull out my mother's list of contacts and find the address of her old friend Hope Struben whose husband, Arthur, died and left the family very well bestowed. I find their elegant and comfortable house seated in Rondebosch, a few miles from the center of Cape Town. When I ring the doorbell, I'm caught off guard by a vivaciously beautiful girl, roughly my age. I collect myself quickly. "I'm Geoffrey Kent," I tell her. "I've travelled here from Nairobi, and I believe our parents are friends."

"Mummie!" Her voice echoes in the grandness of the foyer. "Well, don't be silly," she says with a laugh. "Come in." She turns inside the house and addresses me over her shoulder: "I'm Hillary."

Mrs. Struben makes me welcome and shows me to a room where she says I'm invited to stay as long as I care to remain in Cape Town. I ask her whether she can recommend a mechanic for some work on my bike, and she gives me an address for a reliable shop in town.

Cape Town is beautiful, and I make no secret that my favorite part is having Hillary as my tour guide. Together we visit a Cape Town art gallery, and for the first time I find myself curious about paintings—funny how a budding romance can make even the least likely thing so interesting to a boy. On my motorcycle, we ride down to Cape Agulhas, where Hillary and I marvel at the monument marking the point that divides the Atlantic and Indian Oceans. "Imagine, Hilly," I tell her. "To be here, at the most southern point of the African continent."

"I know," she says. "It feels like standing at the end of the earth."

The bond between us rises like the ocean, too much like a fantasy to be real, and yet . . . very natural and very real indeed. We make a trip to the Strubens' weekend cottage on the coast at Betty's Bay, a bucolic seaside resort on the Western Cape. We spend our mornings there in long walks in the cool of the dawn. During the daytime we swim and lie on the beach, and in the evenings we sit and watch the huge breakers come in from the translucent blue ocean. The days pass so fast I cannot keep track of them.

However, Mrs. Struben can, and does. "Geoffrey," she says. "You've been in Cape Town four weeks, and on the road for nearly half a year. Don't you think it's time you went home?"

Crushed at the inevitability of leaving Hillary, I brush off her question. "I don't know how to get there."

"Well, how did you get here?"

"Mrs. Struben, to tell you the truth," I say, "I don't awfully fancy another four-thousand-mile bike ride back to Nairobi."

"It's three thousand miles, if you do away with all your side excursions."

"All the same."

"Can't you go back by train?"

"If I had the money, I imagine I could."

She thinks for a moment, then says brightly, "I know, why don't you write a story about it? We'll say that you used Shell fuel, and sell it to Shell as an advertisement, and you can use the money to get home."

I write the piece, and Mrs. Struben makes the edits. The gist is that I've been the first person to travel on a motorbike from Nairobi to Cape Town, using—what else?—Shell fuel the whole way down. The advertising folks at Shell are very complimentary about my completing the journey, but they decline to publish the piece.

Cape Town, called "the mother city of Africa," with the backdrop of Table Mountain.

I go through the article and erase every reference to Shell, replacing each one with Caltex. I travel to Caltex's Cape Town operation and request to see someone in their advertising department. Instantly their response is more promising than Shell's: they take photos and schedule an interview with me, and within days they pay me a check for a hundred and fifty pounds sterling, which strikes a chord with me. I remember a girl I met on my travels who had recently worked for the *Cape Argus* newspaper. When I phone her, she puts me in touch with the editor, who, intrigued, agrees to purchase the article and photographs me on my bike.

I phone my parents from Mrs. Struben's house. "I'll be coming home within the next month or so," I tell my mother, leaving my departure date vague.

"Well, if you get back in time," Mummie says, "you could sign up to join the Outward Bound expedition up Mount Kilimanjaro."

The prospect of this suddenly lessens the heartache of leaving Hillary. I decide to travel by boat from Cape Town to Mombasa on the *Africa*, the best ship in the Lloyd Triestino line, Italy's most luxurious cruise fleet. "Don't you think the cabins will be cramped?" Hillary says, and it's clear how badly she wants me to stay.

"Maybe, Hilly," I reply. "But less cramped if I book first-class."

The morning I'm set to leave, Hillary is crestfallen. Mrs. Struben stands by and gives me a hug.

I approach the dock with my motorbike. "What are you going to do with this bike?" the steward asks.

"I'm going to bring it on board."

"You can't do that unless you pay for freight space."

I calculate quickly: paying for freight space will leave me without a single penny. At that moment a large car arrives, and out steps an extravagant-looking lady with a high stack of Louis Vuitton suitcases. The bellmen follow her inside, carrying her luggage.

"She's taking all that stuff on board," I point out to the steward.

"Yes, but she has a suite."

"So have I! And I can carry my bike on, on my own." In no time I strip my bike down, and I make four trips hauling it on board part by part, finally carrying the two wheels in on my head. The staff stand outside my room, eyeing me as I store the entirety of my motorcycle inside the closet.

None of them look very pleased, but none of them try to stop me.

Except for my occasional bouts of seasickness, which I fend off with the staff's daily servings of ginger biscuits and tea, all fourteen days of the cruise are superb—every minute in the lap of luxury: fresh flowers in my cabin each day; afternoons spent playing poker with new friends in the lounge or in the library recording notes about my journey. The first-class dining room is adorned with marble floors, backlit columns, and bottles of red wine awaiting us on crisp white linen each evening. I conclude that what I love best about travel is all the new people one meets—fast friends with open minds, always eager for a laugh and up for an adventure.

On the day before we arrive in Mombasa, I take the parts of my motorcycle out of my room and onto the deck to reassemble it. As we approach the dock, I can see my father on the quayside waiting for me.

From the first-class deck I grin down at him. The expression on his face is genial, but it seems to say something more. When I step onto land, he walks along with my bike and me. "Did you enjoy yourself, then?" he asks.

"I did indeed."

"Good," he says. "If you savor a challenge, then what I have in mind for you next should be right up your alley."

Snow-capped Mount Kilimanjaro, located in Tanzania, has three volcanic cones: Kibo, Mawenzi, and Shira.

Chapter 3

Mount Kilimanjaro

❖❖❖❖❖

1959

I start up my bike and follow Dad's car to the Mombasa Club, where he and Mummie are members. The two of us sit down at an umbrella table on the patio. The breeze blows up from the Indian Ocean, creating a gentle bend in the palms and pine trees. "GJ," Dad says, "I've been doing a lot of thinking these last few months."

I keep my eyes fixed on the lunch menu. "Really, Dad? About what?"

"After the episode at school, we really have to sort out your future."

"Mm?" My gaze stays down. "What have you got in mind?"

"It's something I think we're finally going to agree on." This gets my attention. "First of all, I know how much you love polo."

It's true. When I was fourteen, I learned polo from Major Digby Tatham-Warter, a decorated soldier and good friend of my parents', whom they had asked to train me in three-day eventing. During my first afternoon on his farm in Eburru, a few hours from the South Kinangop, he told me, "Geoff, the truth is, this three-day eventing business is for girls. You're excellent in the saddle and you've got really quick reflexes. Why don't we try your hand at polo? It's a much more exciting sport."

Polo excited me wildly; in fact, it proved to be the single

interest that trumped girls and elephant hair bracelets and motorcycles and all my other distractions. After that day on Digby's farm in the countryside near the Ol Doinyo Eburru volcano, I spent hundreds of afternoons riding ponies and hitting the polo ball with a stick in my hand.

Dad's mention of polo has me. "Now, if you were to join the British Army's Household division—"

"The British Army?"

"—you could play all the polo you want. Why, they've got their own regimental ponies, which no other regiment has. You can ride horses! We all know how you like to ride."

"Yes, but—"

"And you can shoot at Bisley. You're a great shot, Geoff. There'll be training, and expeditions. You love the life of the bush! And you're very Kenyan," he says. "You hate wearing a suit."

This is true.

Well," he continues, "when you're commanding a tank in the desert, you won't have to wear a suit! It just so happens," my father says, "that I have a few brochures about life in the army. Have a look at these and see if they aren't attractive."

I begin to leaf through the brochures, taking note of how tough the young men look, with their helmets on their heads and machine guns in their hands. "Look at these magnificent chargers," Dad says, "and these uniforms. And see, there are the polo ponies."

There are the polo ponies, good God, looking so athletic and so graceful.

"And there are tanks racing across the desert, flags flying, aerials. Why, look at this soldier with a beret on! Oh"—Dad sighs—"and the travel, Geoff. By now we all know how you love travel!"

"Where would I go?"

"You'll go off to Cyprus, and Aden; you'll go all over the Middle East—"

"But—"

"And you'll see Germany, and Italy, and even France. Just look at these photos!"

I continue to browse through, a strange emotion rising: Could I really be excited about a life of discipline? I suppose I could, if it's really alluring as all this. "It actually looks quite good," I muse.

"Of course it does!" Dad says. "And *that's* why you're going to love the British Army."

"Dad—"

"So in just a month's time," he says, "you'll ship off for training to become an officer at the Royal Military Academy—"

"Sandhurst?!"

"Exactly. I would have given my eye teeth to have gone to the Royal Military Academy Sandhurst. But first you'll take a course at the Outward Bound program here in Kenya."

"To climb Kilimanjaro, like Mummie promised?"

"Yes, GJ."

I've studied that mountain to the inch: it stands just south of the equator, across the Kenyan border in Tanzania. There's a history of debate suggesting that the mountain once actually belonged to Kenya, and Queen Victoria of England gave it to the Germans in the late nineteenth century as a response to a somewhat uncivil letter from her cousin, Wilhelm I, the emperor of Germany. The Kaiser's letter to Queen Victoria is said to have stated how unfair it was that England held possession of Kilimanjaro when the great majority of the mountain lay in what was then German East Africa. In response, Queen Victoria is said to have acquiesced and granted Kilimanjaro to her German relatives by giving it to her eldest grandson, Wilhelm II, on his wedding day.

◇◇◇◇

Mount Kilimanjaro has two main peaks, Kibo and Mawenzi, which are connected by a saddle. Kibo is the taller of the two at 19,341 feet. Mawenzi is nearly half a mile shorter, at 16,896 feet. The saddle is about 16,000 feet up; altogether, Kilimanjaro covers 995 square miles of land.

I focus my excitement for the climb by selling off the last of my elephant hair bracelets—lucratively worthwhile—and stripping down my motorbike. I splay out the parts in the farm's garage, cleaning and oiling each one with care. I reassemble the bike and take it to the local garage in the South Kinangop. They spray it with fresh paint, matching the original color perfectly. I polish and repolish the bike until it looks brand-new.

When I'd left the dealer's shop six months earlier, the bike had had almost exactly five hundred miles on the clock. Now there are nearly seven thousand. If I'd never travelled to Cape Town, I might have put on about a thousand. I pop out the glass that covers the odometer, and I tinker with the digits, winding them to read 1,497.

I drive the bike to River Road, Nairobi, where at the sales lot stands the dealer Sohan Singh. He's a handsome, smooth-talking Sikh, his head covered in a black turban, his face covered in a black beard, his city trousers covered to the knee with a clean white smock. "Ah, Mr. Geoffrey! I have not been seeing you for a very long time. What has been keeping you from me?"

"These last six months I have been on safari."

"Your motorbike is looking very fine, Geoffrey."

"I'm glad you say that, Sohan, because I was thinking that I would sell it back to you."

"But why would you want to sell such a splendid motorbike back to me, Mr. Geoffrey?"

"I need to sell it back because my father is packing me off to Sandhurst at short notice, and I cannot have a motorbike there. I'm leaving in a few weeks. I want to sell it as soon as I can."

"I see," says Sohan Singh. "How many miles do you have on the bike, Mr. Geoffrey?"

"About fifteen hundred."

"Fifteen hundred! Where did you ride, all the way to Cairo? Let me think . . ." He drums his fingers on his upper lip, and then says, "I tell you what, Geoffrey. Because I like you so much, I will give you for the motorbike twenty-five percent of what you paid for it."

"Twenty-five percent, Sohan Singh? Not a chance." We negotiate back and forth, until I get him to pay me 70 percent of what I paid.

A week later when the local newspaper runs an article about my ride to Cape Town, Sohan Singh calls my house. "How could you do this to your good friend, Mr. Geoffrey?" he cries. "Don't you know I read the news? Please return at once so we can discuss a refund!"

"Sohan, to date I've bought three bikes from you and you've overcharged me every time because I wanted them so badly. You're well ahead of me in this game, and I'm not about to discuss any refund."

This self-assurance comes in handy again a few days later, when I meet our leader for the Kilimanjaro climb. Major Stroud is a former marine with a pronounced limp, which he explains to us in a pitiless tone is due to a wound from the Second World War. He's decades older than all of us young men, and he possesses an intensity that none of us questions.

The twenty of us take a small bus from Nairobi. The morning's ride is largely quiet, with Major Stroud in the front seat. "Any of you know what 'Kilimanjaro' means?" he says.

I wait a beat, and then raise my hand. "I believe I do."

"Kent?"

"It translates to 'impossible for the traveller.' "

"That's right. It comes from three words in Chagga, which is a local Tanzanian tongue, and it suggests that the mountain

is so great that any man should be warned against even trying it. Most people climb this mountain from the Tanzanian side, but you're about to learn the hard way. We're going to take this thing from the Kenyan side."

"Why?" says one of the guys.

"Because the leopards and monkeys on the Tanzanian slopes would rip us to bits!" pipes up another.

I ignore them in the same manner Major Stroud does—though I do take note that he does not confirm or deny this rumor.

We exit the bus in a place called Loitokitok in Kenya, a shanty village located three hours south of Nairobi, right at the border of Tanzania in the low ridges of Kilimanjaro. "This is it," Major Stroud says. "Toward that hill in the distance is our home for the next two weeks." From these foothills, one beholds the mountain with awe: its ridges appearing in clay-ish hues of pink and brown in the combination of morning light and fog, the vista framed by trees so beautiful that at first sight, the image haunts me.

To train, Major Stroud says, we'll rise at five every morning for a five-mile run. Then we'll return to camp, strip down, and dive into a pool made by a natural waterfall—"Just above freezing point, naturally," he says. "We've got to break you in." At the beginning of our training, our days are spent on exercises and activities that build our strength and stamina—because, as our leader reminds us, once you're on Kili, there's no easy way off.

He pairs us each with a partner with whom we'll spend three days on the lower slopes of the mountain, tasked together with building our own shelter out of giant bladed ferns and a tarpau-

---

PRECEDING PAGE: *A stunning view of Mount Kilimanjaro, which is the highest mountain in Africa and the highest freestanding mountain in the world.*

lin sheet. My partner is none other than a boxing champion in Kenya—a lean, muscular African named Festus. Festus is six feet one inch tall, every ounce of him pure sincerity.

Major Stroud doles out field rations of canned goods, coffee, biscuits, and three wooden matches each. "Lose your matches or get them wet," he says, "and that means breakfast from a tin can and no coffee or tea."

Before we start up the hill, I flag Festus into my tent. "Give me your matches," I whisper. Without question he digs them from his pack and hands them over. Using my razor blade, I slice each match into two halves lengthwise. Then I wrap them up in the cellophane that had been housing the spoon in my pack rations. "Twelve matches," Festus says with a smile.

"That's right," I assure him, "instead of six." I zip my pack. We head off up the hill.

In order to build our stamina, our ascent is divided into four sections over the course of four weeks. The first week we spend mastering the saddle. Major Stroud leads us up and then back down again, four days in a row. His energy and able navigation of the mountain astound me. "Your biggest enemy on this leg isn't the mountain or the conditions," he explains. "On these lower slopes, it's the elephant and the buffalo you'd better watch out for. Any of you know where you'd shoot a buffalo if you came face to face with one?"

"Right between the eyes!" shouts one of the guys.

"Why don't you stick close to me, Collins," Major Stroud says. "It'll probably save your life."

I smile, but only to myself.

The week after we've mastered the saddle, we take it again, now adding a climb directly onto Mount Mawenzi. "Altitude sickness and dehydration will start to thin out the group on this ascent," Major Stroud says. "If you're among the ones who don't make it, you'll see us when we come back down."

From the saddle to Mount Mawenzi lies 1,500 feet of volcanic ash, scree, and snow—zero greenery at all. I take a step forward and sink back three, my feet and ankles now covered in slushy filth. I track Major Stroud's fast progress in spite of his age and his limp. I stay as close to him as I can—keeping my focus on this goal takes my mind off the pain of the climb—and I sip water from my canteen every time I see him take a drink.

The dozen of us who make it struggle for air in short breaths at the top. After a full morning's work to arrive there, we barely stop to admire the panorama of Mount Kibo in the sun. "The air up here is cleaner than anything you've ever breathed," Major Stroud tells us as he turns back down. "Air this pure will exhaust your system—take it easy going down."

The following week we climb again, this time for the rim of the Kibo crater, known as Gilman's Point. I curse my pack—only forty pounds, but without enough oxygen, it feels like two hundred. I keep my eyes on the ground in front of me to focus my mind on something—and suddenly a landscape of ice cliffs seems to rise up out of nowhere. It's gorgeously sharp, a transparent shade of blue. "When people tell you they've climbed Kilimanjaro, they're usually referring to Gilman's Point," Major Stroud shouts through puffs of air, "but to really climb to the very top—the peak of Mount Kibo—you've got to work all around the rim of the crater and make the high point on the north rim. That's Kaiser Wilhelm Spitze."

"We'll climb it next week?" one of my comrades asks.

"I will," says Major Stroud. "But very few of you will get there with me."

Indeed, the next week, we start up Kaiser Wilhelm Spitze—German for "Emperor Wilhelm Peak." "Porters would be good right now," huffs one of the guys behind me, and already I'm sure that leaving my pack behind and carrying a few snacks and two canteens was definitely the right decision.

We take only three steps at a time, then pause for air. As I

Dawn breaks over Kaiser Wilhelm Spitze, Uhuru Peak, the highest point in Africa—19,341 feet.

work to catch my breath, the snowflakes on the ground sparkle like rainbow jewels for as far as I can see. Gazing at the higher peaks still in the distance, I see the snow as thick as clumps of white frosting on the sides of a massive cake.

Every time I look behind me, the group has thinned out and shrunk. Festus remains, but now he's slowed down significantly. "Fatigue is a bear," growls Major Stroud—even he is visibly suffering. After eight hours of climbing with no break, we finally near the top. I look out over the dangerous edge of the mountain and I am amazed by what I see: it's a trampoline of clouds beneath us, as if we were at full altitude in an airplane. *A parachute could be a lot of fun right now.*

There are only six of us present as we make the final summit. My only letdown is to see that Festus isn't among us.

Summiting calls for a celebration.

Major Stroud, taking a celebratory tone for the first time since I've met him, urges us to view the inside of the crater: it's fantastic, with giant glaciers that stand like gleaming islands of ice. Then as a group, we approach the famous wooden sign, its letters carved and filled in with yellow paint:

CONGRATULATIONS
YOU ARE NOW AT KAISER WILHELM SPITZE
THE HIGHEST POINT IN AFRICA
19,341 FT

There's a rumble of victory among us, hoots and full, labored breaths to take in what we've just accomplished. The view that lies before us is all sky and open space. It's overwhelming in its simplicity.

Every sound we make creates a conscious transaction among our bodies, the ground, and the air. It's here, in nature, that we are completely unified with all of life. What more could anyone want than this view? More than accomplishment, it's a deep sense of peace and sheer, absolute freedom. It's the peak of existence, like standing on the roof of the world. I turn to Major Stroud. "Now that we've made it, we get to sign our names in the book, right?"

"Yes, Kent, you do."

I turn for the tin box at the foot of the CONGRATULATIONS sign.

"After you climb this once more."

I stop in my tracks.

"Are you surprised, Kent?"

"No, sir."

"Good. Do that, and your name will exist here for eternity. All right, gentlemen," he calls, "let's make our descent."

In a group, we start back down the mountain. My tracks crunch and pack down the snow. We have three days of rest before Major Stroud summons us for our second climb to the top of Kibo. This time it is easier. We are fitter, acclimatized, and know what to expect. And Festus also makes it to the top.

Finally Major Stroud allows me to sign the book. Kaiser Wilhelm Spitze now knows my name.

Now I am ready for Sandhurst.

Chapter 4

The British Army

1959

S andhurst is an education in many ways.

My father sees me off from the Nairobi airport the day I fly to the Royal Air Force base in Lyneham, two hours west of London. When I finally arrive at the Royal Military Academy Sandhurst in Surrey, my cautious naïveté isn't due only to the fact that at age seventeen, I'm one of the younger cadets to enroll in recent years, but also because my rather untamed upbringing in Africa clearly has been quite apart from the much more aristocratically polished backgrounds from whence my classmates come. One afternoon following our second week of basic training, we're all assembled in a sitting room, waiting to be interviewed to determine whether we'll be accepted into our regiment after graduating from the Royal Military Academy. A jittery group of boys next to me try to control their nerves by comparing each other's wardrobes. "Kent!" one whispers. "Who makes your shirts?"

I turn to him. "Sorry, what's that?"

"Your dress shirts," he says. "Who designs them?"

I shrug.

As a young Lieutenant catching up on my paperwork at GHQ Malta, 1964.

"Well have a look!"

"We're about to be called in to interview."

"Go on, we'll tell them you went to the loo."

I look around and excuse myself into the men's room, and, now curious, wrestle off my shirt to have a look at the tag inside the collar. Inconspicuously, I slip back into the sitting room.

"Well, Kent? Who makes your shirts?"

I lean across confidently. "Van Heusen," I whisper.

The group of them meet eyes with each other and burst into uncontrollable laughter.

Puzzled, I ask, "Who makes yours?"

"Turnbull and Asser—only the finest shirtmakers on Jermyn Street in London!" one says.

"Same!" says another. "Although I suppose Van Heusen *would* suit a Jomo from Kenya!"

A Jomo.

I stare hard ahead, completely incensed. Tears threaten to sting my eyes. I'd shown up the first day wearing a suit that hung too large on my thin frame—"From the finest men's shop in Nairobi," my father had convinced me—only to find that my peers all had theirs custom-made by the high street tailors in London. I'd packed my beloved African bow and arrow with the intent to hang them over my bed in the barracks, but I quickly realized it would only elicit more ridicule. I gather straightaway that if I want to blend in at Sandhurst, I'll have to evolve my style—fast.

I also need to adapt to the academy's hierarchy of power and respect. From the first moment I arrived, the sergeant major told the lot of us on the square, "From now on, I'll call you sir and you'll call me sir, but there will be one difference because *you'll* mean it and *I* won't! Quick march!"

◇◇◇◇

We start marching and don't stop for two years, except to learn military history, current events, weaponry, trench work, map work, assault courses, battle training, and a general academic curriculum akin to a university degree, as well as mastering such chores as polishing boots and brass belts to a radiance I'd never known possible and making the bed with so many fractions of an inch of sheet showing above the top blanket.

Intimidation is part of the training, and for the first time in my life, I'm thoroughly petrified of authority. One day, while we're standing at attention, the sergeant major puts his head up against mine and shouts, "Mr. Kent! Did you shave this morning?"

"Yes, sir!"

"Did you put a blade in your razor this morning?"

"Yes, sir!"

"Well, you look like a ruddy hedgehog!" he shouts into my face. "Go back to the barracks, and shave again!"

I work hard, both to blend in with my fellow cadets and to stand out to our sergeants. By the end of the first year, I'm named polo captain (fortunately, my two-goal polo handicap earned me quite a stronger reputation among my cohorts than my wardrobe did), and by the end of the second year, my social life is so bustling that I nearly get myself kicked out for racing my Austin-Healey—the sports car I bought with my ongoing elephant hair profits—back to the academy after a late-night party with some debutantes in London and my roommate, Patrick Grayson.

I'm extremely privileged that the only disciplinary action I face for my foolishness is twenty-four hours in solitary confinement. I'm still allowed to graduate as a senior cadet, and I'd had no clue that such a bold folly actually could increase my standing as I entered the army itself—nor was I aware that I'd been racing Sir Gregor McGregor of McGregor Bart, an army officer whom most of the senior officers have little time for—especially Brigadier Cecil Blacker.

Because of this, Brigadier Blacker takes a strong interest in me and quietly begins to carve out the path for me to join one of the most prestigious regiments of the British Army. For years he commanded the 5th Royal Inniskilling Dragoon Guards, or the "Skins"—a fine regiment, professional and prominent, sometimes led by military members of the royal family and said to be the nursery for future generals. (Today the Colonel in Chief of the regiment is His Royal Highness the Prince of Wales.) What I particularly like about the Skins is their uniforms: khaki jackets and sharp green trousers. These colors appeal to the Kenya boy in me and show the regiment's historically valorous reputation.

As part of our cavalry training for the Skins, we take three specialized courses to come out as troop commanders, each in charge of three tanks. The first course is in tank driving and maintenance, and the second is in learning the very essential signals used to communicate while driving tanks. Given the months I'd spent the year before with my motorbike as my close companion, I relish learning to drive and maintain tanks, changing their engines, and removing damaged tracks to put on new ones. The third course, in gunnery, comes smoothly enough to me, as I have good hand-eye coordination—usually. We take this course on Lulworth Cove in Dorset, where they teach us to shoot out over the sea to prevent us from actually shooting anyone with our Centurion 105-millimeter tank guns. Some mornings, there's a group of us, including HRH Prince Michael of Kent, who turn up at seven o'clock, bleary-eyed and hiding our good trousers under our jumpsuits after a very late dinner in London with some beautiful young debutantes. "Young sir!" calls out our commander. "At present you're aimed at a freighter that's passing through the English Channel! You're meant to be aimed at the rusting tank hulk in the foreground which is your target!"

"Gosh," I mutter to Prince Michael, who's shooting at the

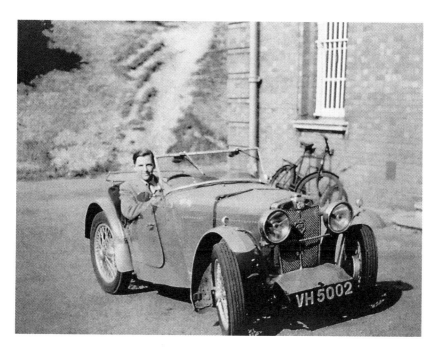

My first car, an MG J2, at the Royal Military Academy Sandhurst.

post next to me. "Did you see what I did? I think that was me who was aiming at the freighter."

"Your barrel looked high to me," he ribs back.

What surprises me, though, is my knack for logistics. My fellow officers loath trekking out in the foggy, damp darkness— "It's four o'clock in the bloody morning!" they moan—but alone with my torch as my only light on the training ground, I examine my map and plan my route to the slightest detail. We have just sixty minutes to reach our commander dead on time, every time, and I vow that if I have to drag my tank there, I'll make it. I log my tank's performance, accounting for any delay that the weather or varying terrains could cause, and build in time for wrong turns and mechanical issues.

By the time they deploy us to Aden in the Middle East, I'm bolstered by my growing reputation for a strong logistics record and my attention to detail. My mother has always said that I'm impossible to satisfy until I've done a job to the best of my ability, always setting myself a very high bar over which to jump.

Our first station proves to be quite a means to cut our teeth. Aden was once a British territory, the capital and chief port of what was then South Yemen situated on the Gulf of Aden near the southern entrance to the Red Sea. *Aden is ghastly*, I write to my parents. *Bare, arid, and hot as hell.* South Yemen is in the midst of insurgency against the British—bombs drop, villagers scurry in chaos, and our job is to keep it all from getting too much out of hand. News arrives not a second too soon that after a six-month deployment there, we'll ship off to Bahrain.

Bahrain is an archipelago-state in the Persian Gulf between the Qatar Peninsula and Saudi Arabia. It too is uncomfortably hot and humid, a depressing flat landscape with nothing but a narrow coastal strip to bring any appeal.

Bahrain is an absolute monarchy ruled by the Khalifa family but bound by treaty to Britain. Oil brings in 80 percent of its wealth, and our job is to protect the regional supply. Every morning we leave our living quarters in the capital city, Manama, and drive two and a half miles to the port of Juffair to board the ship that holds our tanks. Then we sail out and patrol the region, occasionally running drills with the tanks in case we're forced into rapid action.

The assignment itself isn't terribly taxing, but my chronic seasickness makes the days never-ending. When we get the chance to transfer posts, I volunteer, vowing not to complain if I land somewhere flat, hot, and sandy—so long as it doesn't rock.

Hot and sandy, and dangerous as well. Significant quantities of oil and natural gas have been discovered in Oman, and several rebels are hiding out as snipers in the Jebel Akhdar mountain range in the northern desert. We go there to flush them out and force their surrender, and for the duration of the mission we're largely out of contact with headquarters, receiving our food and ammunition exclusively by airdrop.

It's here, in the presence of such real and imminent danger, that I find comfort in the land's beauty in moments of calm. Oman's interior is mostly rocky hills and desert, but there is a strip of coast that is fresh and green, with trees and explosive tropical flowers and sugarcane plantations. This country is another world from Africa, and in the silence of nature, I find profound peace.

Then suddenly, I'm summoned back to Aden to the presence of Lieutenant Colonel Henry Woods, my commanding officer. "Geoffrey," he says, "our regiment has been posted to Libya, and therefore it's up to us to supply the next aide-de-camp to the general officer commanding British troops in Libya and the Middle East, General Frost, whose headquarters is in Malta."

"Yes, Colonel?"

"I've decided to nominate you. Granted, you are not really senior enough for the job, as it should go to a captain—and frankly, I don't think you're up to it—but I'm nominating you all the same."

"Thank you indeed, Colonel . . . but if you think I'm not up to it, then why are you sending me?"

"Because, Geoffrey, you are a good polo player, and General Frost lives for the game. Plus, your attention to detail is tireless, and you're unwaveringly loyal."

"Thank you, Colonel."

"The job also calls for someone easygoing who takes himself seriously when the moment calls for it . . . and the bottom

Lieutenant Geoffrey Kent (second from left) as Aide-de-Camp to Major-General John Frost.

line is, you are good at logistics. General Frost is an absolute perfectionist."

"I'll bear that in mind, Colonel."

"The one final piece of advice I'll give you," Colonel Woods says, "is that General Frost is a fine man—one of the most dedicated servicemen Britain has ever seen—and he is as pleasant to be around as he is brave. But don't make a single mistake, Kent. We're counting on you."

Every soldier knows the reputation of General John Frost, whom Prime Minister Winston Churchill had publicly praised in 1942 after Frost had led a very daring raid during the war to capture the radar equipment at the German-controlled Bruneval radio station in northeastern France. The general's bravest feat, however, was in 1944 when he led the assault on the bridge at Arnhem. Colonel Woods didn't mention this to me—he didn't need to; it's legend enough—but during that battle, General Frost had both of his legs severely wounded and was taken a prisoner of war.

As soon as I meet him in Malta, the image comes together: General Frost's congeniality is as inspiring as his brilliance. "One thing you'll learn about me, Geoffrey," he says, "is that I'm a stickler for detail, and need you to be too."

"Yes, General."

"Whenever one of my operations succeeded, it was always as a result of careful planning. It's a British principle of war: time spent on reconnaissance is seldom wasted. You and I are scheduled to leave Malta at the end of this week to visit King Idris at his palace in Tobruk; then we'll head to Benghazi to visit your regiment. Let's review the itinerary."

I learn quickly how precise the details need to be. "Geoffrey," General Frost might say, "there's a gap of three minutes here between my taking leave of the palace, walking down the steps, and driving off in the car. What happens in those three minutes?"

"Well, General, while you're saying good-bye to King Idris, I shall be fixing your flag to the front of your car."

"Very good, Geoffrey. And how long will it take you to fix the flag?"

"I should allow one minute, General."

"Very good; write that in. And the other two minutes?"

I plan for it all, depending on the situation: the fractions of a minute it could take for him to have a hushed conversation with a private secretary, the moments we might sit in London's rush-hour traffic en route to his plane at Heathrow. General Frost's exemplary service to the United Kingdom and his reinforcement of my work bring out an inspired dedication in me, and I devise a plan.

One afternoon in Malta, I visit Corporal Taylor of the Royal Electrical and Mechanical Engineers. "Corporal Taylor, I'd like to create a mobile refrigeration plant to have a few surprises delivered to General Frost. Would you be willing to help me out?"

"Don't see why not, how big?"

Together we design and build a generator connected to a truck that provides power for a miniature freezer and a fridge. I chill gin for a good martini and stock the fridge with a cold smoked salmon. "Goodness, Geoffrey," General Frost says, "even in the desert at Kufra Oasis we'll be able to enjoy a good drink. Gentlemen, I have to commend you. Very well done." My loyalty to General Frost is cemented.

Our year together in Malta and Libya is intense but interesting, colored by the conversations I'm on hand to witness between King Idris and General Frost. One afternoon, in an official meeting with the sandalwood burning in the background, King Idris in a joking fashion asks the General, "How is it going training my officers?"

"The training is going very well."

"Not too well, I hope," the King chuckles, and then turns rather serious. "There's a young soldier that concerns me," he says. "I hope you aren't doing such a good job that he could lead a coup."

Instantly, I know which young Libyan soldier he's speaking of: Muammar Gaddafi, a young officer who's friendly, a natural leader, and who takes easily to our training.

At the end of my yearlong attachment, the general and his

wife host a farewell dinner for me in Malta. Before dessert, I summon up the nerve to ask the general what he sees in my future. "General, do you think I have what it takes to make a career in the army?"

"You'd be great in wartime, Geoffrey," he says. "But during peacetime, you'd soon grow bored. You're a self-starter, you know that. And just from your love of polo, it's clear how much energy you have."

His wife, Jean, leans in toward the center of the table. "Geoffrey," she says. The candles in the center of the table flicker ever so gently with the genuine intent of her word. "You need a career that will harness all your passion."

"That's right," says General Frost. "Find the one thing that would make you feel as though you've done nothing with your life if you don't accomplish it. It's nice seeing the world, but England is my home. The army will fly you anywhere you like at the end of your service. You have to decide where your home is, as well."

The next day, we arrive at Heathrow together for the last time. I step out, fix his flag on the car, and salute him.

Then I arrange for a Royal Air Force flight back to Kenya.

Chapter 5

Tented Luxury
Safaris

✧✧✧✧✧

1962

In 1952, in an effort to gain independence from England, a large group of Africans band together to take their land back from white settlers. During the worst of the conflict, which becomes known as the Mau Mau Uprising, my sister, five years old, and I, age ten, leave our home to stay in the center of Nairobi with my parents' friend Dr. Flowerdew. When my parents come to visit us, they offer hushed accounts to the Flowerdews about the massacres happening on the Kinangop. "I can't bear to think about what happened to the Rucks," I hear Mummie tell Mrs. Flowerdew in the next room.

"What's happened to the Rucks, Mummie?"

"Geoff, that wasn't meant for your ears," she says. "Darling . . . they've all died."

"The Mau Mau killed them?"

"Yes."

The Rucks were our family's good friends on the mountain, and their youngest son was just a toddler. But even as the attacks reach their most horrific points, my father won't dream

---

Enjoying Sundowners around the campfire in Kenya, 2007.

of leaving the South Kinangop—and my mother won't dream of leaving my father. But when she makes the drive into Nairobi to see us, in addition to donning a hat and gloves, she also has a .32 Beretta pistol strapped around her waist.

In February 1960, the British Prime Minister, Harold Macmillan, gives his famous "Wind of Change" speech in Cape Town, stating that colonial rule cannot go on. Despite the fact that British settlers have put down the uprising, the British government in 1962 gives Kenya self-governance and determines that the farms in the white highlands will be taken away and returned to the Kikuyu. Ironically, because my father knows all the land and all the people in the area, he takes a temporary job with the new Kenyan government to help them decipher exactly which land belongs to which owners in the land settlement. Then, after they have possession of everyone's properties, the new Kenyan government force my parents off the farm they've spent two and a half decades creating.

Fortunately, Mummie and Dad sensed this coming. As they face the prospect of having no home and no income, my father lands a part-time job as a tour guide with a local travel company. Finally something is going well: thanks to his military experience of having been the first person ever to map the route from Kenya to Nigeria, Dad knows the roads and sights of Africa better than any tour guide in the region and is earning a good wage—especially from American travellers, who are known to tip generously when they especially like a guide.

At this point, every few months I'm making regular visits home from the army. During one of these visits in 1962, Dad, Mummie, and I make a decision. We love Africa, and travellers are clearly growing more interested in the place we call home. We three go in as partners, founding our own travel company, with the intent to host safaris around Kenya, and then possibly moving into other areas of East Africa.

By 1965, when I return to Africa for good, friends of mine are leading hunting expeditions, and some of the locals have set themselves up as travel agents, guides, and drivers—and everyone is beginning to make money.

My parents find a house to rent in Rosslyn, one of Nairobi's most genteel suburbs, and I move into the tiny guesthouse on the grounds of their new home.

In a bold move to set the tone for our brand, I use the money the army paid me when they discovered that my working on tanks had left me with high tone deafness to buy a Toyota Land Cruiser—one of the first-ever Land Cruisers sold in Kenya. "Not a single travel company in Kenya even owns its own truck, and you had to go and buy a Japanese one," my father says. "Don't you remember what they did in the war?"

He, my mother, and I spend evenings drinking Dad's gin, developing a business plan, and brainstorming a name for the company that will both sound grand and put us at the top of the yellow pages. Abbot & Kent is a little too sleepy; Aardvark & Kent would make for a horrible logo. And then we all think that "Abercrombie" sounds like someone who is rich and powerful. "Abercrombie . . ." I experiment with it. "Abercrombie & Kent."

Mummie and Dad both look up, turning the phrase over in the silence between them. "I quite like it," my dad says.

"Rather elegant, isn't it?" says Mummie.

Our challenge now is to find clients. After reading an issue of *Time* magazine, I learn that Texans are the richest people in the world. Whenever I station myself outside the New Stanley Hotel or in the adjacent Thorn Tree Restaurant, I find it easy to spot the Americans in contrast to the travellers who arrive from London or Johannesburg. Americans usually carry lots of baggage, and they wear cowboy boots, and sometimes Stetsons.

Americans are very picky about their guides, and my

My first design of a mobile tent, canvas and poles, Ngorongoro, 1966.

friendliness proves to be a selling point—indeed, we begin to magnetically attract business with this approach. As we book our first few clients, I'm motivated to think even more critically about what people really want from a once-in-a-lifetime safari vacation. We've set ourselves apart with a nice truck, and we send our clients out for the day with drinks chilled in our ice bucket. Still, there's so much opportunity for us to stand out. The lodges for nonhunting safari clients are lackluster, sometimes offering only a couple dozen tiny rooms and zero in-suite dining. The last thing a tourist wants to do after a flight from London or New York is to locate an African market and then navigate his or her way around it, looking for a nice bottle of wine or foods that are particularly appetizing.

My idea lights something in me so serious that I know I can't share it with my father. "Let us carry on as we are," he's taken to saying, but I know his true conflict is with how much money we'd need to invest to grow our business into something unique.

While he and my mother are on vacation trekking through the Khyber Pass, which connects Pakistan and Afghanistan, I make a trip to the bank. "I'd like to make a withdrawal from our business account, please."

"How much?" asks the bank manager.

"All of it."

"That's seven thousand pounds, Mr. Kent."

"OK, I'll take five thousand pounds," I tell him. "Leaving two thousand pounds for a rainy day."

I call my old army friend, Corporal Taylor, and inform him that I'm preparing to buy a secondhand army Bedford truck—four tons, with four-wheel drive. "I'm putting in a refrigeration system," I tell him. He agrees to meet me in Nairobi.

We work day and night to build the freezer—five feet long, three feet deep—and we fit the refrigerator with special rubber balances to keep everything steady across rough terrain. When we finish, we drink Tusker beers chilled on ice made from a generator connected to the truck: Abercrombie & Kent is officially the first East African safari outfit to develop mobile refrigeration.

I order tents from Low & Bonar, a Scottish textiles company that makes the best-quality tents for hunters. Then I travel into the city on a shopping spree for beds and furniture, blankets and linens, pots and pans, china and silver, Royal Crown Derby teacups, and, in a nod to my mother, cut glass decanters for the wine and a silver ice bucket.

In our driveway in Rosslyn, I lay everything out and pack it into trunks that I've had custom-made to fit into the back of the Bedford. Then I line the trunks with thick layers of sponge rubber to protect all the delicate items during transport. On the sides of the truck I attach containers for spare fuel, emergency supplies, and first-aid equipment; and, finally, I make a checklist to ensure each item is present. (Imagine arriving at your objective one hundred fifty miles into the wilderness and realizing you've forgotten the toilet paper.)

Corporal Taylor agrees to accompany me to the campsite for two weeks, as do Omolo and Wilfred, the driver I've hired, and Joseph Nduati, the chief salesman from Low & Bonar. We color-code our tent poles for the fastest assembly possible, and then at four in the morning we pile into the back of the truck and trundle out of Rosslyn. To train, we drive out a hundred seventy miles to Lake Baringo in the Great Rift Valley—a spot that I know well from the crocodile-shooting escapades my parents took me on as a child. Its shallowness—the lake is at maximum thirty-nine feet deep—makes it a prime habitat for crocodiles and hippopotami, meaning we'll get the experience of setting up camp in the wild.

When we arrive at our training ground, I pull out a stopwatch, a pencil, a yellow pad, and my whistle. "Logistics training at its finest," Corporal Taylor rags.

Meanwhile I take my place to coach the team on our objective. "We have two weeks," I tell them. "We have to learn to set up camp in under twenty-four hours, and strike it in less than twelve." I click the stopwatch and we unload the truck, the tents going up and down, up and down, up, down, up, down, until the staff is exhausted.

After just over a week's time, we pop a bottle of champagne: there before us stand four tents, each of them fifteen feet across with a veranda six feet deep in the front. In an afternoon's time, each tent can be erected by this, my new staff, to hold an occupancy equivalent of a double room in a hotel. The floor of every tent is covered with a groundsheet to keep out bugs and beetles, then covered again with a beautiful rug. The walls of the tents rise about twelve feet and slope somewhat inward, making the interior feel much like a bedroom. The veranda leads into the living-room portion of the tent, and the entire thing feels spacious and bright, with electric light, bedside lamps, beautiful carpets, and lovely sprung double beds high off the ground.

The lavatories are located outside, near the tents. They consist of long drop holes, about three feet deep, treated with lime and covered with a proper seat—a handsome mahogany box, which totally conceals the fact that there's only a deep hole underneath it. Inside the outhouses are tables carrying current copies of *Country Life* and *Punch*. There's a heap of earth behind the lavatory seat and a little drawing of a rhino on the wall, with the inscription *Rhinos cover it, so will you too, please?* We'll never stay at the same site for more than three days, so the conditions are perfectly hygienic.

Inside the tent we've put lovely Plastolene tubs for women to take bubble baths in, and out back we've put in showers for the men. The showers lie directly behind the tent and consist of a perforated showerhead attached to a large canvas bag that's filled and refilled with heated water, operated by a chain and slung over the branch of a tree. A guest can soap up and pull the chain, then down will come the water at an impressive pressure. When they've had enough, they'll pull another chain, which will cut the water off.

Inside the suite we lay out a bottle of Scotch on ice, chilled martinis, crystal wineglasses, and sideboards displaying fresh vegetable crudités, smoked salmon, and chocolate cake. I look at my men, and we behold the total luxury experience before us. The whole scene is completely ace. I vow that this marriage of adventure and extravagance will be the stamp that Abercrombie & Kent's brand will come to be known by: the Off the Beaten Track Safari.

I leave Corporal Taylor, Omolo, and Joseph looking after camp while I head into town to sort out the final details. I stroll in past the grand columns and coral pink facade of the

Each mobile tent contains a fully flushing toilet, washbasin and shower, and arched, netted windows that allow the breeze to pass through.

Muthaiga Country Club, where my father has recently had me instated as a member. Sipping a drink in the lounge area, I take in the club's incredible beauty: the polished wood shelves and trim, the rich flower arrangements, the stained-glass windows and French doors. The head barman, Francis Maina, calls over to me from the far end of the bar. "Would you like to see the lunch menu, Mr. Kent?"

"Please."

He comes to me, opens the leather binder, and places it between my wrists resting on the bar. I have to control my appetite as I view the lunch menu. Francis walks over to take my order—the usual: potted shrimps in frozen butter on well-done toast, roast beef, and Yorkshire pudding. "I'll start with ice-cold avocado soup with Tabasco sauce," I tell him.

"And to finish? Chocolate pudding with ice cream, or sticky toffee pudding?"

"Chocolate," I tell him.

Abercrombie & Kent needs the best chef in Nairobi, I sit think-ing. *Where will I find a hospitality staff as good as the Muthaiga Club's?* When Francis returns from putting in my order, I lean in. "You're known to be the best barman in Nairobi," I murmur. "If I told you I had a job for you, and that you'd make more money with more interesting clientele and more flexible hours . . . would you come with me?"

His eyes go wide as we exchange a glance. He nods incon-spicuously.

"What about the maître d', and the chef—do you think they'd come along with you?"

Again, Francis nods.

"Give your notice and plan to start in two weeks," I tell him. "And don't say a word to the members."

However, my parents return from their vacation the next week, and my father's gotten wind of it. "You've spent our en-tire savings, you've killed our business, and you couldn't fail to do so before nicking the best staff the Muthaiga Club has ever seen. Jesus, Geoff, have you gone completely nuts?"

"Dad, I've told you that we need to do something to stand out from the competition. It was a risk, but now we've done it, and soon we'll be the envy of every safari outfitter in Kenya."

"Darling," says my mother, "I think the idea itself is mar-velous, but the price of something like this will cost three to four times what we've been charging, at *least*. Where on earth do you think we're going to get clients who can spend that?"

In a huff, my father speeds off—to the club, no doubt—and I look at my watch: the first flights from London and Johannes-burg will arrive in time for lunch. I dash out to the New Stanley Hotel, sit down at my usual table, and order my usual lunch: a milkshake. From my bag I pull my calculator and a notebook and lay out my maps, staring hard.

Then suddenly, I spot a Texan—it's just like spotting a bird. "Forget the milkshake!" I call to the waitress, racing out into the lobby, where I extend my hand to him. "I don't think you're from around here," I say. "Texas, perhaps?"

"How'd you guess?" he says, laughing.

"I'm Geoffrey Kent, I own a safari outfitter in the area."

"Name's Worthing—Tom Worthing." He's more than six feet tall, wearing fine-looking cowboy boots, jeans, a red-and-white checkered shirt, and a Stetson. "And this is my wife, Sara." His paw is friendly, but it nearly swallows me up when he shakes my hand. "Sara and I actually would like to go on a safari," he says. "Which company are you with?"

When I tell him, he slaps his knee. "From what they tell me, you've got the best safari in East Africa!"

"Is that what they say!" I laugh. *Good God, is that what they say?*

"Yep, sure is. Would you set up an itinerary for us?"

"How long?"

"Say, thirty days. We were just gonna step out ta lunch, can you run me some numbers and meet us afterward?"

"Certainly, and might I recommend the Thorn Tree next door for your lunch—tell them Geoffrey Kent sent you. I'll come up to your suite in an hour."

The kind of comfortable, Hemingway-style tent used on a mobile safari—
electric lights, mosquito nets, hot and cold running water—a far cry from
1966.

Thirty days, thirty days. I begin making notes, plotting out the logistics and the costs of fuel to travel. From Nairobi we'll leave to spend four or five nights in a number of different locations, with occasional stays at guest lodges so my team can set up the mobile camp ahead of us. The itinerary will go from Kenya to Tanzania to Uganda, as such:

Amboseli, where we'll camp for a couple of nights beneath Kilimanjaro, then on to Lake Manyara, the only place to see tree-climbing lions. From there we'll visit Ngorongoro Crater, where I've managed to get the first-ever permit to camp at the bottom of the crater, then to the Serengeti for tea with Jane Goodall at her camp—I know her through the Leakey family; she loves to chat with visitors about her work with chimpanzees. Then we'll stay for a few nights in the Masai Mara, then on to Kisumu, where we'll catch the ferry across Lake Victoria to Jinja, Uganda, from which point we'll make our way to Queen Elizabeth Park. From there we will go to the Kibale Forest, where we will spot chimps, and then, for the grand finale of the safari, three nights at Paraa Lodge in Murchison Falls, Uganda. This destination is currently all the rage, as the 1951 Humphrey Bogart film *The African Queen* was filmed there.

I calculate the costs of food—lots of steak, Americans love steak—and good liquor, hospitality staff, housekeeping, transport. I keep the numbers low by planning to host the entire thing myself. I'm prepared not to make a profit—the whole point is to show my parents we really can sell this vacation, keep up my morale, and hopefully grow the word about how excellent Abercrombie & Kent's Off the Beaten Track Safari is.

It comes to $3,235.00.

Damn! The price is still too high. Why didn't I come up with a less luxurious package? I should've thought how I could pare down my staff and plan for slightly lower-quality food and beverage—Americans don't mind a burger every now and then! Just like that, I feel as if I've lost the business.

An hour later, as I knock on Tom and Sara Worthing's door, my palms and forehead are sweating. I'm not sure even a Texan will be keen on the idea of a safari at this price.

"Great lunch, Kent, fine recommendation," says Tom Worthing. He stands over my desk with his thumbs through his belt loops. "So what'll it be?"

I've rehearsed this pitch for weeks, awaiting the right moment to launch into it. "Thirty days, you'll have me as a guide all to yourselves, and you'll see elephants, and rhinos, and leopards and buffalos and lions," I tell them. "The big five! And the birds, the trees, the mountains, the views; why, just wait until you see our camp on the lake—"

"Kent. How much?"

I lay my hands flat on the desk in front of me, as if to brace all three of us. I purse my lips.

I lose confidence and can't get the number out.

Eventually—*finally*—I announce: "It's two thousand, nine hundred and twenty-two dollars."

Tom Worthing's face falls. He looks at his wife, and then turns back to me. "He must be kidding."

I've blown it.

"Kent," he says. "Is *that* all?"

Suddenly, an inspiration: "Each!"

Tom Worthing pulls out his checkbook, scribbles out a check, and hands it to me. "We'll add your tip at the end, if that's okay," he says.

"That will be fine, Tom."

"You see that, Sara?" Tom Worthing says. "Only the best for my lady."

For the first time I realize how to make a good profit.

"Get a good night's rest," I call as they exit. "We'll meet here for breakfast and head out." Then I race to the Muthaiga Club, prepared for what has to come next.

When I pull in, my father's car sits close to the entrance.

"Well, look who it is!" cries one of his cronies as I enter the bar.

"The cockiest safari guide the world has ever seen!" calls another.

"Hey, Geoff, we're all just sitting here with your father toasting you with a drink we've named after your business: an A&K on the Rocks!"

I ignore him and slip a bill to the bartender to take care of my tab. Then I turn to my father and his friends seated at the bar. "Dad," I say. "What's in that new drink? I might serve it at camp."

"Why, it's a delightful mix of gin and bitters."

"Bitters?" There's a ripple of laughter from behind their glasses. "Sounds about right, gentlemen."

Sir Charles Markham, the director of the club, follows me as I head outside. "Geoff," he says. I turn around to face him. "You know that given my friendship with your parents, I hate to have to do this—"

"I understand, Sir Charles. I only came to pay my tab."

"I have to blackball you from the club for six months . . . unless," he says, "you bring back our staff. Then we could call this whole silly thing off."

"That's all right, Sir Charles. I'm so busy with work it could be a year before I have time to come back."

I exit the club and roll out of the gravel lot, back toward the center of Nairobi toward my trucks and my camp and my first luxury mobile tented photographic safari—the first one ever with refrigeration.

When we've secured our place in Africa, I set my sights on other key parts of the world. Fortunately, I have some support.

In the early 1970s, while I'm playing polo in Chicago, I meet Jorie Butler. Jorie becomes my partner not just in business, but in life, as my wife. She's the first handicapped female polo player in the United States, and as I'm on my way to making my dream come true—winning the US Open Championship—her tutelage and advice make it possible for me to make a name both in the American polo scene and in business.

Jorie stands by in 1976 when I play in my first US Open, and in 1978 when the Abercrombie & Kent team is the first to win both the US Open and the US Gold Cup in the same year. It's our shared passion for the sport that first unites us, and it's our love of the world that keeps us together for thirty years.

A natural business mind from a family of entrepreneurs, Jorie sees my vision for the business and knows how to leverage the experience of us both to grow it. She helps me to "go where the fish swim," helps me open an office in the United States, from where the majority of our clientele now come. Our first office is in a barn on her father's property in the prosperous Oak Brook suburb of Chicago where she grew up and where her father runs the world-famous Oak Brook Polo Club. Our office is nothing more than one desk, a yellow telephone, three raccoons, and a blackboard (with white chalk for prospective clients, red chalk when they book). We cater to American clients looking to travel outside the United States, and our US presence expands rapidly throughout the seventies.

In my early thirties, I make my first million dollars. We establish a second American home base in Lake Worth, Florida, next to the brand-new Palm Beach Polo Golf and Country Club in Wellington, where the weather is always good for playing polo and where it's easy for me to catch a flight on the Concorde from Miami for meetings anywhere around the world.

Jorie helps me take Abercrombie & Kent from Africa to

Enjoying Sundowner drinks around the campfire beside the Mara River. There is nothing like a Sundowner in the African bush after a long day.

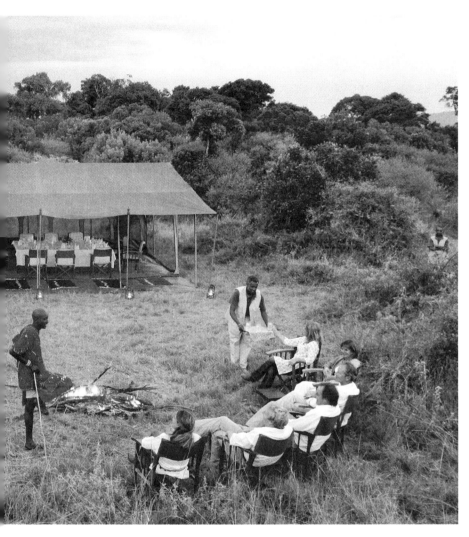

America and most everywhere beyond—and she inspires me to establish a commitment to generating business while also improving the world.

Ultimately, to employ a metaphor that works for both polo and travel—we have a wild ride. For quite some time, I feel as though together, we rule the world.

Chapter 6

Egypt

✧✧✧✧✧

1977

By the late 1960s, our client base has grown, and so have our clients' cravings for highly exotic vacations. After a Kenyan, Tanzanian, or South African safari, they've begun to ask where I might recommend they vacation next.

For some time, I've been fixated on Egypt. Its history is epic, and there is a growing perception in the West that Egypt, with all its mystery and antiquity, could even be glamorous. In the late 1950s, the story of Moses was produced as a major motion picture, *The Ten Commandments*, and then in 1963 Elizabeth Taylor starred in *Cleopatra*—one of the biggest-budget films ever produced at that time. Unfortunately, there's a good reason that very few tourists have ever explored the fabled land of Pyramids and the Sphinx and the magic of the Nile: the Egyptian Minister

It's come a long way since the very first Sun Boat. Cleopatra's Oasis on Sun Boat III provides some of the most beautiful views along the Nile.

of Tourism refuses to give an operating license to any non–Egyptian-owned travel company.

In the 1970s, I manage to operate under the umbrella of an Egyptian-owned company, but I still can't get my own license. Then, in 1981 while I'm playing polo in Florida, I hear on television the news that Egypt's President, Anwar Sadat, has been assassinated. Knowing that an eruption of geopolitical tension scares foreigners away and motivates a nation's government to bring in tourism, I rush to Miami and board the Concorde, which stops in New York and then flies supersonic to London. Within a couple of days, I'm inside the office of the Egyptian Minister of Tourism. "Listen," I tell him, "your President's been shot, the whole world is canceling tours in Egypt. I want a license. You need foreign travel companies now."

"What will you do for me?" he says.

"I will not stop promoting Egypt. But in exchange for my faith in your country, I want an operating license."

Before I leave for the airport, I have a license in hand, and I vow to offer the best Egyptian vacation that anyone has ever produced and market Egypt as a classic destination.

In the sunrise, the Pyramids appear bright bloodred, casting shadows of triangular mountains across the open sand.

The Egyptian Minister of Antiquities accompanies me; both our camels—their legs covered in dust up to their knees—gait slowly over the occasional pile of pebbles, toward the Pyramids and the Sphinx. It's a moment so grand that I might as well be observing the image of us in a film.

As we move in, the sight of the Sphinx haunts me like an apparition, with its arms stretched out like a lion in waiting—and truly, what happened to the nose? Did it erode over thousands of years' worth of windswept desert nights, or could it have been taken in an act of old wartime revenge of some kind? The statue rises up to the sky, and I try to imagine what society must have been like for the people who were living when it was created.

Very few people get to tour the inside of the Great Pyramid of Khufu, but the Minister of Antiquities has made a special arrangement for me. Inside, our voices echo as we wind our way through a cavernous corridor. I peer up: hundreds and hundreds of stairs. My host's shoes click up the first of them, and I start up after him.

I take note of the size of the rocks—huge, perfectly measured and stacked, hewn by who knows how or where. "How did they get all these materials in here?" I ask.

"They were actually rolled in on logs," he says. "This job would have taken thousands and thousands of slaves."

"How could they fit all these rocks with such precision?"

"What's more, Geoff," he says, "is that all the engineering is so perfect that during the day, when the ancient people would worship, all the sunlight would pour directly over there." He points to an altar at the front of a long room.

"Does it still happen today?"

"Every afternoon."

Finally sold on the fact that their country needs tourists, the Egyptians overseeing tourism have organized a top-shelf visit for me. A happy coincidence is that the British actor David Niven happens to be here filming a highly anticipated project, an adaptation of the Agatha Christie novel *Death on the Nile*. David's son, Jamie, had taken our first-ever safari by private carriage and steam locomotive in Kenya, which we called the "Iron Snake." "If you're in Egypt," Jamie says to me, "you must meet my father!" He arranges for David and me to have dinner together on the prow of one of the only two riverboats on the Nile, the *Isis*, managed by the Hilton hotel group.

David is magnificent over cocktails as he recalls stories from the Royal Military Academy Sandhurst—he was known as a fabulous troublemaker there, even when I arrived, two

The first Sun Boat, *inspired by the movie of Agatha Christie's* Death on the Nile.

decades after his departure. He's also generous with insights about his career in film. As the first course is served, he points off in the distance. "We're making this movie on that ship over there," he says. "You see it?"

I turn and find the silhouette of an old steamship in the glow of the sunset. "The one with the funnel coming out of the top?"

"That's the one—beauty, isn't she? The SS *Memnon*. In the film she's called the *Karnak*."

In the film she's called the Karnak. "David," I say, an idea suddenly possessing me, "do you think there's any chance I could go on board?"

"Don't see why not," he says. "When do you think you'd like to go?"

"How about right now?"

He gazes over my shoulder at the boat again, and then nods. "We'll have to get there before the crew leaves," he says, "or there'll be no one to let us on board." We eat our dinner quickly and make our way along the riverbank under the palm trees. The boat is simple and charming, having been constructed in the earliest years of the twentieth century and still so true to the era, with the paddle wheel on its side, clean, curved corners around its front, and one row of portholes to accommodate what must be no more than a couple dozen passengers. We make it no farther than the entry when I know I'm on to something incredible. "David, could you please do me a favor? Get me the name of the owner."

The boat's owner happens to be a very prominent Egyptian. Now better versed in persuading Egyptians to enter into business agreements, I make a few calls and schedule a meeting with him that week. "Here's this huge hit movie that will be released all over the world," I tell him. "Anyone will want to do a Nile River cruise on this riverboat instead of those two Hilton boats I've seen. I'll lease the ship from you in time for the film to come out, then I'll advertise it everywhere: 'Now you can do the Nile on the original paddle steamer where *Death on the Nile* was filmed.'" He agrees, and we schedule a phone call to sort out the details for when I return to Florida.

The cruise is full—instantly. I call Oxford University, aware of an Egyptology expert named Anthony Hutt who could lead talks on hieroglyphics, the history of the cities along the Nile, and Islamic architecture specific to Egypt. "I'm building my business all over the world," I tell him. "I would need to train you to host the trip without me."

"When does it start?" Tony says. "I'm in."

A renowned investment banker from New York has booked the first journey, for a group of a dozen and a half of his friends. On the day of their scheduled departure, I receive a phone call from the still-enthusiastic Tony Hutt. "All the New Yorkers have touched down in Luxor," he assures me, "and they're getting situated on board now."

"Excellent."

Seeing the Pyramids in person really allows you to appreciate their vast scale. They are made from locally quarried limestone and granite.

The Sphinx on the Giza Plateau rests on the west bank of the Nile River. It is 240 feet long and carved out of limestone.

"Excellent, Geoff, it's dynamite! You should see them. They're looking around—'Oh, how wonderful,' they're going. 'Oh, fantastic, why, what a marvelous boat!' Shortly they'll be stepping outside to have lunch under the awnings, and then we'll start the engines and cruise out of Luxor."

"Brilliant," I tell him. "Stay in touch, would you? Let me know how it's going." It's an instruction I'll regret within hours.

Around mid-morning, my secretary, Jeannine Nihil, asks me to take an urgent phone call. "Tony Hutt is on the line," she says. "I think you should take this immediately."

"Put him through."

"Geoffrey?" Tony says. "There's a massive problem."

"A problem?"

"I mean it, Geoffrey. We have an absolute disaster on our hands."

"Tony, what's wrong? Everything was perfect when we spoke a few hours ago."

"Well," he says, "let me tell you what's happened since then. We all get on board, we're sitting around the pool. Then the engines are started. Geoffrey . . . have you actually been on this ship?"

"Have I been on the ship, of course I've been on the ship!"

"Have you ever been on it when it was *moving*?"

"Well, come to think of it . . . I can't say that I have."

"Well, I don't think anyone's started this thing for about fifty years. The engine started up, and this black puff went up in the sky from the funnel, just like a mushroom cloud in Hiroshima. It dropped on them all! It was like a minstrel show! All you could see were their eyes. Everyone was black, Geoff! Completely black!"

I set the phone down on my desk and wrung my forehead.

"Geoffrey! Geoffrey, are you there?"

"I'm here."

"We're all covered in this horrible oily soot that sticks to you—"

"Get everyone cleaned up and off the ship—"

"That would be an excellent strategy," he says, "except there's a problem with the plumbing on the ship."

"What kind of problem with the plumbing?"

"Well, just for example, none of the loos work."

"What do you mean none of the loos work?"

"I mean, Geoffrey, that the *toilets don't flush*."

"So what have you done?"

"The only thing I could do! In the kitchen, the chef had these old empty cans for sliced pineapple, so I set them next to every loo, and I made a little sign: 'Please could you place your toilet paper in these tins?' It's a disgrace, Geoffrey."

More wringing of the forehead, a sigh. "I'll think of a solution."

"The only solution is to fly all these people back to New York, right now, and figure out something else. Trust me: this is a disaster."

Scrambling, my staff in the Unites States hurries to book flights home for the Big Apple Billionaire and all his friends, and we process their refunds immediately. "When Abercrombie & Kent build our own river cruise ship on the Nile," I write to them, "we pledge that you'll be the first guests to depart on it."

We *will* build our own ship, I vow, because we'd sold out the *Memnon* cruise in one go. I'd hit on an idea people wanted, and I had to improve upon my original plan before any of my competitors did.

I hire a native Egyptian boat maker to design a ship I'll name the *Sun Boat*—an homage to the Sun God, Ra, and a boat that will be superior to any other boat that's ever touched the Nile. We design the rooms to provide panoramic views of the riverbank and its palm trees, and the common areas of the ship will contain gorgeous marble detailing. And it will be the first-ever small ship on the Nile with a swimming pool.

The Managing Director of A&K Egypt flies to my home in Florida with a made-to-measure model of the *Sun Boat*. "Let's go outside," I tell him, leading the way. "We'll test it out in my swimming pool."

Down he crouches over the shallow end, setting the model *Sun Boat* into the gently lapping blue. He rises and stands next to me, both of us with our arms crossed to admire our vision—and then suddenly:

Glug, glug, glug, glug.

We turn to each other, dumbfounded. In approximately six

seconds, the model *Sun Boat* sinks to the bottom of the pool. "Oh, no . . ." I moan, my face buried in my hands. We both burst out laughing.

The day comes when we get the *Sun Boat* right, and instantly it's booked to full capacity. I bring in Tim Somerset Webb, who proved himself to the company in a Saudi Arabia endeavor, to oversee our Egypt office and to staff the boat with the best hospitality workers that we can find in that country.

Our premiere cruise, of course, is for the Big Apple Banker and his forgiving group of friends, who are the first to experience Egypt as no one ever has. Clients from the United Kingdom and the rest of Europe book cruises as well, knowing they have just one short flight from their metropolitan area to Cairo before we pick them up on our own buses and drive them to the ship for four days on board and sightseeing on land.

Sun Boat I is such a success that we go on to build an award-winning fleet of luxury cruise ships on the Nile, *Sun Boat II*, *III*, and *IV*. The start of A&K Egypt was more perplexing than the construction of the Pyramids, but soon grows to eight offices throughout Egypt and quickly becomes our most profitable division.

Chapter 7

Southern Sudan

1975

I n the late 1970s, when Heath Manning, my friend through polo from North Carolina, plans a honeymoon with his delightful bride, Bootsie, the game changes for our business.

Heath asks me to accompany him and Bootsie to a place in Africa that is home to wildlife unlike anywhere else. With its vast virgin plains of high grass and its unspoiled habitat for big game of many kinds, southern Sudan is one of the best places in the world.

Sudan has a complicated history of conflict. Heath and Bootsie will almost certainly risk running into complications from civil unrest in the country, and I agree to go as their companion to ensure their safe journey. I bring along Liam Lyn, who trained for nearly a decade to track wildlife in East Africa. Liam served as a guide for such figures as Henry Ford and Roy Chapin of American

---

One of my campsites in the southern Sudan on the way to Juba.

Motors, and he knows every animal in East Africa. He knows where every water hole is and how to approach every elephant, buffalo, lion, and antelope. He knows every bird and every plant in Southern Sudan, as well as those in Ethiopia, Kenya, Tanzania, Zambia, and Botswana.

When we arrive at our destination, I learn that the company that previously brought in most of southern Sudan's travellers has had complications with its license, and Michael Wal, the governor of the Southern Sudanese Regional Development Corporation, says that I can bring my friends in if my company takes over the license. Intent on satisfying Heath and Bootsie's travel plans, I work fast. Then I quickly issue permits to my two newlywed guests.

Unfortunately, this is the last easy transaction ever to happen between the Sudanese government and me. Although we are the first safari company to host an Off the Beaten Track Safari in Sudan—that is, a safari minus hunting—and I want to build tourism by encouraging travellers to "shoot with a camera, not with a gun," it is I who am nearly shot down.

On January 4, 1975, our two Land Rovers set out on the dusty road that runs north out of Nairobi, then passes the length of Uganda to the west and enters southern Sudan. We drive six hundred miles through a spectacular landscape of desert, dry riverbeds, acacia trees, and seas of thick blond grass. Unfortunately, the glorious scenery makes for no easy passage: Our road is no more than a track, with two furrows running along it made by the rare set of tires that come this way. Occasionally the track disappears altogether, obliterated by cattle winding their way to nearby water holes. In some places we have to drive across riverbeds—sometimes sloshing through water, sometimes forging over the hard, dried mud made from the ridiculous heat of this place.

We lose the track at several points, then manage to regain it. Eventually we cross the border from northwest Kenya at Lokichoggio into southern Sudan, in Turkana country. The officer at the drive-through customs checkpoint in Kapoeta is young and intense. I step out of my Land Rover to communicate my authority and greet him in Swahili.

In his long fingers he accepts my passport, then Heath's, looks them over briefly, nods, and returns each to its owner. When he receives Bootsie's passport, he glances it over and moves a step closer to the truck. Through the rear passenger window, he stares into her face carefully. When Bootsie shoots me an unsettled look, I ask him, "Is there a problem?"

He keeps his eyes on Bootsie. "She's wearing a ring and sitting with a man named Manning, but her name here is different. How do I know this woman is not a spy for the CIA?"

I explain that she's not a spy, she's a newlywed wife carrying an old passport. The officer apologizes and shrugs, telling me he's just doing his job. He hands Bootsie her passport and permits us to go onward.

A few hours on as night falls, Liam tells me he's concerned. "Slow down here, Geoff," he says. "I think somewhere we took a wrong turn."

"We've gone a hundred miles since Kapoeta. When did that happen?"

"I'm not sure, but I'd prefer to work it out before the night is black."

Suddenly the headlights of my Land Rover light up a band of human figures walking ahead of us in the same direction. "Bloody hell," I whisper, knowing what we've encountered. "Dinka warriors."

"Oh dear," Liam says quietly. "In full battle gear." He's right: these warriors are carrying spears, machetes, and knives, and are wearing nothing but armlets and white paint from knee to thigh. Extremely tall and thin, and with distinctive features, the Dinka are a tribe of pastoral nomads who inhabit the region along the White Nile River in Sudan.

"How many do you reckon there are?" Liam asks.

"There've got to be about fifty of them."

"Jesus." Just then one of them emerges from somewhere ahead of the phalanx. He presents himself in the headlights.

"Talk to him," Liam says.

"I don't know what they speak," I tell him.

"Try Swahili!" he says. "Try anything!"

I pull the Land Rover next to the men and greet their leader in Swahili. Right away it's clear he doesn't understand, but I continue, using hand gestures to try to express that we've somehow gotten turned around.

"Come," he says.

"What do we do?" mumbles Liam.

"We have no choice."

The leader instructs his band to move on through the high grass. We follow slowly, very slowly, the way ahead obstructed by high grass, thornbushes, and the limbs of fallen trees. In the dark, I shift my gaze frequently to my rearview mirror, checking constantly to make sure our two succeeding vehicles stay with us.

We proceed for an hour—an hour so intense that I barely breathe. Finally, we find that the Dinka have led us back to the main track. I pull up next to them and thank them, presenting the leader with something my father taught me always to carry when travelling in the wilder parts of Africa: a tin of tobacco. He accepts it, very well pleased.

I put the truck back in first gear and move onward, again ensuring our group is on my tail. Just as I sense Liam relaxing for the first time since daylight, there's a thud at the back of our vehicle. The Dinka are back around us, very aggressive, trying to force their way into our trucks. Some of them have out their knives, and some are ripping the canvas canopies of our trucks with their spears. We lock all the doors, rev up the engines, and speed off up the track. Some of the Dinka stay clinging to the roof and sides of the trucks, and some are still trying to get in at the back. Liam forces them off with the butt of his gun as I plow through the ones who have made a human barrier at my bumper. Our trucks roar up through the jungle, crashing over bushes and into trees and bushes overhanging the main track. We go a good ten miles, finally stopping and circling the trucks around a flat space where we put our sleeping bags and build a fire. "Hot dog, Heathy!" Bootsie whispers. "This is some honeymoon!"

Actually no one sleeps that night, or for much of the trip thereafter. Bootsie comes down with food poisoning so severe that her lips turn purple—I never tell Heath, but I'm afraid she might die. We cover her with ice, which seems to help a good deal. We leave and drive farther into Sudan, but the journey only gets worse. The grasslands give way to the dried-up, rutted swampland that the local tribes call the *sudd*. This unpleasant terrain gives off an even more unpleasant smell, fetid and pervasive. By the time we finally return to Nairobi a week later, I realize that the nearly two thousand miles we've travelled have caused my eyes to close up from constant exposure to dust, wind, and sun.

But with a little refining, the trip evolves into a proper adventure. I develop my own camp at Rajef under a big fig tree on a rise about fifteen feet high overlooking the Nile. Michael Wal and his government officials come around for meetings frequently, and the success of the Abercrombie & Kent safari catches the national Sudanese government's attention.

Unfortunately, however, the attention is not all good. In 1979, I'm in Las Vegas at a travel convention when suddenly one of the convention workers approaches me. "Mr. Kent," she says. "I had instructions to deliver this telex to you urgently."

I flip open the envelope and unfold the letter inside.

A traditional village in southern Sudan, with dwellings made of thatch and mud just as the inhabitants' forefathers had built for centuries.

To: Geoffrey Kent
From: Michael Wal, Southern Sudanese
Regional Development Corporation—Governor

Mr. Geoffrey Kent:
We have imprisoned and put under camp arrest all of your
twenty-seven clients which include Lee Radziwill, the Dupont
family and others. We demand your personal presence here
immediately. Do not send anybody to negotiate on your behalf.

I take off to my hotel room and call my lawyer in Nairobi. "My God, what's this about?" I ask him.

"Don't go, Geoff," he says.

"Don't go?!"

"Geoff, if you go, you're finished."

"I have to go," I tell him. I phone my pilot, Jim Stewart, in Kenya. "Jim, I'm coming home from Vegas. I've got to get to the Sudan. Get my Piper Aztec ready and get permission to land in Juba."

"Word's out, Geoff," he says. "Everywhere. They've surrounded all the camps with soldiers from the Sudanese army ... and they want you. Geoff," he says, "I wouldn't go."

"I've got twenty-seven clients from all around the world surrounded by weapons. I have to go!"

"Then let me put it to you this way," he says. "I'm not going."

"You work for me!"

"I resign."

"Jesus!"

I fly to Nairobi and charter a plane and land a day later in southern Sudan. When I reach the bottom of the plane stairs, I'm surrounded by soldiers, and suddenly I remember an old African saying: *When two bull elephants fight, the only thing that gets hurt is the grass under their feet.* It means that when two powerful people argue, they put the well-being of others on the line.

I take a deep breath and vow to resolve this whole thing with as much poise as I possibly can. "I received a telex from Michael Wal," I tell the soldiers, my hair and jacket thrashing about in the wind. They stare at me, motionless, as though there's further need for me to explain what I'm doing. "He told me to come here on my own."

They frisk me, lifting my passport from my inside jacket pocket. Then escort me to a jail compound in Juba, surrounded by a troop of soldiers in our truck holding rifles across their knees. I spend the night in a stale, dank cell, wondering how on earth I'll fix this when I haven't even got a phone.

I am unshaven and shaken up—utterly disheveled—when Michael Wal appears in the doorway of my cell the next morning. A guide slides open the gate and Michael leans his body against it. "Geoffrey," he says with a sigh. He searches the floor weakly for an answer. "This is very bad, Geoffrey."

"Michael," I start . . . but we both know it's useless.

"For twenty-two years," he says, "before you took over the safari licenses, there was a man in Khartoum—"

"Mohammed Osman." I know where this is going—he's referring to the man in Khartoum who held the permits for safari-goers, who received all the revenues from those permits.

"Osman, that's right," Michael says. "Osman has created a bit of a mess with the government. They want more money."

"It's not his money—"

"There's more, Geoff. The radios. You knew bringing radios into your camp was against the law. Now the government here believes you're with the CIA."

I knew bringing radios in was against Sudanese regulations, but I decided to risk it because we couldn't operate the camps without them. "There's no way to communicate without the radios," I explain.

"I'm not the one you have to convince."

"Michael, it's got to be more than the radios . . . this has got to be about money."

He sighs. "Yeah, Geoff, it's about money. Everything's about money."

"Well? What's this going to cost?"

He shakes his head. "I don't know, Geoff," he says. "I'll find out." With his hands in his pockets, he pushes off from against the sliding gate of my cell. He turns and walks out, his footsteps on the concrete my only farewell.

The next morning, I glance up at the entrance of my cell when a figure casts a shadow across the floor. "Four hundred thousand dollars for the Regional Development Corporation [RDC]," he tells me.

"Okay," I tell him. "Okay." I stand, energized by the prospect of a solution. "First of all, I want to be released from this jail. I want to go to my camp on the Nile, and I want to sit under my big fig tree and sort all this out."

"We'll put soldiers around you."

"Put the whole army around me if you have to!"

He stuffs his hands inside his pockets. He's growing impatient.

"Then here's what I want next: I want you to let each client out one by one—all twenty-seven. For each one I'll get a cashier's check given to you. I'll send my plane back and forth carrying a cashier's check to pay the RDC for each camp. Now: In the main camp there's a guy called Charles McConnell—he works for me. Let Charlie go before you let me go."

"Fine."

Over the next few days, they release my guests. One by one, they step out the front door, squinting in the blaring sunlight. The pilot gives me a cashier's check, which I hand to Michael Wal. Then the guests board the plane and fly to Nairobi, from where they connect to flights home.

Finally, after a few days, there's only me. With one hundred thousand dollars left to pay, Michael takes notes as I explain the logistics for the final tradeoff.

"I'll have my plane fly in. Somewhere in that plane will be the final cashier's check—but it will be hidden. Even if you go in there, Michael, you won't be able to find it. Are you still there?"

"I'm here."

"Good. I will stand at the end of the runway, by the big eucalyptus trees—my pilot won't taxi in. You're going to drive me out, with my passport. Then I'm going to get in the plane, I'm going to open the door, pass you the check, and you're going to hand me my passport. And then I'm going to go as fast as I can."

"That simple, eh, Geoff?"

"If you shoot me down," I say, standing down his tongue-in-cheekness, "I've briefed the whole world about this, you understand? It wouldn't be good for you or your country. What do you think?"

"Fine," he says. "Done."

Two days later, the Piper Aztec flies in and stops at the end of the runway. I sit in a truck surrounded by six soldiers, and a driver takes me out. Four soldiers and Michael Wal accompany me as I climb on board the plane. My pilot stares straight ahead, white as a sheet.

I open the window hatch to chat to Michael. "So this is it," Michael says. "Where's the money?"

Fast, the pilot leans over with an old-fashioned razor and cuts open the upholstery of the passenger's seat. He pulls out an envelope and hands it to me, and I pass it through the small window to Michael. "We're all square," I tell him.

"What?"

Then I shut the window of the Piper Aztec so fast it nearly clips his hand. I turn to the pilot. "Balls to the firewall!"

The pilot takes off, right over the eucalyptus trees. I hold my breath and then heave a massive sigh of relief.

That was a near one.

Chapter 8

Saudi Arabia

1975

Following the shakedown in Juba, I decide that it's high time I broaden my business beyond safaris—but doing so to the scale I want will require some serious cash.

Louis Pasteur said that chance favors the prepared mind, and by the late 1970s, it's Saudi Arabia, not some tropical vacation destination, that changes the course for Abercrombie & Kent. Companies related to the oil industry are moving in, and their thousands of workers need someone to make the experience there livable.

That's where I come in: Geoffrey Kent, travel entrepreneur and soon-to-be premier purveyor of desert housing, ice cream, and mobile latrines. When the opportunity comes, I have to recognize the truth: my goal in life is to build a successful company—not just a successful safari company. By the time we're completely up and running in Riyadh, we're highly successful indeed.

I'm sipping coffee at KenCo, the Kenyan coffee shop just down the street from my office in Nairobi, where I always take

Nabatean Tomb in Mada'in Saleh, Saudi Arabia. The tombs are beautifully adorned with intricate designs along entryways and in the curves of the rock.

a morning break. In *Time* magazine, there's an article about a mass of ships stretching out miles into the Red Sea, waiting to dock at Jeddah. They are sitting idle and full of materials that international companies need to come in, to build up and get in on the impending oil boom.

All these companies—run by Americans, British, and Europeans—have won their contracts but are paying hundreds of millions of dollars in penalties for nonperformance because they can't start work; all their equipment is stuck at sea. The port city of Jeddah is developing swiftly, but Riyadh, the capital, has only a small commercial airport and one five-star hotel, the InterContinental, that costs five hundred dollars per night for a room.

Some companies have shipped portable cabin-type housing, which is, of course, stuck at sea, and for hundreds of expatriates who are simply looking to make a good living, the prospect of getting up and running, let alone living comfortably, looks pretty dire.

While I was generating business at my safari camp Rajef in Sudan, I'd made a nice sum of side money when I provided Chevron with a custom-designed version of my safari tents to house their helicopter pilots working on an operation in south Sudan. Now I get thinking: Why don't I develop air-conditioned tents that these companies could fly in? Then they could start work right away, and they wouldn't have all these long shipping delays.

From Nairobi I fly to the United States and set up a meeting with John Daus at Anchor Industries, a tent maker in Evansville, Indiana. We spend a week designing a tent made of heavy material that can be air-conditioned, with the gauze on its windows covered with a white, flexible Perspex acrylic sheet that can be rolled down and up.

Inside we put a proper toilet, an electric-powered shower, and an air conditioner that converts to a heater for use in the cold desert winters. After a month, we put the tent up in our garden in Oak Brook, just outside Chicago: simply beautiful, all lovely light sky-blue on the inside and white on the outside to deflect the sun. Jorie helps move my things into the yard for me to live in the tent, and after a month, I'm sold: I've got to get this to Saudi Arabia. Lord William Coleridge, an old friend who was a very tough paratrooper in our British Army days, flies with me to Riyadh. Immediately we buy a GMC truck and drive into the desert, away from the highways, into an area that's completely isolated. "What about here?"

Bill scans around. "Looks good to me."

We sleep in the tent, waking at five o'clock every morning to dress in our distinguished army blazers and drive an hour into Riyadh for breakfast at the InterContinental hotel—a prime networking opportunity. One morning during our first week there, we get to chatting with an American from Bechtel Corporation, one of the biggest construction companies in the United States. Bill shoots me a look to urge me on. This is our chance. "What do you think of the hotel?" I ask him. "Do you like your room here?"

"It's all right," he says, "but it's *really* expensive!"

"Come have a coffee with us," Bill says. "We'll treat you to breakfast."

"You're having problems with your laborers, right?" I ask.

"These guys can't even start, their housing is stuck at sea!"

Bill and I exchange another glance. "You know what," I tell him casually, "we might have a solution for you. Would you come out with us?"

Within seconds we pay for our breakfast and head toward the door. "Let's go." We trundle out into the desert and when we reach our makeshift camp, he gets out of our truck and marvels at the sight. "Go on," I tell him. "Have a look around."

"If you like," Bill says, "you're welcome to spend a night or two."

"I don't need to spend a night," he says. "I can already tell, this is just what we need. Can you guys do us a spec for a one-thousand-man camp?"

Bill looks at me.

"Sure," I tell him. "Give us a couple of days."

We give him a quote for the tents, for us to hire staff to erect them, for the furniture fitting, and for us to manage the operation with laborers and catering. Within days, we have a deal for one and a half million dollars—as well as a lot of work on our hands.

I run a job advertisement in the *Times* of London and hire a guy named Tim Somerset Webb to be the operations manager, reporting to Bill Coleridge, since I'll now be constantly flying between Nairobi, London, Chicago, and Saudi Arabia. Tim is sharp and likeable, and he and Bill work like dogs in the 115-degree desert heat to erect the tents for Bechtel. With our first payment, Tim and Bill rent a villa in Riyadh—a humble sort of thing, with three bedrooms, a kitchen, a sitting area, and a space out front to park our trucks.

One day Tim takes off for a weekend at Layla Lakes, a two-hour drive south of Riyadh where the waterskiing and camping are excellent. He's pulled over by the police on his way, and when they discover a bottle of homemade wine in his possession, he's jailed and sentenced to a flogging. It costs us twenty thousand dollars to bail him out.

One night back at our villa in Riyadh, we're sweating; Bill and I are preparing for meetings in London while Tim takes a break to sit back and watch the ceiling fan spin. Then he looks at us and says, "This place is like an oven. You know something?"

I keep working. "Hm?"

"I miss home."

In my peripheral vision, I see Bill lift his head for my reaction. My eyes stay on my work.

"Here, there's no women, no drink . . . for God's sake, *Geoff* almost got arrested for bringing a bloody ham sandwich through immigration—"

I sit back, finally in for the ride.

"You know what I really miss?" Tim says.

"Hm?"

"Ice cream."

"Ice cream . . ." Bill sighs.

"Think about it: they're about to become one of the richest countries in the world, and they haven't even got ice cream. Why isn't there ice cream?"

We all three stare at the ceiling fan, caught in the fantasy.

Finally, Bill breaks the silence. "I suppose you can't get ice cream in on ships that are stuck in the middle of the bloody ocean."

The next day when I land at Heathrow, the answer hits me just a few minutes away from my office in Sloane Square. As my taxi rolls along, I spot a Bedford van stopped just outside the gates of Hyde Park. "Stop the taxi," I tell my driver.

"Pardon?"

"Please. Stop the taxi." I climb out and jog across the street, digging a pound out of my pocket. "I sure would love an ice cream," I tell the man in the van.

"Certainly." He pumps me a cone, turns to me out the window. "Fifteen pence, please."

"How does this ice cream work, anyway?"

"Sorry?"

"It's not frozen blocks of ice cream. How does it work?"

"No, sir," he says, "this is a special type of ice cream made just for the vans. We buy the liquid, and we freeze it here in the van."

"You buy the liquid . . ." My plan is beginning to gel.

"It comes in a Tetra Pak, but it's a liquid, like milk. Then it's frozen through the machine, and we squeeze it onto the cones."

"Can you ship this stuff?"

"I can't imagine why not."

"What's the name of the company that makes it?"

"Comelle."

I fly into my office and call Bill in Riyadh. "I want to buy ten Bedford vans."

"Okay . . ."

"And rent the flat next door to the villa, just to park all the vans. Let's get this moving right away." I contact Comelle and place an order for the ice cream, and, after some discussion, they agree to grant me a fifteen-year exclusive license to sell Comelle ice cream in Saudi Arabia.

I hire an ice cream van driver from London and pay him three times his salary. We open with just three trucks in Riyadh's city squares, just to test the market, but by the first week, the lines at all of the trucks wind around the corners and down the streets, and all the locals are reaching into their *abaya*s and *thobe*s to pay three riyals—one dollar—for a cone that costs us just twenty-five cents to produce.

When all ten vans are in operation, we buy fifteen more, and when they're all turning a profit, we buy twenty-five more to open up shop in Jeddah. The mayor of Riyadh phones me. "I want to buy these ice cream trucks from you," he says.

"Not a chance," I tell him. This is my most lucrative cash business to date.

But then, within days, the police of Riyadh are tracking us, pinning us with fines that put a significant pinch on profits. I call the mayor. "You want to buy these trucks?" I ask him.

"Yes."

"Then we'll do this my way." I sell him the business, making a good profit off the vans, and I maintain my license as the sole distributor of Comelle in Saudi Arabia. That is, if the mayor of Riyadh wants to continue selling ice cream, then he has to continue to buy the ice cream—from me.

By 1977, Bill, Tim, and I have been supplying housing and running camps for three years. Saudi Arabia is building up like mad, and we're known around the camps as the good ol' boys. One day, the three of us are inside our truck, and Bill looks out the window. "Everybody's working now, but look at these laborers. They're going to the toilet in the middle of the streets."

"You know," I tell him, "I've been reading. There's something new that's come out—they're actually going to have mobile latrines."

"A mobile loo?!"

"That's right."

"That would be fantastic out here," Tim says. "We'd make a fortune selling those!"

I work fast to book a flight to Chicago. When my plane lands at O'Hare, I book a taxi, and again, I spot exactly what I'm looking for on the way to my office. "Stop the taxi."

"Sorry, sir?"

"I said stop here. Please."

I jump out and run to a construction site that has an aqua-blue pillbox standing tall on its perimeter. "Excuse me!" I call to the foreman. "I've just landed and drank far too much coffee on the flight. Could I possibly use your toilet?"

"Sure," he says. "Help yourself."

I slam the door and look around frantically—there has to be a manufacturer listed somewhere. Then, I spot it: *Satellite Industries, Minneapolis, Minnesota*. I write it on my pad, with the number.

I test the toilet: When I flush, the chemical whirls down. A little lock flips up, I walk out, job done. "How does this work?" I call to the foreman.

He jogs over. "There's a holding tank. We have a contract with the company, we lease these, and then three times a week they come and pump out the sewage."

"Genius," I tell him.

"Yeah, a real relief, right?"

I call Satellite Industries and ask for the owner. "Al Hilde's my name!" he says. "You say you've just come from Saudi Arabia?"

"Indeed I have—"

"Wowee! What's it like—I heard they cut off people's heads there!"

"Yeah, they do," I tell him. "Every Friday."

"I heard they cut your arms off too, is that true?"

"Yes, also on Fridays."

"Wow! I don't think I want to go near that place! No way!"

"Well, you wouldn't have to, but there's a need for these portaloos, and I want to license them from you."

"Let's talk about it, but you've gotta understand: these are my babies! I wouldn't license these to just any old cowboy, Mr. Kent. I have to train you. You've gotta learn how to pump them right!"

Bill Coleridge, Tim Somerset Webb, and I sign up for a three-day training course. There we are, graduates of the finest schools in England and the Royal Military Academy Sandhurst, wearing little round smiley-face buttons that read: *Satellite Industries: Give Us a Whirl!*

"Yeah man, give it a whirl!" says one of our comrades—a farmer and a Harley Davidson enthusiast from Boise, Idaho.

"Tim, how did your whirl go?" I ask in my most educated English accent. "I'm afraid I didn't *whirl* very *well.*"

"What's wrong with you lot?" Bill says. "Why aren't you just whirling like everybody else is whirling? Go on, guys, give it another whirl!"

The exam is a written one, and it is actually very difficult, but when all three of us pass, Al Hilde tells us to saddle up in high rubber boots and gloves. "Okay, fellas," he says. "Today we're gonna learn how to understand the product!"

"Product?" Bill Coleridge says. "Hell, it's crap."

"Don't you ever say that word again!" Al Hilde says.

"What, 'hell'?"

"No! 'Crap'! I don't ever want to hear 'crap' or 'shit,' or 'shyte' or even 'porta-potty' outta your mouth again! Do you understand?"

Bill places his hands on his hips. "So what do we call it then?"

"You call it"—Al Hilde primes his lips for perfect pronunciation—" 'effluent.' "

" 'Effluent.' "

"Effluent."

Bill gives me the look of death. "Fine," he says. "Effluent."

We pass the final stage of training, purchase one hundred units, and buy three pump trucks to ship to Saudi Arabia. "Enough with your city streets being filled with people's waste," I tell the mayor. "We'll supply all job sites with these loos, and we'll be the ones responsible for cleaning up after them."

"I won't allow any company to come in and build unless they've signed a contract to host one of your loos on their site," he says. "It's perfect."

The next year, it becomes even more perfect: Waste Management, a company based in Oak Brook, Illinois, buys our mobile latrine business for enough money to do what I really want to do next: enlarge our travel business in the United States.

There's no question that Saudi Arabia remains a very important location for the world's economy, culture, and religion, among other concerns—not the least of them, travel. In 2004, three decades after my first, shall we say, "enterprise" there, His Royal Highness Sultan bin Salman Al Saud, the head of Saudi Arabia's tourism authority, contacts me to see how I might bring travel there. I fly in for meetings, and meet my guide, Keith Sproule.

We travel all the way to the north of the country, where Saudi Arabia borders with Jordan, to explore the caves of Madain Saleh—and on the way there, we drive through the holy city of Medina which is one of the holiest sites in the world for Muslims, second only to Mecca. We're surrounded by security. "This site is virtually off-limits to infidels," Keith explains, "but His Royal Highness Prince Sultan has arranged for us to have access to it.

Remembering that Prince Charles is enamored with Islamic architecture, I call him from inside the courtyard of the mosque. "You'll never believe where I am, sir," I tell him, and when I reveal my location, immediately he knows it, recalling that the original was designed by the Prophet Muhammad.

"Is the minaret that beautiful blue color, as it always appears in photos?" Prince Charles asks me.

We all look up and, sure enough, it is.

I'm not the biggest fan of across-desert trips—overnight in the desert, anything can go wrong—but my time in the Middle East has given me a special kind of admiration for this region of the world. The sand dunes in Abu Dhabi and Dubai are gorgeous, and the falcons and Arabian horses are all very interesting. I've also made a visit to Jordan and Israel, travelling the same forty-mile route on camel in Jordan as Peter O'Toole did in *Lawrence of Arabia* (to note another early 1960s film that glorifies the wonder of the Middle East), between timeless Wadi Rum (or the granite-and-sandstone "Valley of the Moon") and Aqaba.

I've also toured Israel and its antiquities, even getting a special opening of the room where Jesus held the Last Supper. That was an amazing trip—we held banquets in the desert for dinner, slept in tents along the way, and sang under the stars at night.

The travel experiences of the Middle East are treasures, and it is a place that I find critical for Westerners to visit. I feel very strongly that if more world leaders and decision makers travelled there, there would be less conflict in the world. When we witness with our own eyes the everyday life of people who seem very different from us, we gain an appreciation for them . . . and often find that they are not so different at all.

Canopy detail of the Mosque, Al-Masjid an-Nabawi.
FOLLOWING PAGE: *Al-Masjid an-Nabawi, the Mosque of the Prophet, in Medina. The prayer hall can accommodate more than a half million worshippers.*

Chapter 9

India

✧✧✧✧✧

1979

There are circles of my friends who barely think of me as a travel executive—to them, I'm better known for my forty-year career in amateur polo. At Prince William's wedding in 2011, I approached Prince Philip to say hello and congratulate him on the marriage of his grandson. He asked me, "Geoffrey, are you still playing polo?"

"I'm not, sir," I told him. "I had a rather bad injury a few years back."

"Well, everyone gets hurt playing polo," he said. "Are you still selling those ridiculously priced safari holidays of yours, then?"

We had a good laugh—me even more than him. Here was the boy from Kenya who in his Sandhurst days had arrived at the Guards Polo Club to lease ponies at ten pounds a chukka because he didn't have the budget to ride his own horses—who then went on to captain the Windsor Park Polo Team when Prince Philip's son, His Royal Highness the Prince of Wales, revived the team in 1987.

My polo friends contribute to my career significantly. In 1969, I play in Nairobi with Jai Singh, known among society and royal circles as Joey Jaipur. Joey's brother Bhawani Singh

---

The fabled Taj Mahal in Agra, built by the Mughal Emperor Shah Jahan to express his undying love.

(known to us as "Bubbles") is the Maharaja—the prince—of Jaipur. Joey and I get on brilliantly and, sincerely supportive of what I'm working to accomplish, he introduces me to an Englishman named Jim Edwards. Jim has just opened a lodge in Nepal and is hopeful I can help him brainstorm some marketing plans to attract clientele.

On visiting his lodge, I see the attraction. It's irresistible, easily one of the friendliest, most uniquely beautiful, and vibrant places either of us has ever been. I want in—but to penetrate this area and bring in Western travellers will require us to create a new standard in tourism. Clients need to sense that even if they feel worlds away from home, they're close to a source of help for whatever they might need. We establish Abercrombie & Kent India to accomplish this in India and Nepal.

◇◇◇◇

"Elephant polo?"

"Elephant polo!" Jim Edwards is high energy over drinks in central London. We discuss how to create a spectacle that will get worldwide publicity and draw people to Nepal and his Tiger Tops Jungle Lodge, where guests arrive riding elephants to sleep among the tigers inside rooms built up on stilts. "It won't actually be competitive, Geoff, it's for amusement—think tourism, charity. It will attract fantastic attention."

Jim Edwards admits he's never touched a polo mallet, but I have—and I see great opportunity here. Nepal is a market that's relatively underexposed, as it opened for tourism only in the early 1950s. For some time now, I've had my feelers out for the right way in.

"You'll come and stay at Tiger Tops," Jim says. "There's nothing in the world like it. You'll play some polo, teach me a bit of the game, and make a few new friends. You'll see for yourself how attractive India and Nepal are. Soon Tiger Tops will be a world-famous lodge where you bring your clients," he leans in to the table and narrows his eyes, "and we both make a *lot* of money."

I lean back in my chair, observing how the stars are lining up. Last year, in 1978, my team won the US Open in polo, and ever since, I've received a number of invitations to play polo in India, where the game is a national sport. Joey Jaipur once insisted that if I ever came to India, I'd stay with his step-mother, the Princess Gayatri Devi—better known as Maharani Ayesha—whose husband, the prince, died in 1970.

After my meeting with Jim Edwards, I phone Joey Jaipur. He's enthusiastic to schedule polo games in Jaipur and Delhi and make the arrangements for me to stay at the guesthouse of Ayesha's hideaway mansion called Lilypool, adjacent to Rambagh Palace in Jaipur.

The offer seems surreal: Princess Ayesha is a living legend. She was born in London to royalty from another Indian state, and was a spirited child who was said to be the most beautiful girl in the world. A bit of a tomboy, she captured the heart of the Maharaja of Jaipur when he was twenty-one and already had two wives and two sons. At the time, Ayesha was just twelve.

Her mother and grandmother, both rather progressive Maharanis, worried that if she married the Maharaja, Ayesha would become secluded from society life. She proved them very wrong when she cultivated famously close friendships with some of the world's leading women, such as Queen Elizabeth II and Jacqueline Kennedy.

On my first morning in Jaipur when I arrive for breakfast on her patio next to the swimming pool, Ayesha is dressed in a bright tunic and sits before a generous breakfast spread. "It's so nice to see you again," I tell her. "What a lovely breakfast."

"Geoffrey!" she says, rising from her chair. "Lovely to see you again too." Her lips are full and painted deep violet; her eyes are dramatic. Her hair is sleek jet-black, and it skims the pearls around her neck. Her air is somehow both mysterious and friendly. "Please, sit," she says, and her cook arrives at my side at the table. "Would you get Geoffrey some chai, please?" The cook bows in response and turns inside.

Over breakfast, we chat about the many friends we have in common, all connected through our mutual love of polo. The Princess's husband was a ten-goal player—it's no wonder to me that she knows the sport so well. "It's the start of the season," she says, "you'll play while you're here, won't you, Geoffrey?"

"Yes, here and up in Delhi."

"That's what I hoped to hear."

In Delhi two days later, I find the lobby of the Taj Hotel gleaming with marble accents, gold furniture, and a row of massive chandeliers lining the center of the ceiling. The clerk at the front desk is dressed in full sari, wearing thick gold bracelets on both wrists, and her hair is pulled back, elegant and smooth. "Mr. Kent," she greets me with a subtle accent and a bow. "We've arranged the house car for your stay."

She gestures toward the front door, where I turn to find a gorgeous Mercedes sitting outside. Ayesha must have made a phone call. "The chauffeur will be here for you whenever you like," she says. "Go on and get settled, we've put you in the executive suite with a view of Humayun's tomb. You can have a look about the city any time you like."

When I enter the front portal of my suite, I find that the space is palatial, both in size and decor. Each of the walls has a unique Indian crown molding and an ornate design carved into it, with symmetrical curved cascades that rise up to a point like an exaggerated, perfect flame. Through sliding glass doors is a view of a thick tree line . . . and crowned among the trees is the white marble dome of the tomb of Humayun, the sixteenth-century ruler of the Mughal Empire, which then covered most of modern-day northern India.

I wander out onto the balcony and find a small plunge pool and a full grand garden panorama, a sprawling stretch

I played one of the best polo matches of my career in India, and here I am going for a goal.

of pure lawn and trees. I'd expected a city like Delhi to make me feel trapped within buildings, but this is one of the most serene spots on which I've ever stood.

◇◇◇◇

For the few weeks that I'm in India, luck seems to lead me. Far up north in Kashmir, known for its friendly people, I'm invited to a champagne party on a houseboat on Dal Lake. Back in Delhi, I attend the finals of the Indian Open polo championship compliments of the Maharaja of Jaipur, who is nicknamed "Bubbles" because of all the champagne that was consumed when he was born. Bubbles has gotten me a seat in the VIP spectators' box. Less than sixty seconds into the match, Colonel R. S. "Pickles" Sodhi flies off his horse and breaks his collarbone, and I'm pulled from my seat—reluctantly—to play in the tournament in front of an audience of thirty thousand. Without any changing room, the teams, officials, and grooms form a ring around me on the field, hardly the height of privacy, and pass me a variety of boots, breeches, and a helmet. Finally, I find something that fits and climb onto one of Pickles's ponies.

As much as I'd looked forward to a relaxing day of watching polo, by the end of the match, I've played one of the best games of my career: I score three goals, and we win, four goals to two. On the way out, I go to the hospital and try to hand off my trophy to Pickles Sodhi, who's being attended to by a medical team. "You won it, Geoffrey," Pickles says. "You keep it."

The first week in November, I attend the beautiful camel fair at Pushkar—something biblical. The camels, cattle, and horses traipse out, decorated and colorful as floats in a parade. Street performers entertain on the path, and everywhere I look there's something wild and new to see. When the moon rises, the Hindu women come out and walk about with beautiful pots on their heads. I camp there for three days, taking in the magnificence of the desert lights and shadows, plotting how easy it would be to market vacations to India. *Maharajas, Temples, and Tigers.* We'll be one of the companies that popularizes India and builds high-end tours here.

When I return home to the United States, I meet with Tim Somerset Webb, who's still running our Middle Eastern operation. "We've got to get into India," I tell him. "Without a doubt, it's what's next."

Tim flies out to Delhi and hustles to secure contracts with the Taj and Oberoi hotels. We design a leisure vacation that will attract Western clients in the very months they're looking to escape the cold climates at home. I score a contract with British Airways, booking our India tours—as well as our Egypt and South Africa tours—using their airline exclusively.

We're in business in the subcontinent, and within less

than a decade, our tours are generating such buzz that Prince Charles asks me to show him Nepal. We trek the Himalayas led by Gurkha troops, world-renowned warriors from Nepal who serve as our security and as our lookouts. We trek many miles through the foothills of Annapurna I, the mountain with one of the highest fatality rates in the world, and then we attempt to outdo each other's pace around Annapurna II. "I've heard that there are many people on these trails," says Prince Charles. "Where is everyone?"

"We've got Gurkha soldiers ahead of you, Sir."

The Gurkha soldiers are so brilliantly trained that even Prince Charles is stunned by their stealth. As we enter the forest as night falls, he whispers, "Where have the Gurkhas gone?" In that instant, one of the soldiers flashes his torch to demonstrate his proximity just steps ahead.

India is a charm for us throughout the industry hell that is the Gulf War—it's one of the very few destinations Westerners feel safe exploring. But our charmed streak in India ends in November 1994 when I'm driving from Orlando to Vero Beach and Tim Webb calls my car phone. "Geoff, I'm in Chicago," he says. "I've just gotten in from Delhi."

"How did it go?"

"Geoff, I have really bad news. Are you sitting down?"

"Yes, but driving."

"Geoff, you've gotta stop."

"Really?" *Shit.* I search for an exit, my nerves suddenly spiked. I move onto a wide spot on the shoulder of I-95 and turn on my flashers. "What is it?"

"There's trouble in the India office. There's been big fraud."

"Damn it. Just what I was afraid of."

"They've been embezzling, Geoff—massively. They were taking shopping commissions, they've given kickbacks left and right to travel groups and tour managers."

"How bad is it?"

Princess Diana congratulates Prince Charles and me at the Guard's Polo Club in 1987 on a victory when I was Captain of the Windsor Park Polo Team.

"Bad. We're talking hundreds of thousands—approaching a million."

Outside my windshield is flat Florida road; cars zipping by paying no mind to my worries. The world keeps turning at moments like these, which, in some way, is reassuring. I start up my engine and check my mirrors before veering back onto the interstate.

"Geoff? Are you there?"

"I'm here."

"It gets worse."

"How much worse?"

I hear a sigh through the phone, then, "Geoff, I don't know how to say this: they've burnt the office to the ground."

"*What?!*"

Again I hunt down a wide enough space on the right shoulder to peel off. The car is still running as Tim continues. "They have burnt the office to the ground, Geoff. They burnt it down and flooded it."

"Jesus, Tim!"

"All the computers, all the files. Everything. Gone. They knew they were busted, and as soon as I left, they burnt the whole thing down."

"Get ahold of the staff from that office—"

"There is no staff, Geoff. They've all walked out. They were all in on it."

I roll down my window. I can't get enough air. "Right, you and I have got to get over there immediately. This is the start of the high season, everyone arrives for their Christmas holiday in two weeks. We have to send messages—where?"

"To the London, Chicago, and Australia offices."

"Good. Send messages asking for the names of the groups, the travellers, the itineraries, everything. Get a new team, get them set up in a new office. Work backwards from these itineraries. Did the India office cancel any of the room nights in the hotels?"

"No, I already checked. All the rooms are still booked."

Tim sets up desks in the lobbies of the Oberoi and the Taj Palace hotels and works with the bell desks to funnel all Abercrombie & Kent clients to that desk. He pleasantly explains to our clients that there's been a small accident in our office, and, single-handedly, he manages to salvage the trips.

In January, after the Christmas rush has slowed down, I call him up. "We've worked it up: in the end, the whole debacle cost us three hundred thousand, but it could have been a lot worse, Tim. Well done. Now there's just one thing left to do."

My wife, Otavia, and I were guests at the wedding of Prince William and Catherine Middleton, and from that day forward they were to be known as the Duke and Duchess of Cambridge.

Tim's silent on the line, then: "Yes. I know." He heads to the Oberoi Hotel and enters the office of their most senior sales executive. Tim makes him an offer, and by the time he exits, we have a new managing director in our India office.

Our business in India has run high and steady ever since, thanks in large part to the fact that India tends to be one of the all-time safest destinations in the world. However, in late November 2008, a group of our clients encountered rare danger when ten terrorists set out and besieged a handful of Mumbai's major tourist hubs: cafés, train stations, and luxury hotels. For an entire day, terrified travellers in various locations across the city hid out inside their suites, listening to gunshots and grenades as 166 people—including guests and hotel staff—were killed in cold blood. While some of the hotels under attack prohibited any guests from leaving their grounds, Abercrombie & Kent's India office knew that it was crucial to lift our clients out of the chaos and set them up somewhere safe—immediately.

An Australian Abercrombie & Kent client later wrote to us: "We were evacuated at 4:00 in the morning out of our bedroom window, absolutely terrified, with flames behind us and the sounds of gunfire." Our staff had shown up firsthand to help execute their rescue. "I now understand the value of the A&K cocoon," she wrote. "As I came down the ladder in the midst of the mayhem, unbelievably I saw the yellow A&K sign and heard a voice say 'Are you with Abercrombie & Kent?' It was our guide waiting to take us away to the safety of the Four Seasons. They were the most reassuring words I have ever heard!"

Some international news reports covering the event stated that some native Indians felt devastated and ashamed that visitors had experienced such terror, but unfortunately, as we have seen in New York, Boston, London, Paris, and Copenhagen, no place in the world is safe from terrorists.

Chapter 10

China

◇◇◆◇◆◇

1979

In the late 1970s, when the Cultural Revolution in China ends, I'm attracted to China as clearly things are going to change in a big way.

I'm in Nairobi, having coffee at the Thorn Tree Restaurant, when I read in the *East African Standard* about a pro-Communist group in Ethiopia offering Ethiopian citizens the chance to visit China. I run across the street to my office and book a flight to Ethiopia's capital, Addis Ababa, and stand before the tourist board a couple of weeks later. "I want to join your tour to China," I tell them.

Their response, naturally, is, "But you're not Ethiopian."

I'm prepared. "But I am, in a way," I tell them. "My sister was born here, in Addis." From an envelope I pull out her birth certificate and let them pass it down the table.

The chief of the tourism board glances at the certificate and asks me to excuse myself for a few minutes. When they ask me to reenter, he tells me, "We've decided to give you an Ethiopian visa to travel to China." On the spot I write them a check for the visa and then book our flights—Jorie's and mine—to Hong Kong. Because I know that no other travel executive has spent

---

I was the first Western tour operator allowed to run trips in China, with tailor-made journeys for the individual traveller.

more than two weeks scouting China, I plan a sixty-seven-day reconnaissance, with the final week in Tibet—also a place explored by no more than a couple thousand travellers. The goal is to immerse ourselves in what still stands of the cities, the villages, the history, the food, and the culture of the Middle Kingdom in the wake of the Cultural Revolution—a truly historic journey.

Already from on the plane, Hong Kong is unlike anywhere else I've been. The city is a forest of buildings, and we're flying at a height well below the level of the highest floors of the skyscrapers. As we make our descent to land, my fellow passengers and I catch up-close-and-personal glances into the conference rooms of office buildings—then suddenly our wheels hit the tarmac.

In my head, I rehearse the simple note I'll make in my travel report to the company: *Hong Kong needs a new airport.*

I spend a week in meetings with new contacts like Burton Levin, the US State Department deputy principal officer, and Patrick Macleod, an old friend from the Seychelles. Rain pours from a gloomy sky as we tour the hotels and restaurants of Hong Kong, but I'm pleased that the city is civilized and thoughtfully designed to attract travellers.

The shopping is impressive as well. An antiques lover could get lost in the shops on Hollywood Road, and one afternoon I duck into King's tailors on the first floor of the Mandarin Oriental hotel for a suit and shirt made from the highest-quality English cloth available anywhere. After a week in Hong Kong, I prepare to leave to see Macao, but it's pure disappointment: a monsoon is about to sweep in, and the rain rages. Our trip to Macao is cancelled.

Apart from the weather, the next few weeks are brilliant. As we descend into the morning light of Guilin, a prefecture-level city that sits on the west bank of the Li River, I catch a glimpse of the magnificent karst scenery, where water has weathered the mountains into a landscape of sharp, rocky hills. That afternoon I board a boat for a cruise down the Li River, and my guide seats me at the front table at the very prow of the boat. "This is one of the finest excursions anyone can do in China," he says. The river is set amid jagged vertical limestone mountains that the Tang dynasty poet Han Yu immortalized with these words:

The river forms a green gauze belt,
the mountains are like blue jade hairpins.

As I lunch on chicken, rice, fish with sweet-and-sour pineapple and peppers, mushrooms, and fresh mandarin oranges, I take in the landscape—and it is exquisite. The mountains and rivers of traditional Chinese painting come to life before my eyes, and Ming Dynasty pagodas appear all along the route. There are fishermen wearing pointed wicker coolie hats and floating on bamboo rafts, people clearing river weed and collecting fodder for their pigs, and water buffalo cooling off in the lakes that lie beside the river. I gaze in front of us, to the south, at the jagged peaks of limestone rock, a summit obscured by ethereal mists.

It makes me all the more eager to reach the city of Xi'an for one of the highlights of this reconnaissance: the tomb of the first Emperor of China, Qin Shi Huang Di. The Emperor began building his tomb as soon as he came to the throne in 246 BC, and hundreds of thousands of laborers toiled to finish it before his death. My guide tells me that the Qianling Mausoleum is also worth a visit to see the tomb of Li Zhi, the third Tang Emperor and his notorious wife, the Empress Wu Ze Tian, who reigned from 649 to 683 AD. The route to the tomb, known as the Royal Way, is flanked by towers, obelisks, statues of winged horses and ostriches, ten pairs of standing statues of men with their heads lobbed off, a pair of steles, a

It's always been my dream to see China from the 5,500-mile-long Great Wall.

pair of towers, and groups of statues representing those who attended the emperor's funeral. "As yet they haven't uncovered the actual tomb," says my guide. "But one wonders what treasures they'll find when they do complete the excavation."

After a day touring the tombs in Xi'an, I'm raring for the modern life of Shanghai and its eleven million people. The afternoon that we land, we head straight for a tour of the Shanghai Hotel, which is currently the tallest building in Shanghai at twenty-six stories high. The foyer is as basic as that found in any metropolitan hotel, featuring a marble downstairs and a café and bar area. When the manager shows me up to one of the six hundred guest suites, we're met with a surprise: a pretty Chinese girl carrying her maid's uniform emerges from one of the hotel rooms for a night out on the town. She slides by us in a rush as the manager looks her over, then he shows me to the rooftop, where the view is magnificent and the setting would be perfect for a cocktail party for my clients. Then he takes me for dinner in one of the private banquet rooms, and as we eye the menu, he reveals, "In Shanghai, you have to try the Peking duck."

"Why's that?"

"Everyone here knows that Shanghai Peking duck is much better than Peking Peking duck."

He's right. In addition to the Peking duck, we order boned chicken drumsticks lightly fried, accompanied with a poached quail egg on a wheat toast round and medium-sized freshwater crabs. This is the best I've eaten in the few weeks I've been in China, and the next evening when I eat cream cakes and cream puffs and chocolate éclairs at the Peace Hotel, it's clear why Shanghai is known for its fantastic cuisine.

From Shanghai it's a short drive to Suzhou, a two-thousand-year-old city known for its artisans' wares. Our first stop is at the Suzhou Embroidery Research Institute, established in 1957 with over 300 people working in design, embroidery, and silk tapestry. As I tour the institute with the director, Madame Qian, I take note that the students are almost all university-aged women who will train for nearly a decade before they take jobs in factories or stay on as designers at the institute. They show me the projects they've worked on for the last six months: silk pieces with reverse embroidery and double-sided embroidery, delicate details, and bright color. There's a particular work of roses so well defined that I'd almost like to pick a bouquet of them right out of the fabric.

My next port of call is one of the only four sandalwood factories in all of China, at Suzhou's Northwest Street 58. Here

Sailing through the Three
Gorges on the Yangzi River—
Qutang, Wu, and Xiling—the
most celebrated natural wonder
in all of China.

they make the traditional sandalwood fans that many Chinese women carry to cool themselves.

In the shop, I observe as the workers cut out the intricate fans on their handmade fretwork saws, and in the next room, as they use a hot electric stencil to engrave the fans with images. At the end I make my way into the sculpture room, where they complete the fans and carve the handles. The whole process takes twenty days for a sandalwood fan and up to two months for an elegant ivory fan.

After my tour of Suzhou I board a boat on the Yangzi River for a cruise through the Three Gorges. I take two weeks to make my way to Beijing, allowing for plenty of time along the route to tour agricultural areas—the State Market and Free

Market in Wuxi are unique representations of how the government has assigned land to farmers, for example. After a hair-raising ride over narrow roads and small humpbacked bridges, I reach the gorgeous West Lake in Hangzou. I'd read in one of my guidebooks:

> *One of the most beautiful sights you will see in China is the sun rising over West Lake. Make an effort to rise early to see the first rays touch the lake. You will not be disappointed. The sun will disappear from time to time as the slowly receding mist lifts and is carried skyward.*

But when I wake at six thirty the next morning and look out of my hotel window across the lake, I see gray clouds diffusing themselves under a milky white sky. The branches of the willow trees sweep unwillingly toward the lake; the gentle leaves of the lily pads tousle in the wind. After a morning tour of the man-made islands on the West Lake, I beg off for Beijing, where I'm eager to visit the Forbidden City. On the flight there, however, I find myself in debilitating pain. Just as the flight crew announces we'll be making our descent, our hostess walks down the aisle serving each of us a candy. Curious to sample a Chinese-style sweet, I untwist the wrapper and tuck the small cube inside my cheek, discovering a flavor exquisitely similar to a buttery English toffee. Unable to reserve my fondness for the treat, I bite in with gusto and suddenly clench down in pain. Now I remain calm as I remove the toffee from my mouth, embedded with a gold filling that my dentist promised would never need replacing.

I wrap the gold filling in a napkin, and, upon landing and checking into my hotel, I phone the China International Travel Service to help me locate a dentist. A young man named Jimmy calls for me at the hotel and drives me to a hospital—an entirely Chinese place where the receptionist asks me to pay a deposit of one American dollar before she escorts me down a long corridor into the dentist's surgery space.

Slowly, I glance around: the curtains hang halfway off the rods, the medicine bottles—most with the caps off—are scattered on the counters, their liquid contents spilling onto the floor. The drill looks like something designed by Heath Robinson, the English cartoonist and engineering illustrator. I lean toward my guide. "Could you tell these two nurses, please, that I do not want the dentist putting any injection inside my mouth?"

"These two women *are* the dentists," he says.

"Excuse me, ladies?" I say. "I'd like to make it clear that I do not want either of you, or anyone, putting an injection of any kind inside my mouth." I pause for a moment. "Please."

Their eyes go blank over their face masks and they look toward my guide. In Mandarin, he puts forth a somewhat hesitant explanation of what I've just said, and there's a sudden explosion of argument. I observe as there are shouts, dental instruments pointed in the air like threatening pistols, arms wielding, and, at one point, I think, almost tears. "Doctors!" I shout, pulling the napkin from my back pocket. "It's only a filling!"

At once, everyone calms down. One of the dentists turns to the counter and silently begins mixing up a paste. The other points me into the chair, as if to say, *What meltdown? Please, sit.* She glides onto the wheeled stool and says something in Mandarin. I flinch as one of them clicks on the lamp over my head. Before I can crane my jaw the entire way, there's a hand rammed inside my mouth and another one jamming my new filling home. In my peripheral view, I note as a foot pedals like crazy to run the drill. "Finished," says Jimmy. "Well done, Mr. Kent."

At reception, I pay my bill: two dollars and fifty cents, American.

When I finally reach the Forbidden City, I'm enthralled

by its beautiful courts and its atmosphere of mysterious history. The sheer scale of the place with its nine courtyards is astounding, as well as the fact that in the time of the last emperor, regular people were not allowed to enter it. The China International Travel Service has arranged for us to take an incredible tour into places few people had ever been before.

The Great Wall, though, is staggering. The whole thing is built wide enough for ten horses to stand side by side on top of it. How could humans build this, with its scale and massiveness, walling off China from the nomad hordes? The whole visit is a wildly cultural experience—not my typical type of adventure, but incredibly unique nonetheless.

We spend our last morning in China touring Chengdu, the capital of Sichuan Province known for its industry, its reserves for giant pandas, and the fact that in the thirteenth century, Marco Polo noted it as a place where a young man could get very lucky with the ladies. Apart from the prospect of bringing special clients to see the pandas, we find the city rather disappointing: with its own Imperial Palace, Chengdu was once thought beautiful enough to rival Beijing, but it turns out that most of the lovely sites were destroyed during the Cultural Revolution. In the afternoon, we take to shopping, and Jorie loads up on oranges and tins of fruit, a loaf of bread, smoked oysters, pâté, and steak fillets in soy oil with chilies and a small bottle of Chinese red wine.

We rise at four in the morning for our six thirty flight to Tibet and take off, as is typical of Chinese airlines, at ten thirty a.m. After an hour in flight, we start to cross the Hengduan Mountains—nearly five miles high in one spot, and with magnificent glaciers and snow-covered peaks. Rolling clouds hover beneath the mountains in an azure sky. We snap photos and make a note to instruct clients to do the same, as this view is especially unique thanks to Tibet's position as the highest region in the world.

The sun shines marvelously, assuring us that we've made the right choice to come here, and another hour after soaring over the mountains, we spot the landscape of Tibet—desolate, as I might have predicted—crossed by the crystal-blue Yarlung Zangbo Jiang River, which is one of the sources of the great Brahmaputra River.

When we land at one thirty in the afternoon on a hard-topped strip in the town of Gongkar, the deputy director of the China International Travel Service meets us and escorts us to the Chinese Army jeep that awaits. "And our luggage?" Jorie asks.

"It will arrive in Lhasa in separate transportation," the director tells her.

Jorie shrugs and climbs into the vehicle. "Let's hope so," she says. "All my warm clothes are packed away."

Our driver, Keping, leaves the airport and moves at a steady pace until we're stopped by a roadblock. "The Chinese army is dynamiting the road," our driver says. "Trying to make it bigger for more tourists to come through."

Keping rolls down his window and yells an exchange with one of the road workers. He sighs, rolls the window back up. "I'm sorry, Mr. and Mrs. Kent," he says. "He's saying that we have to wait until eight o'clock tonight to get through."

Jorie and I look at each other and start laughing. "What else!" I cry.

"Ah," she sighs, leaning against her headrest. "At least there's fresh air," she says. "No pollution, no cigarette smoke like in China—"

"And no bus full of people that use yak butter for deodorant!" says Keping. He rolls down the window again, waves the road worker to the vehicle. They exchange more words, escalating into what sounds like a rather involved argument. Finally our driver starts the vehicle back up. "I'm going to try and get through anyway." He drives slowly as workers shove great boulders aside. "I told them I'm driving the man who's going to bring Tibet the tourists they're making these roads for!" he says.

A gang of probably fifty workers stands at the top of a hill and greets us, and we return the wave. *Drive*, I will Keping. *Keep driving.* If any of the workers above makes a wrong move, the rocks they're guarding could tumble down and crush us in a second.

The driver negotiates one more dynamite explosion and then sails on toward Lhasa, stopping at a fourteenth-century monastery for us to capture some photos of the structure, with its bright red and cobalt-blue beams, murals depicting Buddha's disciples, and a stupa containing the ashes of the monastery's founder with a gold leaf–covered statue of Buddha.

"Keping," Jorie whispers as we enter the east altar room, "what is that scent? I've been smelling it since we landed at Gongkar."

"The smell like bad cheese and animal fur?"

"Well . . ." she says, "yes."

"That's yak butter! People in Tibet use it in everything—tea, deodorant, everything. What you smell now is this." He points into a pot of oil holding a wick. "They even use it for candles."

"I don't think I could ever get used to that," Jorie says.

"Don't worry," Keping says. "Some of us don't either!"

The shadows and light are magnificent as we cross the landscape and spot red and white gleaming on the far horizon: it's the Potala Palace, indicating that we've reached Lhasa. Keping crosses his way through the city streets and parks outside a rather official-looking building. "This was the provincial administrative headquarters before Tibet opened back up to tourists," he says. "But now, this is your guest cottage."

When we enter, he brings us coffee, tea, and hot buttered toast. "I can't wait for a bath," Jorie says, entering the bathroom. A minute later, she shouts. "Geoff? Is Keping still there?"

"I'm here, Mrs. Kent!"

"There's a problem," she says, ducking her neck around the doorframe to face Keping. "I think the boiler needs turning on."

"Oh no, Mrs. Kent," he says with great concern in his voice. "We never give clients a hot bath on the first night."

Jorie closes the bathroom door and opens it again, exiting in a white robe. "Pardon?" she says. Her arms are crossed tight against her.

"We would never let you have a hot bath on the first night, Mrs. Kent."

"Now just a minute," I pipe in. "Why's that?"

"We are very worried about your wife's welfare, Mr. Kent."

"And?"

"And if she takes a hot bath, she could catch cold!"

"Keping!" she says. "We are twelve thousand feet above sea level in early November. The sun will go down within the hour, *and* our luggage is stuck somewhere on a road that's being blown up with dynamite between Gongkar and Lhasa!" She approaches him slowly with her hands on her hips. "When an American woman tells you she wants a hot bath, she really means *that she wants a hot bath.*"

Alarmed, Keping backs out of the room slowly. "I'll be right back with a kettle!" he yells, and takes off down the corridor.

Jorie closes the door and collapses onto the bed. "The first ones in," I tell her, sitting down gently at her side.

"The first ones in," she sighs, turning toward me to prop herself up on her elbow. "Tonight I'll be the first one *tucked* in."

There's a knock on the door. "Mrs. Kent, your water!"

I open the door to find a woman standing outside, her smile as delicate as the rest of her. "It's warm, sir," she says, and I thank her sincerely.

Jorie rises, accepts the kettle, and slips into the bathroom. "It's warm, dear!" she calls, and she returns from the bathroom with new energy. We opt for dinner in our room—beef and fresh vegetables clearly flown in from China for our visit—

and retire to bed in a freezing cold room, wearing the same clothes we'd worn all day—our luggage is still stuck on the other side of the blasting area near Gongkar.

In China and Tibet, there is only one official time zone for the entire country, and so the farther west one gets, the later the sun rises and sets. When I wake at eight o'clock, I call for a coffee and part the sheer curtains to find light cast across the land from a sun not yet visible. There'd been a snowstorm in the night, and the red-brown Himalayas are sprinkled in white—a precise contrast with the blue sky beyond. It's unfathomable to me that for so long, so many travellers have missed out on this experience—a sight both splendid and humble, both completely natural and utterly perfect.

It's a view that will stay with me as one of the most memorable, grounded moments in my life.

The morning to follow remains every bit as inspired. As we approach the Potala Palace, the sun pierces the clouds and spotlights this, the Dalai Lama's winter living quarters, which was first built in the seventh century. Keping drives us onto the sacred mountain, Red Hill, where the two main palaces are situated. The immensity of the place is incredible: more than one thousand rooms soaring to thirteen stories and expanding to nearly a million and a half square feet. Keping ushers us through two chapels; the second of them, known as the Hall of the Sacrifice, contain stupas that house the salt-dried and embalmed remains of some of the Dalai Lamas. The stupas are decorated with what are literally tons of gold and precious stones. At their bases are lamps of yak butter oil that keep the stupas ablaze at all times and throw glimmers and shadows across the shrines. There are groups of primitive-looking people circulating in the chapels with us, each carrying a container of yak butter. "Who are these people?" Jorie asks.

"These are pilgrims who come from the northwest of Tibet,"

Inside the Forbidden City, a series of palaces and courtyards that was home to the imperial courts of the Ming (1368–1644) and Qing (1644–1911) dynasties.

Keping says. "They live in small tents and lead a nomadic life, tending to their goats and their yaks."

Jorie clicks her camera, capturing remarkable images of the pilgrims bowing and praying and spooning their yak butter oil into the bases of the stupa lamps to keep the candles burning.

Keping leads us throughout two more chapels, one of which was the cave of the god of mercy, built in the seventh century on the rock of the hill, which now serves as its floor—it's the oldest building in the Potala Palace. "You notice that in each chapel there are these story paintings mounted on silk brocades that hang from the ceilings. They're called *thankas*, and they're hundreds of years old—"

"And so beautifully preserved," Jorie says.

"That's actually because of the cold, dry air up here on the hill," Keping explains. "The same is true for the murals you see on the walls, despite the fact that they range anywhere from three hundred to thirteen hundred years old."

"Fascinating, isn't it, dear?" Jorie says.

I nod.

"You're quiet," she says.

"Just taking it all in."

"Geoff . . . are you all right?"

"I'm actually not feeling all that well."

"How about some Potala holy water, Mr. Kent?"

"Thanks, but no," I tell Keping. "I don't think another cold bath will help, even if it is with holy water."

"No, Mr. Kent," Keping says. "Come, follow me quickly through the seventh chapel and then you'll see what I mean." He locates a tea room where Jorie and I take a seat, then he returns. "Potala holy water is green tea, Mr. Kent. It will help you stay hydrated—very important here on the mountain." Jorie and I both sip cups of tea, which are very welcome indeed.

Then Keping leads us to another wing of the Potala Palace. "Of the sixty-four palaces here," he says, "this, the White Palace, is the room where they hold ceremonies each time a new Dalai Lama is chosen."

"Chosen?" Jorie says. "I thought the Dalai Lama was a hereditary title."

"It's a common misunderstanding, Mrs. Kent, but to become the Dalai Lama is a chance experience." He goes on to explain that when a Dalai Lama dies, it's here that the names of infants, born at exactly the moment of his death, are placed in a gold vase. The successor is chosen when the ivory stick with his name on it is randomly pulled from the vase. The baby who's the lucky winner represents the Dalai Lama's reincarnation and therefore becomes his successor. Until that baby turns eighteen and comes to the throne, the country is ruled by a regent king, who is often the previous Dalai Lama's son.

"Geoff," Jorie says. "Still not feeling well?"

I shake my head. "A headache."

"Chest pains, Mr. Kent? Nausea?"

I hate to admit it, but I do. "A little."

"Geoff!" Jorie cries.

"It's altitude sickness, Mrs. Kent, don't be alarmed."

"But Geoff's so fit!"

"Lhasa is the highest capital city in the world, and we've been up here all day. Let's quickly go visit the Jokhang Temple," he says. "Then you two can go have a rest."

Outside on the beams and porches of the temple are a wealth of decadent carvings in brilliant colors. Inside we find it lavishly decorated, featuring a gilded bronze statue of the Jowo Shakyamuni Buddha sitting on a golden throne. Legend has it that the statue was brought to Lhasa by the Chinese princess Wen Cheng in the seventh century when she married the king, Songtsen Gampo, who first unified Tibet.

"It's all very fascinating," Jorie says. "But why don't we get back to the cottage?"

We have a mediocre dinner in the dark, due to one of the frequent blackouts that come from the lack of oil. *It is very important*, I write in my diary, *for all clients to bring a torch with them to Tibet.*

"A 'torch'?" Jorie smiles slyly over my shoulder. "For the American brochures, why don't we call it a 'flashlight.' "

I awake the next morning with a fiendish sore throat and a headache—all the signs of a real dose of the flu. "Maybe no wonder," I muse out loud.

"The altitude?"

"No, the hundreds of pilgrims that streamed past us in those tiny rooms with their noses running!"

We leave at nine o'clock for what's to be the most rugged day of our entire tour of China and Tibet: a 168-mile trek west to the city of Shigatse. Shigatse is the second city of Tibet, and only a handful of Westerners have ever been there. Our journey in the army vehicle is expected to take eleven hours, but thirty minutes into the trip, when we make our first stop, we're impressed at the time we're making: already we've reached a colored portrait of the Sakyamuni Buddha carved into the stone of the Himalayas in the seventh century and painted on and off since then to ward off evil spirits within the valley. "This was supposed to take an hour for us to reach," Jorie says.

I make a note in my diary about logistics and pledge to watch our driver's speedometer.

An hour later, at ten thirty, we cross the bridge over the Zangbo River and start to ascend the summit of the mountain pass called Gampa-La. Climbing to the top is slightly hair-raising as we overtake trucks on blind corners. "These drops are totally vertical for thousands of feet," I tell Jorie.

"Not recommended for a client who doesn't like heights," she agrees.

But at the top of the Gampa-La, at nearly seventeen thousand feet, are the most stupendous views of the Zangbo River and the beautiful turquoise lake Yamzho Yumco.

At one thirty, we stop for a picnic lunch beside the river with a large mountain range towering above us. We then start out again, and the closer we get to Shigatse, the more and more we have to share the narrow dirt roads with the stream of donkeys and mules that tow small graders with blades to flatten the roads. "Oh dear," Jorie says, sighing. "The dust . . ."

We close the windows of our jeep and stop at three thirty in the afternoon in the small town of Gyangze, with its fortress on a hill and a long wall surrounding it. Keping offers to show us the local temple, but with more traffic and army trucks heading toward Shigatse, the dust problem is growing unbearable. Not a good journey for anyone to make in summer months! I write in my diary: *At the moment, at the start of November, the temperature is cool enough for us to close the jeep windows . . . but in the summer, a person would nearly suffocate.*

We reach a turnoff to the Indian border, meaning we're only 250 miles away from India. "Jorie," I whisper, "this means we'll arrive at Shigatse in time for tea."

She looks at her watch. "True, it's nearing five o'clock." She looks up at me with wide eyes, knowing what it means: our driver has made an eleven-hour trip in eight hours.

When we enter our hotel suite, we find that it's merely a converted army barracks. It consists of two double rooms separated in the middle and a small alcove containing two washbasins and some towels. There is no running water. If that's not bad enough, the lavatory facilities are simply open pit latrines, dreadful-smelling things, and I borrow a stick of Tiger Balm and Jorie's Chanel No. 5 to alleviate the experience. "If I wasn't sick before, I definitely am now," I tell her. As I stagger to bed with a damp cloth on my brow, it's clear that I'm running a fever.

I wake the next morning with a raging headache. After
the staff delivers coffee and toast with honey—cheering me
up considerably—Jorie takes the morning excursion on a yak
boat down the Yalu Zangbo River, boarding the boat ten miles
north of Shigatse. I take to bed until lunchtime, finally rising
to sit in the sun like a great monitor lizard until Jorie returns
for our afternoon tour of Tashi Lhunpo, the monastery built
in 1447 that is considered to be one of the most beautiful re-
maining examples of Tibetan architecture.

Situated against brown hills, the monastery glows vivid
white and orange in the hot sunlight. Our first stop is inside the Chapel of the Future Buddha, featuring a Buddha
statue that was built in 1914 of copper, gold, and brass with
1,400 pieces of diamonds, coral, and jade that construct his
sparkling third eye. We tour the monastery's library with
its seven hundred books on the sciences, the Ganzhur holy
scriptures, and swastikas on the floor—a sign of good luck
in Tibet. We view a stupa containing the Fourth Panchen
Lama, then follow ancient cobbled pathways between
winding adobe walls, passing monks wandering to and fro
in their saffron-colored robes and headdresses. We come
to an area of the monastery with a thousand Buddha statues
and a printing press, where I ask the monk printing money
to print out a few extra yuan so I can leave an offering at
the monastery before I leave. "I don't think he understands
you," says our guide.

"Thank goodness," says Jorie.

Our guide takes us into the tea rooms with five enormous
bronze caldrons holding yak butter tea for the monks . . . and
then into the most fascinating place we've seen in all of Tibet:
the chanting room. It's the oldest building in the monastery,
and beautifully embroidered scrolls hang from the ceiling
and rows of seats are set in squares, with the whole room being
bisected by pillars. Seated throughout the room are chanting

monks, led by a senior monk who tolls his bell, a symbol of wisdom, at auspicious moments.

From the chanting room we move into a foyer where a monk stands preparing an offering to Buddha made of yak butter and barley flour. This room is even more stunning than the great chanting room, which our guide explains is because it's a room meant for the highest-ranking monks. There's a great deal of bell ringing, drum beating, and cymbal clashing.

We return to our sparse room, and we suddenly feel that it is all worthwhile—the wild, dusty drive, the gray barracks, and the nearly inedible food we've tried to eat all week.

Just as I'm dozing off, there's a flash of light through the curtains and a blaring noise. "What on earth . . . ?" Jorie says.

"Is that the radio next door?"

"Call the front desk."

"I'm sorry, sir," says the young man who answers the phone. "On Friday nights, there's the Chinese cinema."

"What time does it end?"

"Usually around midnight."

Jorie stuffs the pillow over her head and moans.

It's not an easy job being the first to bring tourists to a section of the world that has had its reasons for keeping foreigners out— but by 1994, we see how our efforts in places like China have really made an impact. Bill Gates, passionate about travelling and learning about different cultures, contacts us to organize an itinerary for him to visit China. He and Warren Buffett are planning a trip together, and they will be bringing along a group of their friends and revered business acquaintances. Keenly aware of how important this trip will be to both them and us, we dispatch Gerald Hatherly, our A&K China specialist, to lock down all the arrangements and special requests.

We want to plan a trip that's more than just the "standard"

China itinerary. The Gateses haven't been to China as leisure travellers, so we design a trip that introduces them to China but also gives them access to some locations that are off the beaten path and very intriguing.

It helps that Mimi Gardner Gates, who is married to Bill Gates's father, is an eminent China scholar. Mimi approves of the inclusion of Urumqi, a region that's rarely traveled but so rich in sights, sounds, and life, and also Dunhuang, which means "Blazing Beacon"—a reference to its once glorious status as a major center for trade and culture over 1,500 years ago.

Therefore we plan a China itinerary that touches on the classic regions that make China such a magical destination: Beijing, capital and city of historic monuments; Xi'an, one of the great cradles of Chinese civilization; and Guilin, the living landscape painting. To this we add the Silk Road cities of Urumqi, Turfan, and Dunhuang because of their place in China's ancient history, and also because they are wonderful examples of just how diverse and how unusual China is. The average traveller may not know that the world's second largest desert is located in China or that the greatest concentration of Buddhist cave art is found in the shifting sands of China's vast northwestern desert; or that in Turfan there were ancient Silk Road cities that had Nestorian Christian churches, Manichean temples, and images of Greco-Roman deities.

To complete the itinerary, we add a cruise along the middle reaches of the Yangzi River through the Three Gorges—a region that is celebrated by the Chinese. The Yangzi is the "mother river" and it is truly the lifeblood of the country, with more than four hundred million people living along the river's course. It accounts for 35 percent of the country's most productive agricultural land, and it has always been a natural barometer or metaphor for what it is to be Chinese—stoic yet passionate (just like the swirling waters of the gorges), and also deep and enduring.

So, combining these diverse elements we design what we feel is the ideal China trip.

I'm especially pleased with the way Gerald and his team plan to introduce the Gateses to the Three Gorges of the Yangzi River, which was one of my favorite experiences on that first reconnaissance. It so happens that their visit will coincide with the Three Gorges Dam Project, approved in 1992 and now well underway. The project has generated worldwide interest and is likened to being "the Great Wall across the Water," and Bill Gates makes a request that we offer some informative briefings on the project that cover the planning stages, the costs, the environmental impact, and the social issues that are front-page news.

The cruise on the Yangzi will make for a wonderful interlude during the trip so the party can relax and enjoy themselves. We're able to charter MS *East Queen*, the best boat on the river, and as the cruise director we arrange to bring on board the great Bill Hurst—the finest Yangzi River specialist. Gerald also pledges to carve out time for the group to swim on the Shennong River, a tributary of the Yangzi, with crystalline mountain waters.

The Gateses' group also hopes to ride on the train that Chairman Mao Zedong, who lived from 1893 to 1976, rode when he made his national tours of China. The train sits in Beijing, not used by foreign travellers, VIP or not. Gerald and Austin Zhu of the China International Travel Sector sit down for meetings with the Ministry of Railways, and after six months of conversations to and fro, they obtain official permission to host the Gates group on Chairman Mao's train from Dunhuang to Urumqi.

Once the official permission is granted, I agree with Gerald

Holding a giant panda in Chengdu, and wearing special clothes to protect it from infection, 2010.

that we should hold a banquet for the Ministry of Railways to really seal the deal with the top officials from the ministry. At the party, Austin and Gerald find themselves seated in a private room with a group of older men, all dressed in Mao suits and clearly all figures from the Great Proletarian Cultural Revolution.

They engage in rigid small talk and rather stuffy formalities, until bottles of Maotai are placed on the dinner table . . . then the toasting begins, and soon these stiff comrades are fast friends, and the evening becomes a cloud of drunken toasts. "Sing for us!" cries one of the railway executives. Gerald and Austin glance at each other in despair. "I hate singing," Austin whispers.

"We need this train for Bill Gates," Gerald replies. They

break into their best karaoke Chinese songs, and before the night is finished, there are more than a dozen grown men dancing the foxtrot. "If it will get A&K the train for Bill Gates," Gerald says to me the next morning, "then why not."

On their stop off the train in Dunhuang, the group requests a Western meal. The chef at the Dunhuang Hotel has no idea how to prepare something Western, so Gerald takes off for the local market to find potatoes for French fries and good ground beef. They chop it up with a cleaver and find bread for buns to serve hamburgers—the first ever served in Dunhuang, it turns out.

However, the greatest feat of all occurs when vital concern is given to Warren Buffett's fondness for Cherry Coke. Gerald and the Managing Director of our China office, Patrick Macleod, meet with the Coca-Cola distributors in Hong Kong to discuss how A&K can provide Cherry Coke to the Gates party at each of their stops: in Dunhuang, Urumqi, on the Yangzi River, and Guilin. Fortunately, they learn that there is some stock in Hong Kong, and it's sent out to these destinations exactly per the group's itinerary. All goes wonderfully, Gerald reports, except in Guilin, where the Cherry Coke is not delivered to the Gateses' private boat for their highly anticipated cruise on the Li River. Gerald sends the group off down the river on their boat. Then he returns to the pier and awaits the grand delivery, which arrives within a couple of hours.

After some cajoling and negotiations, he finds a small motorboat that will carry him fast to track down the Gateses' boat. He races past almost three dozen boats down the Li River, calling out and signaling to the Gateses' craft when he spots it. Finally, when Gerald transfers the Cherry Coke on board, there is great clapping and cheering from Warren Buffett and the entire group.

At the conclusion of the trip, the Gates family and Warren Buffett tells us that A&K is "simply the best way to travel."

Chapter 11

Uganda, Rwanda, and the Democratic Republic of the Congo

✧✧✧✧✧

1985

In 1980, my father—the man who'd introduced me to travel and the early business partner who so often had doubted my aspirations—dies. It stirs me in many ways. Over the years, we'd had so many conflicts; but we always shared a deep, meaningful bond over our love for two things: my mother, and Africa.

My sister, Anne, and I establish a grave site not far from my first safari camp. It overlooks the Masai Mara, and on two giant boulders we place separate plaques for each of our parents. His reads: *John Kent: His footprints across Africa became our roads.* It so happens that at this time, an opportunity to preserve some African wildlife comes my way. The whole thing started in the mid—1960s while I was accompanying an art dealer from New York on a game drive. He asked me whether I'd ever be willing to locate some

Coming face-to-face with a gorilla in Bwindi Impenetrable Forest, one of the richest ecosystems in Africa both in animal species and plant life. A life-changing moment. Don't make eye contact!

pieces for his gallery—in specific, he was looking for some ancient artifacts that he'd heard could be found only in the far reaches of the Congo.

With my colleague Tony Church, who was leading our early horseback safaris at the time, I loaded up two Toyota Land Cruisers and take off. "This is no small errand, Geoff," Tony said. "This is a right expedition. Have you ever been to the Congo?"

"Sure, I went with my father when I was ten."

"Well, that was sixteen years ago, and loads has happened there since then. That whole area has been ravaged by war. Where will the job take us?"

"To the southern end of Lake Kivu—"

"Lake Kivu, it's deadly there! Black Jack Schramme and his gang of mercenaries razed Bukavu to the ground last year, it's like a shelltown now. What's he willing to pay?"

"Seventy-five thousand dollars."

"Seventy-five thousand?" Tony exclaimed. "Just to do the reconnaissance?"

"Yes."

"Well, I suppose we'll end up a little richer, or dead. Let's go!"

Tony and I drove through Uganda's great game park of Murchison Falls, then west to a location in northern Uganda called Pakwach. There we crossed the Nile at a spot my father had discovered years ago and then drove into the Congo, stopping off at the Ituri Forest to visit their legendary pygmies and for a look at the Okapi, a rare and secretive antelope-looking creature with a brown body and legs striped like a zebra's, which can usually be spotted only in a camp kept by scientists.

Heading south, we finally arrived at Goma at the northern end of Lake Kivu. When we finally reached our ultimate destination of Bukavu, we found it indeed to be like an apocalyptic movie set. We drove past the remains of buildings and over potholes as big as craters until we finally spotted someone walking in the town. He pointed us toward the road to locate the Warega tribe, and, sure enough, some days later, there we discover a huge supply of tiny elephant statues, moon shapes, and miniature daggers made of amber-colored ivory.

Mission accomplished! I know my art dealer friend will be thrilled with this information. I mark the spot carefully on my map and say to Tony, "Let's get back to Bukavu."

By way of celebration when we return, we find a nightclub where we can get a beer, and a fellow patron strikes up conversation with us. He is from Belgium, though he's been living here with the gorillas for years. "Guerillas?" Tony said. "Sounds a bit dangerous!"

"No," said the Belgian. "Gorillas—I live with an actual troop of gorillas."

I pound my chest with my fists. "Gorillas—like these gorillas?"

"Yeah," he says. "I'm a scientist. Adrien Deschryver." He holds out his hand. "Pleased to meet you "Would you like to see my gorillas?"

We nod.

In the early hours of the next morning, we climb into Adrien's four-wheel-drive Austin Champ, sipping brandy and ginger ale, as Tony and I search like fools for some hint of a gorilla. Just as the sun rises, Adrien stops his vehicle. "We'll have to trek through some pretty thick rainforest jungle," he said. "Watch for snakes. There's a lot of them."

After an eight-hour trek, Tony finally asks, "Where's your camp?"

Adrien points ahead. "Just there."

There, before us, are about ten gorillas. Tony and I watch in disbelief as our new friend approaches them and makes himself at home. The big male silverback pounds on his chest. The babies thump their tiny chests as they make mock charges along the branches above us. They look excited to see him. He stands there, laughing at our reaction, as if we were the odd ones.

I fly back to New York to report our findings to my client and organize a meeting with a film producer who I know well. "You've got to make a documentary about these gorillas," I tell him. "No one in the world apart from this Belgian scientist has ever seen them."

I start to market gorilla safaris in the early 1970s as part of my Off the Beaten Track safaris, and soon an anthropologist, Dian Fossey, asks to see me.

Dian Fossey meets me at the table I've gotten us inside the café at the Goma Hotel. "Look, Geoff," she says. "I know you're anxious to show off the gorillas to your wealthy clients, but I want you to stay out of my territory."

"*Your* territory?"

"I don't want my gorillas to be disturbed when tourists come along, you see." She explains that she recently lost one of the gorillas to which she was the closest, and she's afraid that if we bring people in, the gorillas will become too trusting of humans—even of those who want to poach them.

"These are not *your* gorillas, Dian," I tell her. "Tourism has the potential to save those gorillas and provide jobs."

"Geoff—"

"Their habitat will be destroyed unless they can prove themselves financially worthwhile to the community. Jacques Cousteau said it, Dian: 'People protect what they love.' The locals will protect the gorillas from poachers if they can earn a living from the people who want to *watch* the gorillas."

She disagrees vehemently, stands up, and storms out of the hotel.

A few years later, in 1985, I'm in my office in Nairobi when

Bwindi Impenetrable Forest in Uganda is home to half of the world's surviving population of mountain gorillas, estimated to be less than 800.

I learn that Dian Fossey has been killed in Rwanda. I realize how terribly off the whole affair went, how Dian and I actually had the same intention to save the gorillas, just two very different approaches.

The following week I get a visit from one of my old army mates, now working for MI5—the British equivalent of the FBI. "We've got an interesting trip tomorrow," he says. "I'm going in with a bunch of SAS guys. We think we have a lead on who's going to be the next President of Uganda."

"I certainly hope it's General Museveni," I tell him. "President Obote is killing thousands of his own people! Someone's got to clean up all the unrest in that place."

Gorilla family checking out the gift shop at Sanctuary Gorilla Forest Camp.

"The most I can say right now is that we are going to see Museveni," my friend says. "Would you like to come?"

We fly from Nairobi to Uganda and meet up with Museveni, surrounded by members of his force. He's just as he's always pictured in the media: wearing combat boots and a wide-brimmed jungle hat. He's friendly and inquisitive as the SAS team checks in to ensure he feels he's got enough security for the upcoming election. After an hour or so of cross-armed talks and occasional bursts of laughter from the group, the SAS disperses toward the fleet of trucks we drove from the airport.

This is my chance. Standing alone with Yoweri Museveni, I introduce myself. "Once you become President, which I'm sure you will do," I say, "you've got to come with me. I'm involved with the gorillas in the Congo, just past the Nyiragongo Crater and the Parc des Volcans. On the other side of that park is the Bwindi Impenetrable Forest, and there are meant to be many big families of gorillas on the Ugandan side."

He looks at me thoughtfully, trying to understand what I want.

"Those gorillas have never been habituated," I explain, "so when you become President, let's see if we can't make it a park and habituate them."

"The election is next month," he tells me. "If I'm fortunate enough to be elected, do come and see me in Kampala."

Sure enough, in January 1986, Museveni assumes the office of President of Uganda. Immediately I make an appointment to leave Nairobi and visit the statehouse in Kampala, just as he invited me to do. "I'm interested in helping you protect these gorillas," he says. "But I'm wondering, in your work, what can you do for Uganda?"

"That's just it," I tell him. "If we create a park where the gorillas will be protected, then I'll bring my clients here to see them. I'll bring you tourism dollars—your communities will flourish."

"You'll see to it that our people make money? If that's what you're saying, then as many people as possible should come and see the gorillas."

"No. We have to make it low-impact, high-yield. You have to believe in me: if you bring loads of people in, they'll hurt the gorillas and destroy the forest."

"That makes sense," he says. "But how can our people make money?"

"You can charge hundreds of dollars per license to track a gorilla, and the community—not the central government—will sell the permits. Within a few years, it will bring hundreds of thousands of dollars to Uganda. Best of all, the gorillas will be protected."

He ponders it, then finally speaks. "One last thing, Geoff: If we establish a park, what will you do?"

"Here's what I'll do: I'll build the first luxury camp in the Impenetrable Forest at Bwindi, and I'll assist in the habituation of the gorillas."

"I'll give you the exclusivity, Geoffrey," he says. "If you do what you say, this will help everyone."

"I agree," I tell him. "Most importantly, the gorillas."

Within a few months, we sign the deal, and the development of our gorilla camp at Bwindi is underway; I dispatch my son, Joss, to build the camp. In 1991 the Bwindi Impenetrable Forest becomes a national park, and we're booking so many reservations that we have a years-long waiting list. Right away we habituate one troop of seven or eight gorillas, and with all the momentum coming at us, I hire a Kenyan named John Webley to open an A&K office in Kampala.

A few dozen clients visit the park each season, and they're falling in love with these gorillas, whose communication is so similar to our own. Our guests have the opportunity to observe a band of gorillas in their natural habitat—eating, grooming, vocalizing—for one hour each day. A videographer captures footage of one guest as the gorillas are patting his head in a good-morning welcome—a video that quickly goes viral on the internet.

It's all running perfectly except for one rather unsettling aspect of the whole project: to open a national park to protect the gorillas meant that any humans who were living within the habitat have to be relocated—if humans stay, they will hunt the wildlife. Worst of all, the only humans living there happen to be the Batwa pygmies, an ancient tribe of African hunter-gatherers who had lived in the area for thousands of years. We are concerned—not just for where they'll have to move, but for their overall well-being.

Few of them have ever seen a doctor, and some are in rather dangerous health.

We work with an American doctor and his wife, Scott and Carol Kellermann, to provide medical care. It begins with an open-air clinic under a tree. Our guests meet the Batwa and learn about their traditions: how they live and hunt, their ancient legends and traditional songs, and their use of medicinal plants.

In the years to follow, that little medical clinic grows into a fully fledged hospital. Three hundred patients come through every day, and we've worked to develop a school there as well. Today, our guests have contributed more than $1.18 million to transform the clinic into a regional hospital with an operating room, a maternity ward, a children's ward, a neonatal unit, and a nursing school. Bwindi Community Hospital serves more than thirty thousand outpatients annually and has reduced infant mortality in the area by an estimated 50 percent.

Protected in the park, the gorillas thrive and Bwindi Impenetrable Forest provides a safe haven *for more than half* of the world's critically endangered mountain gorillas.

Chapter 12

Galápagos Islands

❖❖❖❖❖❖

ECUADOR, 1988

I've always said that seasonality is the biggest killer
in the tourism industry. In almost any given destination, you can run at full capacity for four months
of the year, and then you're half empty or less for the
other eight months. So as we continue to develop vacations beyond safaris, I think long and hard about the
locations where the weather is reliable year-round.

At this point, I've learned well what Americans desire when they travel: they prefer to stay somewhat close
to home and, when possible, close to their own time
zone. Wouldn't it be great, I realize, if I could get a ship
to the Galápagos Islands? Americans will feel somewhat
at home in this archipelago so very near the equator;
it boasts gorgeous weather twelve months a year, the
temperature growing just slightly cooler from June to
November, when the Humboldt Current flows north
from Chile to Peru. Up until the seventies, only scientific expeditions really had been to the Galápagos, and

---

*This striking bird, the blue-footed booby, spends its days
scanning the sea for food, returning to land to nest and to carry
out the foot-stamping mating display that makes it a favorite of
Galápagos visitors.*

Sea lions basking in the sun. The social sea lion hardly bats an eye at human visitors. When not congregating on the beach, sea lions are swift, powerful swimmers, navigating pounding surf with ease as they search for sardines, their main food.

most people still associated that part of the world with hard-nosed science and Charles Darwin's natural selection research on board the *Beagle*. I've always imagined the islands must be spectacular—amazing fish, beautiful reefs, volcanic areas, hundreds of birds, seals, and penguins that follow the cold waters north from Antarctica—and that it would be possible to take it all in while feeling completely safe. Also, the Galápagos Islands have been protected by the Ecuadorean government since 1934, so the animals are relatively unafraid of hunting or disturbance from humans.

This would be the perfect vacation spot for families, I muse: children will be captivated to learn about the distinctive, colorful wildlife that inhabit the islands; and with so many islands for our ship to cruise around, parents will have plenty of chances to rest and recharge.

Then in the 1980s, Prince Charles introduces me to his close friend Gerald Ward, the godfather of Prince Harry and a fellow Sandhurst-trained former soldier. In 1988, Gerald and his lovely wife, Amanda, tell me they're interested in taking a vacation that is totally off the beaten path. Because of our mutual interest in sport, I know Gerald loves the outdoors and animals. It hits me: this is the perfect opportunity to introduce the Galápagos as a luxury destination. I accompany Gerald and Amanda Ward to the Galápagos Islands—a new adventure for them, as well as a new one for me and just about anyone.

Off the main island of Santa Cruz, we board a private yacht that's fully stocked and self-contained, all ready to house us for an entire week, as good as if it were a safari camp. "The generators for the scuba tanks are here?" I ask the captain.

"The generators are here, Geoff. They're charging the cylinders now."

"Excellent, well done. And our instructor?"

"We wouldn't leave without Carlos, Geoff. Your naturalist is on board, too."

Brilliant variety on this trip—we'll spend mornings on land touring most of the nineteen main islands with our naturalist. The captain says the island of Santa Cruz, an inactive volcano, is a must-see for its lava tunnels. Over lunch on the first day, the naturalist tells us all about the Galápagos penguins and the giant tortoises. "The tortoises are the biggest living tortoises in the world," he says, "often five feet in length and over five hundred pounds." The Wards look at me with wide eyes when he explains that the giant tortoises can live to around one hundred years old. "They're old devils, sometimes their faces look like little old men," he says, and they were once so populous that the Galápagos Islands became their namesake. "It's surprising how few people know that 'Galápagos' comes from the word for 'tortoise,'" he explains. "It's an Old Castilian word that the Spanish explorers used to describe the abundance of the reptile on these islands." The animals in the Galápagos aren't at all afraid of humans—in fact, he says, as we walk along the beach, we'll actually have to step over the sea lions. They're completely unthreatened by humans, and in between mating and swimming in search of sardines, they love to relax and catch some sun.

"Not the worst existence in the world."

Gerald and Amanda look at me and break into laughter, which pleases me all the more.

"Whoops," I tell them. "Did I say that out loud?"

"Geoff," says Gerald. "I'm curious. Which animal or bird would you most like to see while we're here?"

"That's easy," I tell him. "The blue-footed booby on Espanola Island."

The blue-footed booby is wild, and I don't just mean it in the undomesticated sense. I've read that their name comes from *bobo*, a Spanish word for clown, either because of their huge, brightly colored feet or because of their peculiar mannerisms. When a male blue-footed booby is courting a female, he slowly lifts his legs, one and then the other, in the oddest mating dance. Then he stretches his wings wide to show off how broad and strong he is, and he brings her a gift of little twigs as a promise that he's capable of building a good nest for their young.

The female, however, keeps her eyes mostly on one thing—his feet. It's not because bigger is better in the double entendres of Galápagos wildlife; it's because the brighter his feet, the healthier he's meant to be. The blue-footed booby's foot color is an indicator of fertility, and the duller his feet are, the poorer potential the female will believe he has to give her babies.

In the afternoons when the water is calm, we'll dive among the marine life and coral reefs, so compelling because of the difficult time they have surviving in this part of the world. The Galápagos happen to sit at the intersection of several different types of currents, bringing a variety of water temperatures through, with the warmer temperatures typically making it more difficult for the highly sensitive coral to adapt and situate themselves there. El Niño in the early 1980s wiped out much of the coral population, which is thought to have originated millions of years ago, and because of the wealth of shellfish, sardines, and anchovies in the Galápagos, overfishing has affected the food chain and caused sea urchins to graze hungrily on the coral without allowing enough time for the coral to recover. Acidity in the water is equally as concerning—since the industrialization of the twentieth century, the waters in this area have ended up with one quarter of the world's carbon dioxide, which is choking the coral.

Our first afternoon out on the Pacific, Gerald and Amanda elect to lounge on board to get over the jet lag of their flight from London. As we suit up on the deck, Carlos, the diving instructor, harnesses his cylinder on his back and tells me, "You don't want to wait another decade and hope to see this coral." I fit my goggles and put on my wet suit and attach my tank. As we transfer into a smaller Zodiac boat, I know that if we'd sat back much longer to take this trip, the most vibrant corals of the Galápagos would be gone.

"Now, Geoff," Carlos says, "I know you've done this before, but I have to remind you that this is a drift dive. When we get let in, the current is going to take us down, and you'll barely even notice it. You don't have to do much work."

"Right, I follow."

"Okay. I just had to make sure that's clear. We'll be down about a hundred twenty feet, so just remember to keep your eyes on me. Watch for my signals."

I nod. One hundred and twenty feet is not an extreme dive, but it's nothing a beginner would attempt.

We fall backward off the sides of the Zodiac into the ocean—Christ, for as sunny as it is here, the water is freezing!—and immediately we are among what must be thousands of brightly

colored, tiny fish. When the fish scatter, I spot my first reef: it looks like a great green boulder decorated in yellow and fluorescent-pink moss. Carlos is close at my side, and I give him a thumbs-up. So far, so good.

The fish are everywhere, practically raining on us, in bright, reflective red, nature's romantic contrast to the royal-blue depths of the ocean. They swim down, they flutter aside, they swirl away and scatter from us. When Carlos catches my glance again, he points up. My gaze follows his signal, and there they are: hammerhead sharks, directly above us. There must be two dozen of them, floating in a slow circle—a necklace of moving sharks. The instructor gives me the A-okay sign, letting me know we're completely safe. I've been told there's never been a shark attack on a human in the Galápagos. A considerable percentage of the world's fish come from this area, so sharks don't have much reason to prey on us—there's already plenty for them to eat.

The hue of the water grows darker, the neon surface grows more distant, and I know we must be just a few minutes from our maximum depth. A pair of dolphins dances by us, their white bellies catching rays of light beamed down from the surface. Schools of fish appear and disappear again, as if by magic, and a stingray gracefully flaps and floats its way by us. Sea lions greet us, comical little wigglers, not unlike circus seals—one can easily imagine them balancing a ball on their noses. Then, a shark: classically gray and self-assured. He glides by closer to the ocean floor, most likely in search of a late lunch. The ridge between its back fins makes me suspect that it's what is known as a Galápagos shark. Carlos watches, motionless . . . in turn, the shark ignores us entirely.

The knowledge of this seems to liberate me completely. I

PRECEDING PAGE: *The volcanic island of Bartolome in the Galápagos.*

get Carlos's attention and point down. *I'm going farther*, I signal to him. He nods his head exaggeratedly and then pumps the Stop signal at me with his hands, as if to say *Just take it easy*.

Down, down, down I go, the water ever richer in its color. The most tranquil feeling washes over me, a sort of deep-sea euphoria. A shark swims over my head and for a moment I consider swimming up to him, going face-to-face. The instructor said, after all, that the sharks here won't do anything.

Instead, I let the water carry me some more. When I look up, the sun is but a faraway thing. *This is the perfect existence*, I think. It's as though I'm drunk on happiness; it occurs to me that in another life I must have been born with scales and gills. The water feels like paradise—even the temperature here is just right now.

I could stay forever.

Just then, there's a tug. It catches my attention—something's got my fin. Keeping my senses, I navigate a slow, calm turn, so as not to startle whatever this creature is. Then the tug is harder. I jerk around, and it's Carlos. He stares at me through his mask. *What?* I ask him, holding up my hands.

He points to his wrist. *Time*, he's telling me. *You're running out of time.*

I want to go deeper and deeper. I gaze down, and in my peripheral vision Carlos waves for my attention. Now he's tapping his wrist, hard.

He's serious.

We swim toward the surface. Carlos moves at a pace that seems urgent, about a dozen feet ahead of me, and then he stops. When I reach him, he signals for me to stop. We stay there for several minutes to clear our blood of nitrogen—otherwise, we risk getting the bends, or decompression sickness, a condition that raises the blood to a temperature that can cause crippling or even death. Then he starts up some more and motions for me to follow. We pause again, head farther upward yet, and repeat the pause another time. Moments

TOP: *This brilliant-hued crab occupies rocky coasts feeding on algae, its strong legs keeping it firmly rooted against crashing waves.*
BOTTOM: *My wife, Otavia, and I with a giant tortoise in the Galápagos Islands. Can you believe this giant tortoise is more than 100 years old?*

later we surface. Carlos grips the edge of the Zodiac. "Grab the boat, Geoff," he tells me.

"I'm fine," I answer, lifting my mask to rest on my forehead. "Just give me a minute."

"Geoff, you had a moment down there. Do me a favor and grab the boat just until I know you're steady."

He seems alarmed. I extend my wrist and get hold of the edge of the Zodiac, the rest of me still treading gently in the water.

"The raptures of the deep got to you," he says.

It's a beautiful phrase. "The what?"

"'The raptures of the deep.' Nitrogen narcosis. The gas in the cylinder—it got to you."

"Was that what that was?" I ask him. "My God, I got carried away!"

"Literally!"

"Literally."

"That can kill you." He's chuckling now, maybe only to lighten the scenario. "It's a good thing I was there."

"I didn't even feel it. I was just so"—I watch my free hand float with the motion of the water in front of me—"happy."

"That's it," he says. "It goes to your brain and numbs your perception that anything is different. That's why I didn't want you to go too far down. The deeper you go, the greater the effect."

"I knew we were coming up in stages to prevent the bends, but—"

"I'm sorry I didn't mention the raptures of the deep, Geoff. I thought you knew!"

"It's a good thing you were there; I never go diving without an instructor." I take a deep breath, regaining my bearings. "Wow."

We're lifted back into the Zodiac and I'm utterly wiped out. "How was it?" ask Gerald and Amanda, who are lounging on the deck.

"Breathtaking," I tell them. "Truly."

Chapter 13

Oman

1992

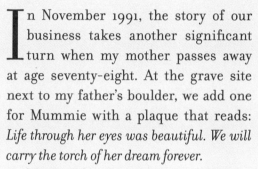

In November 1991, the story of our business takes another significant turn when my mother passes away at age seventy-eight. At the grave site next to my father's boulder, we add one for Mummie with a plaque that reads: *Life through her eyes was beautiful. We will carry the torch of her dream forever.*

Mummie's take on my accomplishments had always been much more favorable than my father's, and a few years earlier in the late eighties, she'd witnessed the pride of her life when I captained the Windsor Park polo team of His Royal Highness Prince Charles, winning most of the major trophies in England and playing in the finals of the 1987 British Open.

Fort Al Jalali, built by the Portuguese in the 1580s, protects the entrance to the harbor of Old Muscat.

At the same time, my community-minded and conservation projects such as my collaboration with President Musevini in Uganda put me on the radars of other world leaders to whom I have some ties. Prince Charles is certainly one of them. Another happens to be Qaboos bin Said, His Majesty the Sultan of Oman.

My friendship with His Majesty the Sultan originated in our British Army days, when we were considered outcasts by our more upper-echelon colleagues. Along with our brother officer, Tim Landon, Qaboos and I were not "landed gentry"— that is, we hadn't been born to upper-class parents in England. What many of our classmates were not particularly aware of was that Officer Cadet bin Said was in fact the son of the ruler of Oman. We stay in close touch with each other, and Tim and I are stationed in Oman in the 1960s.

In 1970, there is a successful coup and my old Sandhurst friend becomes the ruler. Tim Landon stays on as his right-hand man and becomes known as Brigadier Landon. In early 1992, His Majesty the Sultan Qaboos bin Said asks me to pass along his invitation to my polo teammate the Prince of Wales for a visit to Oman. In turn, Prince Charles—a lover of history, archaeology, and nature—accepts graciously, and His Majesty the Sultan bin Said sets us up with all the arrangements and generous accommodations for a whirlwind three-day visit.

After my morning run and a hurried job of packing, I place a call downstairs to the front desk of Claridge's Hotel at 9:15 a.m., just to be certain that I don't delay the 11:00 a.m. Royal Flight from Heathrow. Leonard, my driver, assures me that he knows where the airport's VIP suite is—"Just at the south side terminal, past Terminal Four. It's all signposted," he promises. As he pulls out onto Brook Street from the hotel, I relax into the backseat and pull out a stack of notes to review on the ride to the airport.

As we near the south side terminal, it's clear that there's zero activity. "This isn't the terminal they use anymore," says an airport employee in an orange vest, squinting in at me through my driver's window. He goes on to give Leonard a completely twisted stream of directions, and a lump of panic forms in my stomach as we enter a long line of standstill traffic.

As we inch closer to the next gate, employees are hooting and making Do Not Enter hand motions. "That bloke gave you the wrong directions," says one of them. "The VIP suite for the royal party is at the other end of the airport."

When we finally find the VIP gate, security is very, very tight. "We have your name," says one of the guards, "but we don't have the correct number of your car."

"That's not my problem," I tell him. "I provided all the necessary information yesterday." The guard gets on his radio, and after a couple of minutes of reading the details from my passport to his colleague, he finally motions me through.

Before us, sitting on the tarmac, is the most beautiful DC-8 jet airliner I've ever seen. "Is this the Sultan's plane?" I call to the pilot, who's standing in the doorway of the aircraft.

"No, sir," he says, "this is actually the runabout. His Majesty the Sultan's premier aircraft is actually a 747."

"Let me guess: custom converted."

"Indeed," he says with a grin.

Leonard helps the airline crew load my bags, and, forever vigilant with logistics, I review the next three days' itinerary with a careful eye to the hour-by-hour plans. When Prince Charles is surrounded by history, it's important to mind the time—at moments, I've seen him grow so passionate that his entire party has rushed to make up for lost minutes.

Within fifteen minutes, the motorcade with the Prince of

Wales arrives, and Prince Charles greets me and kindly asks me to join him in his section of the plane. On board, we explore the seating arrangement: an office full of its own electronic equipment, an ultraprivate seating area, a fantastic master bedroom and bathroom, and a separate first-class section for His Royal Highness's staff.

Prince Charles and I spend the first forty-five minutes of the flight catching up on work and life, and then we take to our respective tables and pull out some work. A short while later, the flight attendant wheels out lunch: a trolley full of lobster, caviar, and fresh vegetables that Prince Charles has brought from Highgrove, his house in Gloucestershire. Eating in leisure, we watch our seven-hour route on the television monitor: we've already crossed half of Europe, and we're about to fly right over the top of Romania and then on down into the Persian Gulf.

When we land at Seeb International Airport at ten o'clock at night, the Prince of Wales is met by a guard of honor. With a warm handshake, my old army chum Tim Landon meets me at the bottom of the steps, and there in front of us sits a fleet of identical blue Mercedeses. "Just think, Geoff!" he calls to me. "If you'd never left Oman to be General Frost's aide-de-camp, you might have gotten my job, and all this would be yours!"

We share a good laugh and a hearty handshake. "All in all, Tim, I'd say things have turned out all right for us both."

"Without a doubt," he says. "His Royal Highness the Prince of Wales will ride in the white Jaguar in front. You and I will go in the first Mercedes right behind him."

When Tim and I served in Oman together in 1964, the city of Muscat was composed of not much more than Fort Al Jalali, and the dirt airstrip where our Beverley military plane would land. Thirty years on, as we exit a high-level overpass on the

Playing a polo match with Prince Charles as Captain of the Windsor Park Polo Team.

highway, bank buildings brighten the night, and the windows of high-rise apartment buildings glow warm with electricity.

Twenty minutes later we enter the Al Bustan Palace hotel, and the octagonal ceilings inside the five-story lobby soar high as a temple. We check in, and the Sultan's staff pass around special badges for us to wear at all times. Tight security surrounds us as we pass through the marble-framed archways of the slick, wide foyer, making our way to the royal suite, which the Sultan has had prepared for Prince Charles's party. We drop our bags and immediately make gin martinis, and I wander out to the balcony: Beneath the suite lies a great lawn with a walkway lit by palm trees and glowing founts of water. Our view looks out onto the Sea of Oman and a silhouetted view of the jagged Al Hajar Mountains, which stretch far up north to the United Arab Emirates.

After the rest of the party retires for the night, I head to the executive center, where I work until three o'clock in the morning.

The next morning, the Royal party heads to the Omani cultural museum at Fort Al Jalali. I stay back to eat a late breakfast with the British Ambassador, Sir Terence Clark, who confesses a flub the Sultan's staff made as they prepared for Prince Charles to visit. "Bit of a nightmare last week," the Ambassador says. "Last week, the Sultan sent out at least a dozen bulldozers to clear the ground for the Prince's camp—"

"No . . ." I stare at him wide-eyed, quite certain where this is going.

"Indeed," he says. "They wound up bulldozing sand in the archaeological digging area *and* a part of the turtle breeding area."

Don't tell Prince Charles, I warn him. He's a steadfast nature lover and would be horrified. When the Prince returns from his museum visit, we head to the Sultan's secret camp on the beach, where the famous Omani sea turtles nest.

When we land, the area looks like a beachhead from the Gulf War: four-dozen vehicles, three camps, and a fleet of helicopter gunships. While the Sultan's staff set up for a barbecue, Prince Charles and I venture off for a walk on the beach. Within minutes we discover what appear to be the wide tracks of armored cars, and it dawns on us that these must be the tracks of the famous hawksbill sea turtles that make their way annually from the Red Sea to the beaches of Muscat.

Over a breezy dinner on the beach, one of the Sultan's guides explains that the turtles in Muscat are extremely solitary and spend all their lives at sea, meeting exclusively for the purpose of mating. The female leaves the water only every few years to lay her eggs high on the beach. When she finds a depression in the sand, she claims it and digs a deep hole. Then, crouching hind-end down, she takes a few intense hours to herself and deposits her clutch of eggs. "How many does she lay?" I ask our guide.

"One hundred fifty at a time."

There is an instant roar of disbelief among us men. I envision the plight of the determined female turtle, all alone with a great shell on her back, her abdomen heavy with babies, using the claws of her great flippers to dig her hole and relieve her body of her eggs. Too often, her labor is in vain: a fox or a monitor lizard will sniff out the yolk-rich eggs, and very few of the baby turtles ever survive their fifty-five-day maturation period to reach birth.

The few hatchlings that do make it crack from their shells employing great strength from their tiny flippers. Then as a frantic little group they emerge, producing a stampede of miniature tracks in the sand as they race from their hole to the water, where they'll have to avoid predators like crabs, birds, and mammals. Out of every ten thousand eggs that a mother turtle lays in her eighty- to one-hundred-year lifetime, only two or three of her young will actually reach twenty or thirty years of age to produce their own offspring.

The guide tells us that as if those threats aren't enough to endanger the life of a newborn turtle, the hatchlings find their way to the water according to only one critical influence: the brightness of the sky over the water. This first journey to the sea is important in calibrating the turtles to a magnetic orientation, allowing them to return decades later to the area

An ad I did for Rolex at the same time as golfer Arnold Palmer and skier Jean-Claude Killy.

where they were hatched so that they can breed and hatch their own eggs.

At midnight when we've all retired, I call to Prince Charles's tent. "Don't stay up reading all night," I tease Prince Charles. "Your headlamp could plant the wrong signal inside the mind of a young turtle. It will be searching for you its whole life!"

"I don't think the hawksbill sea turtles of Oman have the range to swim to Gloucestershire," calls Tim Landon.

"We do have a tight day tomorrow," I tell them. "Six hours of touring to fit in before our five p.m. flight home."

The next morning, I step out of my tent at eight o'clock sharp, a beautiful clear morning, as I wade into the sea—bracing and warm. Afterward, I shower and meet everyone for a quick breakfast before we climb a concrete staircase onto the Sultan's helicopter pad. "Have these steps always been here?" I ask one of the Sultan's staff members.

"No, Mr. Kent!" he answers proudly. "His Majesty the Sultan had these put in just for His Royal Highness's visit!"

We board our helicopters for a short flight to the top of the Jebel Akhdar mountains, where I was stationed in the army.

We fly along the walls of Wadi Tiwi—*wadi*, I remember from my army days, being the Arabic word for "valley"—getting a spectacular view of this gorge in the middle of the mountains.

There's a high wind when we reach the site where the Sultan has arranged for us to visit some recently discovered tombs. The pilot maneuvers deftly and apologizes when we land a few minutes late. It's fine, I tell him, but we've got to mind the time this afternoon to make our five o'clock departure flight for India.

"There's nothing that will delay us this evening, sir," he says.

Just then, Prince Charles alights from his helicopter, sets

his hands on his hips, looks around, and says, "This is not exactly like Gloucestershire!"

The tomb site, rather barren, lies 5,500 feet high in the mountains. The area features not much more than a dome-topped tower surrounded by an intricate series of large boulders, clearly the tombs, which our guide says would have been laid here starting in 3,000 BC and continuing over the following thousand years. Under study by a team of archaeologists, the tombs lie in various states of repair. The craftsmanship and detail, I can see when we inch up close, are superb.

From there, we seek out my old stomping ground at the very top of the Jebel Akhdar mountains. When I was here on mules three decades ago, there were no roads or electricity—but now as we walk through the village centers, there are telephone lines hung above the mud houses and TV screens flashing on the walls inside. When we reach my old base on the plateau above the village of Saiq, it too is hardly recognizable: in the old days, the base consisted of nothing but a few huts, a football field, and a viewing platform dais for the inspecting officer. Now there are an impressive modern headquarters, sophisticated artillery ranges, and paved airfields.

From there, we make our way to a region with high cliffs—and I'm delighted how I remember these walnut trees with hearty nuts, and the pomegranate trees flowering with lively pink blossoms. Prince Charles finds a steady place on the mountain track to sketch—he says he loves to draw not just for creativity's sake, but for the calm it gives him to survey the scenery, hear the noises, and smell the air.

I take off alone on a quiet stroll. When the breeze blows, I also take in the air. It carries down scents from the contoured fields where onions and garlic grow, just as it did in my army days. In the fields sway tall strands of wheat and the tiny purple flowers of the alfalfa plant. Oman never felt much like home when I was stationed here, but I'm comforted that some parts of the country have remained untouched.

Heading back, I call to Prince Charles. "Sir, we'd best get a move on. It's nearly time for lunch."

"Right, Geoff, just let me finish this one branch . . ."

"Fine, sir." I check my watch: the afternoon is escaping us. I watch His Royal Highness as he tilts his head in thought. *What a crazy life this is*, I realize in a sudden surreal moment. As a boy, I never could have dreamed that one day I'd accompany the Prince of Wales to visit my old Sandhurst friend, who's now the Sultan of Oman, in one of the most ancient lands in the world. I never even knew to imagine that Prince Charles—such a good-natured, considerate, and influential man—would be one of my close friends.

Visibly satisfied, he rises from his folding stool and walks toward me, smiling. "Come on then, let's go," he says, breezing past me toward where our cars have driven up to fetch us.

Our drivers locate the elegant guesthouse where the Sultan has arranged our lunch. Prince Charles had made a special request for a light lunch of vegetables and salad, but when we sit down, the Sultan's staff serves us with something much different: a seven-course meal with smoked ham, grilled red snapper, beef, mutton, and chicken. After a dessert of Omani dates, I sit back in my chair. "Had enough?" says Tim Landon.

"I feel like a sea turtle without the ability to lay any eggs."

Everybody laughs. We drink the last of our coffee—rich and strong—and meet our cars to make our late-afternoon flight. On takeoff, we have another good laugh when Prince Charles and I glance toward our escort helicopter. Evidently, there was some confusion on takeoff, and instead of the gunship guarding our flank, it has ended up on the wrong side. We are looking directly into the barrels of their guns! The pilot quickly realizes the mistake and moves into the correct position.

In the meantime, I glance at my watch. We're twenty-five minutes late, a logistic that I never would have compromised in our army days. Today, however, our timing is perfect: the sun sets over the sandstone cliffs, the mountains casting intense shadows over the sleek green ribbons of alfalfa growing in the field beneath us.

After our whirlwind three-day visit, I reflect that as a young man on a mule, the young Lieutenant Geoffrey Kent of the 5th Royal Inniskilling Dragoon Guards never could have known that one day he would return to accompany His Royal Highness the Prince of Wales in such style with a flotilla of helicopter gunships! In the end, it's an old army friendship, and another destination, come full circle with significance to my life.

Floating in the Dead Sea, the lowest point on Earth at 1,378 feet below sea level. This is a memorable experience for travellers to the Middle East.

Chapter 14

Papua New Guinea

❖❖❖❖❖

1993

A t this stage, Abercrombie & Kent has moved into a variety of corners of the world, and I'm conjuring my next vision. For thirty years we've been showing people some of the remotest places on earth, but now I want to bring the world to people who don't have the opportunity to travel. I'm primed for my pitch when I meet Mark McCormack, the founder of the benchmark talent agency IMG, at a Wimbledon party in the early nineties. "Mark, let's create a TV series together," I tell him. "I want to take viewers inside the world's most unusual locations."

Mark puts me in touch with the producer Charlie Lafave, and together we determine that the best way to do this will be to follow celebrities to the places they've always wanted to travel. We line up Lauren Hutton, whose all-American natural beauty made her the highest-paid model in history in the 1970s, to star in an episode. The series is titled *To the Ends of the Earth*. "And when I say go for exotic," Mark says, "I mean go for it." We ask Lauren where on earth she'd go if she could choose any location. "Just dream," I tell her.

Crossing a river to Timburke Village.

The stunning masks at Karawari, which are used in rituals, dances, and fertility ceremonies.

She says she wants to locate the remotest human tribes on earth.

Our timing is right on. Since the late eighties, American and European tourists have grown hesitant to leave the safety of home. Ronald Reagan's bombed Libya, apartheid's been happening in South Africa, India and Pakistan are fighting over Kashmir, and Egypt has suffered its own internal struggles. In 1986, I'd done a reconnaissance to Australia with the intention to employ one of my sales and marketing philosophies: "Go where the fish swim." We'd been attracting more and more Australian travellers. I've been eager to push into a still-unspoiled land in this same area, one with tourism opportunities that weren't yet in full swing. For Lauren, I know just the place: *To the Ends of the Earth* would be filmed in Papua New Guinea.

"You're sure you can get us in, Geoff?" Charlie the producer says on the phone. "Keep in mind this is a fifteen-person production crew."

"As long as the crew and the actors are fully committed, my team will get you in." Having already spent some time with Lauren, I'm confident she will be perfect. She loves motorcycles, the outdoors, and even diving.

Caroline Wheeler, my right-hand woman, voices some doubt. "Don't you want to take them someplace where Americans would actually want to holiday?" she asks me. "When most Americans hear the words 'Papua New Guinea,' they think of the Rockefeller boy who disappeared there. Maybe dial back on the intensity, just a touch?"

"It's Papua New Guinea or nothing," I tell her. "Mark Mc-Cormack said 'exotic,' and we're going to give him exotic. Mainstream television viewers have never seen a place like this."

"Yes, Geoff," she says with a sigh. "Perhaps there's an excellent reason for that."

After ten years' working with me, Caroline knows I can't be deterred—though as my team and I begin to lay out the itinerary, I do begin to wonder whether we're pushing the bounds a touch too far. Papua New Guinea is home to some of the most secluded indigenous people on the planet: there are valleys and villages where many of the inhabitants have never even laid eyes on a white man, and it's known that some of these natives still practice rape, cannibalism, and headhunting as part of their everyday life. Even if these accounts are slightly exaggerated, the lifestyle in this country could put many viewers off: the men and women live completely separately from one another, and they meet up only for sex. The women wear nothing but grass fronds on their lower halves, and the men who live in the highlands are called "wigmen" for the elaborate wigs and masks they wear. Apart from that, their normal wardrobe consists of not much more than penis gourds. "Lauren Hutton is a feminist, you know," Caroline chides me.

Denying my rising doubts, I respond: "And I'm not?"

Further complicating our planning is the fact that there are hundreds of tribes that speak almost a thousand different languages—none of them English—and that many of the villages that neighbor each other fight frequently over their livelihood of kina shells and pigs. The managing director of our Australia office, Anthony Hyde, agrees to meet me in Papua New Guinea's capital, Port Moresby, where with Charlie Lafave we board a boat on the Sepik River to make our way inland.

When a Land Cruiser picks us up in Mount Hagen early that evening, I know we've hit on a location that will render Papua New Guinea unforgettable to TV audiences. Winding down rutted dirt roads, we encounter groups of men with wide, rugged faces standing outside their longhouses, which are built up on stilts. The men eye us suspiciously, and the director pulls his baseball cap farther down on his head. "Papua New Guinea was the last place that Rockefeller kid was ever seen alive," he says. "People say he was eaten by sharks, but the way these guys are checking us out, I'd say he was eaten by them."

"When was that?" Anthony says.

"It was 1961," I tell him. Having taken David Rockefeller, Sr. on safari since the 1960s, I knew the story well. "But that was in West Papua, on the Indonesian side of the island."

"Are you sure Lauren Hutton will be up for this?" Anthony asks. In response, the director gazes out of the Land Cruiser, clearly wondering the same. Anthony stretches his neck forward, pulling a pair of binoculars from his bag. "There's smoke ahead," he says. "What do you suppose it could be?"

"Would you like to go have a look?" I ask the director. He nods.

Our driver turns to me. "Mr. Kent, I wouldn't advise that we drive into this," he says. "There could be trouble."

Before special gatherings and seasonal events, a Huli Wigman (pictured here with me) will spend hours preparing his costume and make-up, complete with a ceremonial wig and accessories.

"Turn off your headlights," Anthony tells him. "They won't be bothered by us."

We forge ahead slowly for a few minutes and make a turn around the corner. "Back off a bit," I tell the driver, and he slowly reverses the truck and tucks it back into a space where we're protected by bushes.

"Are those spears landing in the road?" says the director.

"Arrows," I tell him.

"Good God, it's like a movie set," he says.

Our driver shuts off the car, and we all watch in silence. One group of men fires arrows at another group, and the second group charges the first. Suddenly there's an arc of fire sailing through the air, and a grass house goes up in instant flames. In a frenzy, both groups of men scatter away. With our headlights still off, our driver takes us down the dusty road, through the smoke and destruction. "I really don't know if Hollywood's ready for Papua New Guinea," Anthony says. I stare ahead at the road, ignoring him completely.

When Lauren lands in a twin-engine propeller plane, we begin to film on location. The production crew follows us around a village that borders the rain forest, and as Lauren takes it all in, they murmur words such as "dangerous" and "primitive." Lauren smoothes her hair and jokes about the cruelty of not having brought a stylist to the most humid climate on earth. "When is the rainy season here, anyway?" Charlie Lafave asks me.

"It starts in December."

"And ends?"

"In March."

"Ah."

As if on cue, a heavy blanket of rain drops from the sky. The film crew scrambles to cover their equipment with a tarpaulin sheet, and Lauren and I dash from the field toward the forest in hopes of being sheltered by the trees. "Spider!" she cries.

"You told me you were tough!" I tell her. "You ride motor-bikes and all that!"

The next morning we were running short of food and wanted to get to the next location. We climb onboard our twin engine Norman Islander.

As the pilot goes to fire up the engine, the right one starts—but the left one doesn't. "So," says Charlie, "it looks as though we are marooned! How will we ever get in a spare part?"

Then I had a great idea. I remember the model planes I had when I was young. We used to put a string around the propeller boss to get them started.

I run for the lake and get a rope from a canoe. I holler to the men watching: "Come! Help us!" They follow me to the plane and help me run the rope around the boss of the propeller. "They don't speak English, Geoff!" Anthony yells.

"Then I'll teach them to count! *One!*" I lead. "*Two! Three!*" With the rope over our shoulders, we run as fast as we can. Suddenly, the propeller whips around, and with a loud bang the engine catches and starts.

"Amazing," Charlie Lafave says, turning to the film crew. "Did you guys get that?"

The next day in our new location we're coming back from a village, and our guide says to Lauren, "You see the women here, Ms. Hutton, how one breast is often much larger than the other?"

Lauren looks up, looks around at the women rearing their children and watching us from their homes. "Well I hadn't noticed," she says, "but yeah, you're right! Why is that?"

"Well," says our guide, "the most valuable thing they have are pigs, you see. If they don't want to risk a young piglet being pushed off the sow's teats by the other piglets, then they'll nurse the piglet themselves."

Lauren goes completely berserk. "That's one of the wildest things I've ever heard!" she says. "Are you making this up?"

Market in Kamindibit Village—I still have some masks in my collection.

"No, Ms. Hutton!" says the guide. "I'm not making this up, it's true!

"Geoffrey, it's true?"

"It's absolutely true."

When we screen Lauren's adventure, we decide to film another episode, this one starring the actor James Brolin, who wants to see a leopard in the wild. *To the Ends of the Earth* airs on the USA Network in 1994. The series receives two nominations for the Cable ACE Award, considered to be the cable counterpart to the Primetime Emmy Awards. To this day I like to look at the footage again and relive those one-of-a-kind adventures.

Chapter 15

Alaska

❖❖❖❖❖

1997

It's no secret that one of my longtime dreams was to conquer America—both in polo and in business. After *To the Ends of the Earth*, I begin to focus on experiential travel opportunities that don't require our American clients to travel internationally. That is, Abercrombie & Kent will make the United States as exciting a destination as many of the foreign locations our clients explore. To create the ultimate American escapade, we scout out wide, open spaces, a distinct cultural experience, and, most important, a total wilderness getaway. I worked to develop the early flying safaris in Africa, and the idea dawns on me: *Let's start flying safaris in America.*

And so, in the summer of 1997, Jorie and I fly from Florida to Anchorage, Alaska, to begin a two-and-a-half-week reconnaissance of

My first glimpse of Alaska from the plane, an awe inspiring wilderness.

a location where, as I note in my diary, one can have total isolation. Alaska is one mission that turns out to be as much play as it is work: our backwoods quest certainly brings out the love of the outdoors in both of us. It also thrills me with both the all-American exploration *and* the business opportunities to follow.

The Regal Alaskan Hotel in Anchorage is not the quietest of places, situated only ten minutes from the airport, with aircraft and floatplanes flying incessantly overhead. However, the hotel lobby does seem to be an excellent spot for pilots to meet women. "Is there a beauty pageant here or something?" I ask the clerk at check-in. "What are all these pretty women doing here?"

"No, Mr. Kent, unfortunately not," he tells me. "These are the pilots' wives." He leans in and lowers his voice to a hush. "This area has a lot of widows."

"Oh dear, you've got to be joking."

He shakes his head. "You'll see: in Alaska, you fly from city to city, often very low through the trees or over water. We have one of the highest plane crash rates anywhere. Already two planes have gone down this year."

"It's only July."

He twists his face in a wistful way, as if to say, *I know.*

As Jorie and I travel to our suite, I recall an aviation rule of thumb that I learned in the army: "There are old pilots and there are bold pilots, but there are no old, bold pilots." When we reach our room, I wrestle out my diary and write:

IT IS VITAL THAT A&K CONTACTS THE LOCAL TOUR OPERATOR IN ALASKA TO MAKE SURE THAT WE GET THE NAMES OF PILOTS WITH THEIR COMPLETE HISTORY. ONLY THEY, THE ALLOCATED PILOTS, SHOULD BE USED FOR CLIENTS AND NOBODY ELSE.

This is essential . . . can A&K please activate.

As a result of the noise from the airport, we're up by seven o'clock on our first morning in Alaska: Thursday, August 7, 1997. We have coffee delivered and work to reorganize our luggage—with the cold-weather gear that we've packed, we have far too many bags! "I'll get that for you," says Michael, the concierge, when he arrives at our room alongside the waiter carrying our coffee. "Mr. Kent, where are the two of you headed today?" Michael asks.

"We're off to the Pribilof Islands." Jorie's first wish was to go birding on Saint Paul and Saint George, the two islands of the group, which lie to the southwest of the Alaskan mainland.

Michael doesn't quite see the appeal. "The Pribilof Islands? What on earth for?"

"Well, I suppose we'd like to go and see the wildlife."

He shakes his head, as if trying to shake off my foolhardiness. "And how long will you be staying?"

"Two days."

8.3 million acres in Alaska were set aside in 2010 as a polar bear sanctuary to help protect these magnificent animals from extinction due to melting sea ice.

"Well, please don't spend any longer than that!" he cries. "And I hope you don't get socked in!"

"Socked in?"

"The weather!" he says. "It's a perpetual natural disaster!"

"It gets that bad, does it?"

"You do know that Pribilof experiences horizontal rain, don't you, Mr. Kent? It rains constantly there, and the wind is so violent that it turns the rain so it comes at you sideways!"

Jorie pauses from fastening her scarf around her neck to give me a glance. *What can we do?* her eyes ask me.

"If you don't mind, Michael." He obliges and takes a load of our bags. Far too late for the concierge to talk us out of this now.

By the time we board our plane to Saint Paul, it's sufficiently evident that perhaps Michael was correct: the weather is one of the key determining factors for travel in Alaska. We're scheduled to depart on PenAir flight 4250 for Saint Paul Island, but by the time we're situated in our seats, our pilot announces that the weather is turning so rough that we have to take on extra fuel and fly via Dillingham to avoid the torrential rain. "What will flying via Dillingham do?" Jorie asks our stewardess.

"In the event that we reach Saint Paul and can't land because of bad weather," the young woman replies, "we should have enough fuel to return back here, to Anchorage."

We exchange a glance. *Oh dear.*

The four-hour trip is incredibly scenic, with particularly heated excitement when, to the north of us, we see Mount McKinley, the tallest mountain in North America, towering to 20,320 feet. The stewardess leans down to us, her eyes fixed out the window. "You're lucky," she says with a smile. "Only one-third of summer visitors get a chance at that view."

Jorie grips my arm with a thrill. "We can take Mount McKinley off of our 'to see' list now."

The Pribilof Islands are famous for their rugged natural beauty, their large seal populations, and their migrating birds. The four islands are volcanic in origin, and only two of them are now inhabited. When we land on Saint Paul Island, the largest of the Pribilofs, Sean, our local guide, explains that the island is located 300 miles west of the Alaskan mainland and 240 miles north of the Alaskan peninsula. It's also within the eastern Bering Sea archipelago, which, to my shock, I learn is actually *west* of Hawaii!

We drive out to Reef Point, a sanctuary famous for its fur seals. Saint Paul is home to rookeries that draw nearly three million birds, and the island is also home to eight hundred thousand fur seals, which migrate every spring from as far south as the Baja California Peninsula. This is probably one of the most concentrated numbers of mammals anywhere in the world, obviously nearly equal to Kenya's wildebeest migration at one and a half million. However, all of the mammals in Saint Paul gambol in the sea and on the beaches of this one small island, with the males sliding around on their flippers staking their claim of the women. The male fur seals collect a harem of up to eighty females, which obviously produces some adorable cubs.

Just as we're about to leave, a beautiful Arctic fox crosses our path, only a few feet ahead of us. Sean tells us that he recently saw a bald eagle take one of these foxes, swooping right out of the sky and picking him up with its talons. "There's a bald eagle right there," I point out as we reach the harbor. The two of them glance up to discover the bird standing on top of a crane.

"It is indeed," Sean says. "It's rare to see them this up-close—deceivingly dangerous predators!"

In the afternoon, we drive through the town of Saint Paul, fascinated by its cultural heritage. The Aleut community here is the largest in the world, making this an area that is richly influenced by its Eskimo origins. The Aleuts migrated over the land bridge between Asia and North America toward the end of the last ice age and were the first human inhabitants of the Aleutian Islands. Today they comprise a large segment of this village, with its tiny population of five hundred people and its two homegrown industries: halibut- and crab-fishing, and tourism.

Driving through the village, we observe how quaint and simple life is: there's a pub, two policemen, a stoplight, and a deli. We drive past the town's only school just as the children, sturdy-looking with their round faces and heavy coats and boots, are exiting for afternoon dismissal. Sean also points out the Russian Orthodox church, explaining that in the late 1700s, the Russian navigator Gavril Pribylov became the first European to discover these islands. He had followed Aleutian legend in search of fur seals, which he and his men hunted and took home to sell, and in return, they left their Orthodox faith. Fortunately today, fur seal hunting—a barbaric act that involves the clubbing of seals and their pups—has been outlawed, except for the Aleutians who are allowed to hunt two thousand of them each year as part of their staple diet. There aren't many foods that I won't at least try, but I couldn't imagine anyone hurting one of those sweet seals.

That night back at the abode, we're amazed that one can literally sunbathe in one's bed, as the sun hovers until midnight. The next morning, we wake up at sunrise: seven thirty, on the dot.

On the way out, Sean points out the false arnica flower, bigger and brighter than a daisy, and another radiant yellow flower. "That's an Arctic poppy," he says. "Don't pick it, Mrs. Kent!"

Jorie looks at him, alarmed. "Why?" she asks. "Is it poisonous?"

"Not very, but it's an old Alaskan wives' tale: if you pick the Arctic poppy, then today it will rain!"

"Well by now, I ought to have a bouquet of them!" she says.

We huddle under the hoods of our jackets to beat the rain toward Sean's truck, and quickly he scans the radio stations to locate the forecast. "Northeast winds throughout the day," says the meteorologist, "with periods of rain and fog." But on our way past English Bay, the sun beams down on the beach's thick, grassy sedges. "This whole island is only about three thousand years old and is thought to have been home to the last of the mammoths," Sean says. "You see the cone of the volcano over there, and those rocks below it that look like cannonballs?"

"Yes," I say. Jorie glares through her binoculars.

"We call those 'splatterbombs.' "

" 'Splatterbombs!' " She's delighted. "It reminds me of the time Geoff and I camped overnight at the foot of the Nyiragongo crater in the Congo as it was erupting. Geoff said it was like a flaming soufflé!"

Sean stops his truck on the high cliffs for us to take a long walk. We stop to study the only tree on all of Saint Paul Island, the Creeping Prostrate Willow tree, which is no more than half-foot high and grows parallel with the soil. We trudge past the rare globe wormwood, stretched tall and flowering as bright as a berry, and stop to view some red-legged kittiwakes with their chicks, some rosy finches, and a tame young rock sandpiper, which runs just in front of our feet.

A short distance later we happen upon a group of blue-face foxes nimbly running across the tops of the cliff, daring the precipices in search of fresh bird eggs.

"Look there," Sean says. "That's Rush Hill, the highest point on Saint Paul Island: six hundred sixty-five feet. If we were to spot any reindeer, it would be from right here."

"How many of them live in this area?" Jorie asks.

"There's a herd of several hundred, which were first introduced in 1911. During the occupation of the army in World War II, they killed them all but a few. In 1951 they were reintroduced . . . and now there are far too many."

We return to the airport for our four o'clock flight to Katmai

The Atlantic puffin lives most of its life at sea. Its short wings are adapted for swimming with a flying technique under water. In summer, the puffin's beak is red, blue, and yellow and explains the bird's nickname of the "sea parrot."

National Park & Preserve. "You're staying at Kulik Lodge, is that right, Mr. Kent?" one of the airport workers asks me.

"Yes, that's right."

"I'm sorry, you'll be about an hour behind. The charter plane that the lodge has sent for you had to make a stop on the way here."

"More fuel in case the weather strikes, I suppose?"

"No," he says. "Another pilot has died. They needed to carry his body home to Saint George Island for the burial."

Incredible, the risks these pilots have to take.

On our eastward flight toward the volcanic landscape of Katmai, our captain points out Augustine volcano, which erupted a decade ago. He was around to see it and says that the ash blew up to forty thousand feet! Indulging our intrigue, he flies around its perimeter and shows us several fissures where the smoke remains wafting high.

We fly over beautiful country with snow-topped hills, landing after an hour's flight on the Kulik Lodge's rough pebble airstrip. Out come a handsome, hearty couple—presumably Bo Bennett, who manages the lodge, and his wife, Amy. They escort us into Cabin 11, where the owner, Sonny Peterson, joins us. His father founded this famous lodge in 1950. "Be prepared," Sonny says with his tongue in his cheek. "I understand tomorrow will be your first ride in a floatplane."

"That's right," I tell him. "We can't wait to learn to cast."

"For now, settle in and then join us for dinner in the dining room," Amy says. "We have a classic Alaskan menu to welcome you."

We get into our cabin and turn to wash up. "Geoff," says Jorie. "Have you got my bag?"

"No, I don't think so . . . wait a second, both of my bags are here—"

And the realization strikes us: the bellboy at our hotel in Saint Paul had taken both of *my* suitcases and had left Jorie's. "No suitcase," she says.

"And no clothes."

"It's rather cold here . . ." She breaks into a wide smile, and I know exactly what she's got up her (rather drafty) sleeve: she gets to squeeze in a shopping trip before our day of fishing tomorrow.

In the lodge's office, Amy Bennett gets on the radio to the tour operator. "Is there no telephone anywhere on the property?" Jorie whispers.

I shake my head. "Evidently not."

"So you think it could come in on the next flight?" Amy says, sliding paperwork to me across the desk. "Your fishing licenses and registration cards," she whispers, covering the radio's mouthpiece. "If you'll fill them out before you leave today, please." She turns her voice back to the radio. "But the next flight doesn't arrive until tomorrow afternoon!"

Jorie wanders to the window that looks down to the front of the lodge. "Geoff!" she says with a gasp. "Come, look!" There, down in front of the lodge, stands a burly brown grizzly bear looking for fish in the stream.

"Sonny will take you out to Brooks Falls in the floatplane today," Amy calls. "The truck's waiting out back to take you to meet him!"

We take off from the nearby airstrip, and for once, the weather is glorious.

Sonny flies us over the rivers, where we witness flashes of red resembling coral thick in the crystal streams. "This is a salmon run," Sonny says. "It's especially red right now because they're spawning."

We fly over emerald-green lakes with backdrops of snow-capped mountains, and we pass over a series of rocky lakes studded with spruce-clad islands stretching to the far horizon—beautiful and unspoiled. There's also a crater lake that's a different color than the other bodies of water—much more opaque. Sonny tells us that it's because of the glacial sediment and volcanic ash. We were now at a mere thirty-five feet.

We land at Brooks Falls, between Naknek Lake and Lake Brooks, in Katmai, and immediately it's clear why the lodge there is famous for its bears. A bear—a male—stands on a bridge, making it impossible for us to cross to the lower river platform. "You don't want to get near him," Sonny says. "The rule is to stay one hundred yards away from a sow, especially if she's got a cub with her. For the bears, stay back fifty yards."

"That one looks hungry," Jorie says.

"Yep, and he knows where to find the salmon. From late June until late July, the largest sockeye salmon run in the world takes place here. The bears have a helluva feast. By now, he oughtta be migrating downstream with his cronies, though."

"That's where the fish have gone?" Jorie surmises.

"That's right," Sonny says. "He won't find them here . . . and when these guys get hungry, they'll eat anything: dead fish, rotting grass, moose calves, even their own cubs."

"Goodness!" Jorie says. "How big are their cubs?"

"One tiny pound," Sonny tells her. "You can hold one in the cup of your hand."

"And how big is that one?" I ask, pointing toward the bridge.

"He's probably between nine hundred and a thousand pounds . . . but in March, when he wakes up from napping all winter, stay *faaar* ay-*way*. He goes down to seven hundred pounds, and let's just say he's grocery shopping. There have been businessmen who have come in the spring and been delayed getting home from here by a couple days," Sonny says. "You do not want to get in the path of a hungry bear." He secures his ball cap down on his head. "Well, not much more we can do here if we can't get from A to B. What do you say we get back in the plane and see what we see?"

We take off again, heading through the Valley of Ten Thousand Smokes toward Katmai Volcano, whose last eruption in 1912 led to its reduction in height from 8,000 feet to 6,715 feet. Sonny zips the plane into the volcano's crater and shouts to us over his shoulder, "I landed a plane in here once!"

"We believe you," I tell him, "but let's not try it again!"

Before us stands a verdant green mountain capped by a snow-white blanket and specked with spots as black as ants. "Caribou!" Sonny says. "There are just a few dozen of them here, but they're part of a herd of thousands!"

He takes the scenic route back to Kulik Lodge, and Jorie and I cannot believe our eyes. The river below us is full of signal-red salmon on their annual run. They arrive from the ocean bright silver, and they turn red just prior to spawning. Then the male and the female lie on their sides and make a hole with their tails among the rocks at the bottom of the river. There

the female deposits her eggs and the male fertilizes them. Together, they cover up the hole and move on upstream to repeat the process time and time and time again. Sadly, Sonny tells us, at the end of the spawning process, both male and female die and create food for the bears, the rainbow trout, and, of course, for their own baby salmon when they hatch—just part of nature's cycle.

Therefore, the rainbow trout here are massive, which no doubt contributes to the huge success of Kulik Lodge.

The next morning we wake at seven o'clock to a light rain. Optimistic that a drizzle won't sabotage our day of fishing, we dress excitedly. By the time we enter the dining room for breakfast, though, the wind is shoving the rain at us in gusts of forty miles per hour. For the morning, we hide out in the dining room, telling stories until noon, when lunch is served: excellent spaghetti bolognese, a delicious salmon pâté, reindeer sausages, and peeled shrimp.

We return to our cabin to haul ourselves into our waterproof waders and boots. Vic, our guide for the day, awaits us down at the beach, where we climb into his small boat and go roaring up the Kulik River for our day of fly-fishing.

For the first twenty minutes, Vic teaches us how to cast—not an easy thing with the wind ripping at our poles. However, we both get the hang of it, and Vic sets us loose to start fishing. "If you'd like a little luck," Vic says, "try fishing with this."

I take the fly from his grip. "What is it?"

"A famous fly-tier made it, it's a special fly. We call it the bunny hugger."

"The bunny hugger?" Jorie says.

PRECEDING PAGE: *It is thrilling to watch pieces of tidewater glaciers break off in the afternoon sun. This calving can be very dramatic and create large waves.*

"Yes," Vic says. "Yesterday, someone caught ten fish in an hour with it!"

"Go on," I tell Jorie, "take it."

"Why?" she asks. "You think I need the help?"

"Well, I suppose if you catch a trout, I can take the credit for having given you the bunny hugger!"

"And if I don't?"

"Then I've still given you the best fly with which to catch one!"

"Oh, I see, it's a win-win for you!" she says.

Vic puts Jorie in the river first. As she begins to cast on her own, he comes down to me—and, on my very first cast, a rainbow trout hits the dry fly. "Quick! Reel it in!" he cries, but the fish escapes and swims away.

All afternoon we stay there fishing, wandering slowly downstream and casting. It's certainly an interesting sport, standing up to your waist in freezing cold water, the rain and drizzle beating down on you, the howling wind, and basically for minutes on end . . . no action.

Then all at once, I hear a shout from upstream: Jorie's got a trout. "I've caught him!" she shouts. "I've . . . almost . . . caught him!" Then suddenly, her expression is as vacant as her hands as the bunny hugger swishes toward me, just out of arm's length. The fish—a huge rainbow trout that leaps high in the air on its way downstream—has bitten the bunny hugger right out of Jorie's hands and escaped.

"Poor Jorie!" Vic calls. "You lost your trout *and* the bunny hugger!"

We laugh, Jorie the good sport included, despite the loss of her bunny hugger, and meander farther downstream. "At this point it's more for the sake of the experience than the fish, wouldn't you say?" Jorie says, and just then there's a tug on my line.

"Vic!"

"Reel him in, Geoff!" Vic cries, and the three of us clamor in great excitement as I try to reel it in. This time the fish comes within ten feet of me, and then at the last minute he's able to toss the fly.

"Let's call it a day," I say. "We've given it a good go."

"One more cast," Jorie says. "For good luck."

We cast, wait patiently—and again a pull on my line. This time, I reel him in like the dickens, with whoops of joy when I get him with success. "This is probably the biggest one all day," Vic says, unhooking him from my line. "He goes about two and a half pounds."

"Not bad for our first try, Geoff!" Jorie says.

Quite pleased, I have to agree. "Not bad at all."

"Okay," Vic says. "Go on. Let him go."

I take a good, long, longing look at my fish . . . and I toss him back downstream.

"Catch and release is a bear, eh?" Jorie says, patting me on the back in half-joking empathy.

"Having admired my trophy, I was happy to send him on his way," I reply. "Not much, I hope, worse for the wear."

"Indeed," she says. "Honor prevails."

When we return to Kulik Lodge, we pack hurriedly and visit the gift shop to buy some beautiful walrus ivory and a carved mammoth tusk. "You're sure that it's all right?" I ask Amy Bennett.

"Mr. Kent, these are *only* carved by the Aleut people. I promise you it's totally controlled."

We seek out Sonny Peterson to pay our fond farewell, and he tries to insist that we spend another night. He's quite prepared, he says, to kick clients out of our cabin.

The Alaskans are so welcoming, like all pioneer people. "I'm going to miss this place when we return home in a few days," Jorie says.

Bo Bennett stands assuredly outside our floatplane to check that we're safely ensconced after we board. "This weather is especially horrendous today," Bo hollers inside, as I glance up front to see who our pilot is.

Just then he turns around to me. "I've been flying the valleys around these parts for eighteen years," he says. "I promise, Mr. Kent: you two are in good hands."

The floatplane runs up and then lifts off ground, and when we've cleared the trees, I glance at the speedometer: one hundred and forty miles per hour. The pilot hugs the contours of every valley, dipping just fifty feet above the valley floors at some moments.

After just over two hours, we arrive in Fairbanks, where the local agent—very on top of all the details—takes our luggage and checks us into our rooms at the Princess Riverside Lodge, one of the newest hotels in Fairbanks, located on the Chena River.

In the room we have a picnic lunch before a phone call causes me to rise. "Mr. Kent, I'm so sorry," the local agent says. "There's a possible change of plans, which I wanted to run past you before we shuffle any logistics." She informs me that Bob Schuerman, the chief pilot and general manager of Frontier Airlines, has offered to take us in his own private aircraft tomorrow afternoon. "You'd be heading up to stay for a few days at Iniakuk Lake and visit the Yukon territory, which is an experience all of its own," she says. "Bob called just to say how he'd love some time to meet with you and Mrs. Kent, but a plane ride north does so much more justice to the area than a restaurant or conference room."

"Let me speak with my wife," I tell her, "but this sounds fantastic." Twenty-four hours later, Jorie and I are headed out the front entrance. "Back to the airport!" says our driver, taking our luggage for the van.

"Can you tell we can't get enough Alaska?" Jorie replies.

At the airport, we're delighted to discover that Bob's plane is one in which we've both always wanted to travel: a Grumman G-44 Widgeon, which is a smaller version of the famous Grumman Goose. It's a totally amphibious aircraft that was built during the Second World War—an antique and lovely old lady.

With no hesitation, Jorie hoists herself up front. "An aspiring copilot, I see?" Bob says, taking a rib out of my athletic but unassuming-appearing wife.

"Actually I'm a licensed pilot," she says, acquainting herself with the controls. "Always wanted to fly one of these things."

With astonished eyes, Bob turns to me in the back. I adjust our bags around myself and give him a closed-mouth grin. "My American girl," I tell him. "We're both licensed pilots, so I suggest she fly the first leg and I'll fly the second."

With that, he guns the engines.

We hurtle down the runway and lift off, heading toward Iniakuk Lake. I take out my guidebook: the lake is sixty miles above the Arctic Circle in the Brooks Range, near the boundary of the Gates of the Arctic National Park and Preserve. This is an area where there are no maintained roads, no telephones, no TV or radio stations, no restaurants, stores, hotels, or gas stations; and no emergency services are available, no hospital, ambulances, police, or fire stations. Unless visitors arrange for someone to rescue them, no one will. People still freeze and starve to death in remote cabins in this wilderness. Months may pass before their bodies are found. "Bob, it sounds like a free-spirited place we're headed," I call up front.

"I'll say!"

"A real experience in self-reliance—"

"Or should we say suicide!" he says.

But one glimpse out the window proves the allure. The mountain scenery is beautiful, blazing with colorful lichens and wildflowers. "Go on, Jorie, you take it," Bob says. For the next hour, Bob and I discuss opportunities to collaborate in Alaska as Jorie expertly pilots us north.

She and Bob combine forces to take a detour around the dreadful weather, and after two hours, we descend for Iniakuk Lake. Together, Jorie and Bob make the landing—an absolutely spectacular feat. In floatplanes, obviously the two floats hit the water first, but in the Grumman Widgeon, the main hull is first to meet the water. A massive wave crashes up over our front windows as we hit the top of the lake and skim along nosefirst.

Then Bob powers up the engines, which turns our plane into a high-powered speedboat. He accelerates until the hull with its floats rises out of the water, and when he arrives at the shore, he puts down the main wheels to bring the aircraft up onto the banks of the lake. "The Iniakuk Lake Wilderness Lodge," Bob announces. "Unlike any place else you'll ever stay."

As we deplane, three figures approach us on the bank. They introduce themselves: Pat Gaedeke, who owns the Iniakuk Lake Wilderness Lodge, her son, John, and their well-known resident pilot, Don Glaser. "The Silver Fox!" I call to Don as he approaches to shake my hand. "You're a legend, what is it? Thirty-five thousand hours of flying time?"

"Thirty-seven thousand," he says with a flattered laugh. "Not that it's like me to brag."

No bragging necessary. Don's experience only further complements the distinction of this lodge, which is 100 percent solar-powered. Staff arrive at the plane to port our luggage to our private cabin on the other side of the river. Bob bids us farewell and says he hopes to see us again soon, then Pat ushers us to the main lodge for dinner: grilled salmon followed by the best freshly picked blueberry pie I have ever tasted. The bread is spanking fresh, having been baked on the premises that afternoon.

"Pat, is your husband no longer around?" I ask her.

"No," she says. "Six years ago we lost him in an airplane crash."

"I'm so sorry," Jorie says, visibly moved by Pat's disclosure.

"Thank you," Pat says. "John and I manage. Bernd first brought me to this area twenty-four years ago on our honeymoon, and we so fell in love with it that we just never left. We pioneered Headwaters Lake together—in fact, you'll see it. The people in that area call it Gaedeke."

"What did you put there?" I ask her.

"Bernd built some of the homes as specs and sold them, and he built us our own cabin. It's a three-bedroom cabin with a fireplace." She smiles. "Anyway, just wait until you see."

"I can hardly wait," Jorie says.

"As long as I'm in Alaska," Pat says, "I feel him with me all the time. This lodge is his legacy. I'll keep it going as long as I'm able."

After dinner, Pat lightens the mood when she and her son show us into the main lodge's storeroom. "Would you look at this?" she says, flipping on the light. Inside, the window is broken and a huge piece of paneling has been ripped from the wall.

"Who did this?" Jorie asks.

"It's not 'who,' " Pat says, "it's 'what': a black bear!" The bear broke in early this morning, she says, and we scan the damage: the chest refrigerator is destroyed, as though the bear had climbed on top and jumped up and down on it. "It ate *everything* from inside," she says, "including three boxfuls of Eveready batteries." The only things it left, she says, were two tins full of mushrooms and chili peppers.

"Not much of a vegetables fan, I suppose," Jorie says. "My heavens, can you imagine the stomachache?"

The next morning, we call for John. Since there are no roads, he comes and ferries us across the street to the little boat, which takes us to the terminal of the local airport, where

Don Glaser's Cessna 185 floatplane awaits us.

We take off on a lake over a mile and a half long filled with crystal clear, smooth water. Don flies us over Takahula Lake—turquoise and glorious—and Don says that here, guests love to board inflatable canoes and float down the river to be picked up again in five to six hours' time. "That should go on A&K's list of excursions," Jorie says. "A nice piece of soft adventure."

From there, the plane begins to climb. "Next site, the Arrigetch Peaks," Don says. "We'll fly up seven thousand feet. This is sure to be one of the highlights of your time in Alaska." We sail over the glaciers, up, up, and up; and some of the walls of the peaks are as thin as razor blades, honed over the millions of years by glaciers. At one point, we reach a sheer vertical wall dropping 1,500 feet beneath us. Don continues to thread his way through the peaks, reading my mind when he says, "In my twenty years of flying these parts, I've never had a single crash."

"Engine failure?"

"Just once," he says. "But I was able to glide it and land."

Over the ridge to the north of the Arrigetch, great excitement: a group of chalk-white dots on the green hills. "Dall sheep!" Jorie cries, and we count them, fourteen in all. Dall sheep are the only wild white sheep in the world, and native to Alaska and Canada's Yukon Territory. "We are now north of the sixtieth parallel," Don says. "This is Alaska's ultimate wilderness."

"How far does it stretch?" Jorie asks him.

"Are you ready?"

She nods.

"Eight million acres."

From here, Don takes us to the lake at the headwaters of the Alatna River, informally known to the locals as Gaedeke Lake, after Pat's late husband, Bernd. It seems he's sent us a happy omen when we discover our quest: the caribou migration.

I've read up on the caribou. Along with the deer and the moose, the caribou is one of the few species to shed their antlers completely. Both males and females have antlers, which begin to grow in late spring and are shed later in the year. They strike a strong resemblance to the fabled reindeer, and they are close cousins, but somehow the caribou appears stronger and more regal.

The tundra is dimpled with their tracks, and it reminds me of the Serengeti, its myriad spiderwebs across the land where the wildebeest trek in their migration. There are herds of caribou beneath us, easily in the hundreds. Don explains that when they're all assembled, the main migration numbers four hundred thousand in this western Arctic herd.

Don lands us on Headwaters Lake and leads us to the cabin that Pat Gaedeke's husband, Bernd, built for them. He walks inside to make coffee and light the fireplace, and Jorie and I take a seat on the cabin's front porch. "What a place," Jorie says. "Here we are, actually in the Arctic—"

"A hundred ten miles *north* of the Arctic Circle," I add.

"This is the sixty-seventh parallel," Don says, handing each of us a steaming mug. "You're having coffee on the Continental Divide. Looking to our north, all the rivers run to the Arctic Ocean. To the south, all the waters flow to the Yukon River—"

"And from there to the Bering Sea?" I ask him.

"That's exactly right."

"And to think that Pat's husband established all the homesteads in this area," Jorie says.

"Can you imagine?" I ask her.

"Pioneers," she says. "We know something about that, don't we?" We watch the caribou roam all around us, and a red Arctic fox crosses and comes within twenty feet of us. Finally, Jorie rises to go birding. Don takes a seat on the porch and talks me through the commercial plane routes to Iniakuk.

At two in the afternoon, we take off again and fly three

The Pribilof Islands are home to birds found nowhere else, also known as the Galápagos of the north.

---

hundred feet down the valley. As we fly over Pat's cabin, we spot a large solitary bull moose beneath us, and then . . . a brown grizzly swimming off one of the banks, just yards from where we'd been sipping coffee. Don banks around, and we watch him walking onto the shore—a marvelous brown figure silhouetted against the white beach.

From there, we go to the Kobuk River for one very Alaskan final adventure: a canoe ride. On this, a beautiful and serene afternoon, we row all the way to the rapids, where we turn around and spend a few moments on a sand spit. We take photos of each other and when we look up, there's a flock of Arctic loons flying over our heads. "Impossible to believe that we're only two hundred miles from Fairbanks, isn't it?"

"No roads whatsoever," Jorie answers, "and the only access is by floatplane . . . not even an airstrip." Thanks to that, this

A floatplane, the Land Rover of Alaska.

area probably will never be spoiled like so many other national parks.

Don allows me the chance to copilot with him back to Iniakuk
Lodge. The three of us strap in and idle around the lake for thirty
minutes to let the engine warm up, then we throttle full bore, and
a thunderous roar shatters the lake and the whole valley. Streams
of spray hit us, and we're climbing like a Spitfire.

What a sensation.

No sooner do we level off than Don swings the whole stick
and column over to me. "You're trained, Geoff," he says. "Go
on, fly us!"

We soar down the valley, bank the Cessna, and Jorie snaps
photographs out the window. I hand the stick back to Don, and
we buzz the lodge cowboy style just before we land on the lake.

The morning of August 12, before we leave the lodge, I sit
down for a meeting with Pat Gaedeke, who tells me she is open

to do anything it would take to work with Abercrombie & Kent. "You'll be a great success in Alaska," she says. After breakfast, the rain is pouring and the visibility is zero, but Pat's son knocks on our cabin door and says Don has spotted a way out for us to get to Juneau.

With rain pouring off the windshield, Don revs the engines and we take off into no more than three hundred feet of visibility. We crawl at eighty miles an hour and try one valley—no good—just a black wall of mist and fog. Don eases around and goes up another valley, slowly, until finally there are some shafts of light. Finally, the visibility opens to half a mile. Jorie turns to me and lets out an inconspicuous exhale—she'd been holding her breath, but now we're in the clear.

We transfer at Bettles to a commercial flight to Juneau, a city that's flooded with sunshine and cruise ships. We check into the Westmark Baranof Hotel in the heart of downtown Juneau. Our final dinner is an incredible surprise: excellent salmon ravioli followed by halibut with a delicious black olive sauce and fresh, fresh zucchini. The chef comes around, informing us that he's working to bring better food to Alaska. Maybe this is the start of a new trend.

The morning that we prepare to fly home to Vero Beach, I catch up on the *Wall Street Journal*: corporate legal battles, union workers fighting for health care benefits, a company that's running tests to potentially manufacture bulletproof jockstraps for the military. Immediately I think back to Alaska, how we could leave our cabin doors wide open and find everything as we'd left it. What a contrast to experience the difference between Alaska and the "lower forty-eight"—or, as we know it, the real world.

Chapter 16

The North Pole and Antarctica

✧✧✧✧✧

1999

Business takes a treacherous turn come the mid-1990s. Until now, 70 percent of our business has been to Egypt and East Africa, but after George H. W. Bush declares war in the Gulf, very few of our clients are keen to travel anywhere near the Middle East.

It so happens that in my life, I need a new frontier to conquer as well. In 1996, I suffer a near-fatal polo accident that crushes not just my face, neck, and spine, but also my hopes to continue in the sport I'd been playing for more than forty years. The worst consequence of being forced to accept that my time as a champion on the ponies is over is that I become a bear to live with. A broken man, Jorie might have been able to nurse back to wellness—but a broken spirit, no woman can fix. Polo was my passion, and without the daily adrenaline rush, I'm growing bored living in Florida.

Divorce is on the horizon and my business is on life support. Approaching the twentieth century, if hell were a location that I could pinpoint on a map, I could guide the first tours into it—I'd been there, and I knew the place better than anyone. I

On my way to the North Pole.

need to take some serious risks to get my power back, and I ask myself, *What would it take for me to be on top of the world again?*

Then I realize: I could *go* to the top of the world.

Maybe I could even bring business there.

With fast research, I learn that there's an expedition to the North Pole in July 1999—the last cruise of the century. With an optimistic resolve to brave what's next in our marriage and our business, Jorie and I make a reservation, and we share ideas about the possibilities of opening the North Pole to clients. *This* would be a new location to crack, we know, no matter how impenetrable the location seems to most.

I quickly learn, however, that nine feet of solid ice is pretty impenetrable.

I predict that our twelve-day journey to the North Pole may be one of the most lunatic endeavors on which we've ever set out. But, there's no denying that a journey on the Arctic Ocean would give any man new energy—or, at the very least, one hell of a story.

The itinerary reveals that we will depart on an icebreaker from Murmansk.

This should have been my first clue.

Murmansk is Russia's largest submarine port and, frankly speaking, a horrible Communist naval city that lies in the Russian Arctic, north of Saint Petersburg and just east of Finland. After one night's stay in delightful, orderly Helsinki and a two-hour flight to Murmansk, I take a morning bus tour of the city to kill time—and am immediately troubled to see how the Soviet Union has fallen apart. Factories sit idle. Hulks of old vehicles lie scattered aimlessly. The tour guide on the bus explains that Murmansk took a tremendous hammering in World War II—after Stalingrad, Murmansk was the second-most-bombed city in Russia.

Considering the city's location on the Arctic, I'd expected that it would be cold, but instead it is a brilliantly hot day. The people of Murmansk are sunbathing on the hills and next to the

The Radio Room at Port Lockroy, Antarctica. During the Second World War, the British established a secret base here. Wireless telegraphy by Morse code was used for routine communication and was the only form of communication with the outside world in the winter.

ponds, looking like seal colonies with their white bodies spread out against the rocks and the water. Even with the temperature blazing, the city itself feels frozen—both in its sentiment and in the less-desirable days of Eastern European politics.

I'm enthusiastic when it's time to exit the bus near the Murmansk harbor. From there we'll set out onto the Barents Sea, which opens to the Arctic Ocean north of Finland and Russia. Now, of all the vessels I've travelled in or worked on, I don't know much about this particular icebreaker, and when I spot the black-and-bright-red ship with the jaws of a shark painted on her bow, I determine that it may be a good thing.

Familiar with my work in the travel industry, the captain, as bearded and brawny as King Neptune, comes out to welcome me. Once I've found my way around his robust Russian accent, I come to decipher what's unique about this ship. "She's called *Yamal*," he says. "It's the Nenets word for 'the end of the earth.' " He's referring to the language spoken by the indigenous Nenets tribe in northern Arctic Russia. She's a nuclear-powered Russian icebreaker, he continues, more than 500 feet long and 160 feet keel to masthead. She cruises at an average of eighteen knots on open water, three knots through ice with one propeller—that has three blades, each blade weighing ten tons. *Ten tons.* The design sounds somewhat archaic, but on the other hand, what would I expect for a journey to the barest point in the world just to see what's there?

Before we embark, I travel to the helm and look down, noticing how sharply pointed the bow is to drive directly into packed ice. The front of the ship will hit it hard, and the bow of the ship will crawl fast up over the ice and crush it under the boat's weight. Considering the mass of our three propeller blades alone, I have to trust that this boat's got things under control.

When I reach my cabin, the accommodations on board strike a very Farthest North feel: The rooms are bright and spacious; the decor is basic and clean. The blinds and curtains are the thick European blackout kind, which makes sense as even nighttime in the North Pole will shine with daylight. Impressed, I figure that I've roughed it much worse than this, and it will feel fantastic to climb into a cozy bed after a day out exploring a land off the beaten path.

Off any path, really.

The engine revs beneath us and I start immediately off the deck, toward the cabin level. At first it's pure pleasantry and smooth sailing, until just after lunch when I hear:

Baaaahhhhhrrrrm

PKOW!

My God, I tell myself, *we're going to die on this thing.*

Crunch-crunch-crunch-crunch-crunch.

The ship lurches again, and for another few seconds we're moving steady.

Then:

Baaaahhhhhrrrrrm
PKOW!
Crunch-crunch-crunch-crunch-crunch.

The *Yamal* blasts and rumbles with the work of its mammoth propeller. I step out of my cabin, searching for life. Down the wood-paneled and brightly lit corridor, I spot a maintenance worker who is examining what looks like a fuse box on the wall. "Excuse me," I ask him. "Are you busy?"

"No, sir." He closes the panel and braves the thunder under our feet to approach me. In sincerely intended English, he asks me: "Is there a problem?"

"I believe I booked one of the antinoise cabins."

"Yes sir, you're in one."

Baaaahhhhhrrrrrm
PKOW!
Crunch-crunch-crunch-crunch-crunch.

He laughs. "You'll adjust, Mr. Kent. Would you like to see how it works? I'll show you the engine room."

I pace behind him through the corridor to a dimly lit stairwell, then down a steep spiral staircase. He opens a portal door into what looks like a nautical factory.

Everything inside the engine room is supersized. Two cylindrical nuclear reactors lie as the engine room's centerpiece, creating a level of noise that I haven't experienced since my time driving tanks in the British Army. "Is it normal for the engines to sound this loud?" I shout.

"Yes, sir!" he tells me. "They're producing enough energy to light a city the size of Paris!"

"My God," I murmur, the vibration in my throat as the only evidence I've just uttered a word. The power is impressive, but the noise is enough to drive a man insane.

"We're thirty feet under the waterline," he hollers. "Don't worry—if there were a problem, we could insert control rods and the chain reaction would stop in half a second!"

The crew from Sports Illustrated *setting up to photograph Kate Upton for the cover of the 2013 swimsuit issue, the bestselling magazine in the world.*

"Literally?"

"Yes!"

The thought is hardly more comforting. He leads me around the engine room, hollering over the nuclear-powered raucousness to explain the different pipes and meters and switches. The engines are so well protected with steel and concrete, he says, that even if a small airplane were to crash into the ship, the engines would almost certainly remain unaffected. He shows me the water desalination system— "If we were to get stuck on board," he says, "we collect some seawater from the Arctic Ocean and distill it for bathing and drinking."

"Let's hope that doesn't happen."

He laughs. "We always hope!"

He leads me to the massive fuel tanks, explaining how much money they save compared with vessels that are run on diesel. "When is the last time you all would've changed the fuel?" I ask him.

"Last week," he says. "Before that, probably 1995."

"How much would it cost to build a ship like this in the US?"

"In the US, five hundred million dollars. But the nuclear reactors have to be reprocessed every three years. That costs three million."

"Every time?"

"Yes, sir."

"What's the thickest ice this ship has seen?"

"She's only meant to break through five meters when she's moving—but I know for a fact that she's broken as thick as nine meters."

"Isn't that bad for the boat?"

"It's not good, sir. Sometimes there's no other way."

When I head to bed that night, I realize that one does not exactly *hear* the noise of the ice breaking as much as one *feels* it. As the captain drives the ship, she mounts the ice and smashes downward in one shuddering, violent crunch. The clash penetrates the ship's thick steel hull and travels all the way to the bridge deck, enveloping those at the helm. It's a piercing sensation, a thud and a grind all in one.

Under us, the ship backs off, lurches, heals, summons her strength, and thrusts itself onto the ice once more. Friction-reducing bubbles hit from her flanks as the sound resounds throughout the ship. Finally we are free . . . free at last . . . until the next pressure ridge.

I begin to wonder how I'll manage this for twelve days. The ship bounces backward and forward, large, thunderous jolts as the icebergs crash into the hull. All the time I'm seesawed and whiplashed around my double bed.

It's a nightmare.

I search for a thought to bring me peace, and finally, I think of the few thousand people who have ever visited the North

Pole. I think how the first explorers to come this way froze just for the sake of arriving here, losing their limbs to frostbite and sometimes their lives, and doing it all with great honor. I remind myself that I knew when I signed up that this really is an expedition, not a vacation cruise.

I spend the next three days working quietly in my cabin and taking advantage of the open-deck policy to climb up to the bridge any time a crew member comes over the speaker system to announce that Arctic wildlife are in view. We seem to be moving at a pitifully slow pace, and during his smoke break, the first mate tells me the ice packs have thickened significantly. We are travelling at only one knot an hour, and sometimes even less than that. On occasions the *Yamal* even has to stop, back off, rev its engines, and go at full speed into the pack ice. I watch, entranced, as huge ice floes are pushed sideways. Certainly it would be impossible for the ship to break through if they didn't drift. As it is, all twenty-three thousand tons of the ship power their way into the ice floes, creating a new passage through the fissures and cracks, like a pattern of frozen spider webs.

As we move farther north, the temperature drops steadily—today, thirty degrees Fahrenheit. The captain has announced that from this point, he highly recommends we wear a parka, gloves, and a balaclava to step onto the deck, but I'm surprised that I don't find it all that horribly cold. With my vision shielded from the sun, I look out over the Arctic landscape, searching for polar bears or their footprints.

The cetacean biology lecturer on board offers a presentation on the beluga whale, also known as the "white whale" for the pure color it turns in adulthood, and as the "sea canary" for the noises it makes underwater, which are so high-pitched that they're audible both above and below the sea's surface. He tells us that the beluga lacks a dorsal fin, which would get in the way under the ice, and that it possesses a flexible neck because the vertebrae are not fused. It's difficult to spot the beluga, he says, among the floating ice or whitecaps, and the best way to do it is to scan the water and waves for a white arc that appears, grows, shrinks, and then disappears. He tells us that if the conditions are calm and quiet, we might hear the "blow" of air when a beluga exhales from several hundred yards away.

There's a helicopter on board, which we fly once a day above the ship—quickly, because in minus eight Fahrenheit, the chopper freezes almost as soon as we take off. During our quick flights, we track the *Yamal*'s progress and view the polar bears that stretch their necks when they see us hovering. Their fur is a soft shade of yellow against the perfect white of the snow, their eyes and noses like the coal buttons on a snowman. Their walk reminds me of a male lion, graceful and seemingly self-aware, even with those giant webbed paws that give them a paddling effect when they swim. Back on board, we step onto the deck of the boat with binoculars for a glimpse of the adorable waddling seals.

The Arctic air rushes at us so fast that it nearly chokes me, but when I manage my breath, what comes over me is a sense of exhilaration that I haven't felt since the last time I climbed on a polo pony almost four years ago.

After our fourth day in the Arctic, we passengers gather at the windows to take it in: at 5:10 in the afternoon, the captain announces that his compass indicates that we're here. "We've reached the geographical North Pole," he says. "Ninety degrees north, the exact top of the world—the very spot where the earth's imaginary axis of rotation meets the surface of the planet." The crew leads our entire group out onto the deck, passing around champagne. Amid dazzling sunlight, sparkling ice, toasts, and cheers, I'm pulled away from the crowd toward the railing. Above the crystal blue-and-white glaciers and a solid ground of ice flies a black guillemot, a seabird that looks, dives, and waddles like a skinny penguin with a long, slim black beak. It's extremely rare to see this type of bird anywhere, and especially at this latitude. I take it as an omen of luck. Perhaps I'm finally turning a corner in my life. Perhaps this journey will help me turn my life around.

At the North Pole, the sun is seen to circle the horizon without setting for six months a year—then twilight descends and six months of night begins. That evening at dinner at the captain's table, we learn that there is actually more than one North Pole! The geographical North Pole, at 90° north, is the place where in any one day the heavenly bodies circle at nearly the same height above the horizon. However, the magnetic North Pole is the place where the horizontal pull on a magnetic compass needle is almost nil and the needle will swing around trying to point downward. At this location, the earth's invisible magnetic rays all come together. The exact geographical position of the magnetic North Pole moves from year to year around the Canadian Arctic. "Right now, it's seven hundred fifty miles from the geographical North Pole," the captain says. "But in another fifteen years, it will be about six hundred miles from where Sir James Clark Ross located it in 1831."

This place may be freezing, but it's thoroughly fascinating. We spend the next two days trekking outdoors, wandering among the pressure ridges and spotting wildlife with binoculars. I'm taken with the great pillars of ice, with their cracks and chasms, the huge holes in them that lead down into the blue.

The blue. There are so many shades of blue, the way the light pours into the ice and the ice pushes the light right back out. There's a range of hues from aquamarine to sapphire, dazzling and rich like none I've ever seen.

Back on board, we get good Russian caviar, cheeses, and soups for lunch and dinner; we also get the choice between Russian lessons, which I skip, and lectures from Arctic explorers and experts. Often I eat with Fred McLaren, the president of the Explorers Club, who tells me that as a naval submariner, he made three Arctic expeditions. On one of them, he was the first person ever to arrange a baseball game at the North Pole. The pitcher stood on the North Pole, and the aim was to hit the ball over the international dateline in the hopes that the ball could be caught yesterday and thrown back into tomorrow!

Fred's tone is a little more somber when he discusses how climate change is affecting the European Arctic seas. The oceans play a crucial part in absorbing carbon dioxide and redistributing heat, and the European Arctic is one of the world's most important areas for deep cold water formation, a fundamental component of global oceanic circulation, and of global and regional climate regulation processes. Very sadly, current models predict that climate change will cause the temperature in the Arctic to rise to approximately twice as fast as the global average, which will affect land systems. If such warming reduces the snow and ice cover in the Arctic, the high level of solar energy reflected back into space from this region would in turn be reduced, and more solar energy would be absorbed by earth. Plus, deep water formation might also be reduced, and the ocean's capacity to store carbon dioxide would lessen.

This scientific understanding—albeit, still somewhat limited—does hit home with me. Fred tells me that the oceans have already risen a foot in the last one hundred years, and studies indicate they will rise between two and a half and six and a half feet by the year 2100. The effect is picking up frightening speed. He also says it is a fact that the ozone layer as a whole is getting thinner all the time, and it is only because of this very ozone layer that humans are able to exist on Earth. The disappearance of the ozone layer in itself is incredibly serious. I make note to research the topic some more when I return home and somehow get efforts in place to reduce A&K's contribution to the problem.

As we spend our very last day at the North Pole, members of

Spotting polar bears from a helicopter.

the crew are playful, stepping onto the ice, hollering and slid-ing around like children. "You're the adventurer, Mr. Kent," says the captain. "Why aren't you out there?"

"Actually, I was thinking about a swim."

"A swim!" he says. "Fancy jumping in that ice cold water!"

"How cold is it?"

"Point-five degrees Celsius," he says.

Quickly I work it out: It's close to thirty-three degrees—one degree Fahrenheit above freezing. "You know what?" I ask him. "I'm so happy we made it here, I'm going in."

"I'll make you a bet."

"Go on."

"You'll have vodka with me, and then you'll dive in."

"Done."

"I haven't finished yet, Mr. Kent," he says, narrowing his eyes. "*No wet suit.*"

"No wet suit!" It's a schoolboys' dare, pure male foolish-ness. "And if I freeze to death?"

"An icebreaker maneuvers better than any boat in the world!" he says. "If you go under, we'll come and get you."

I weigh a doubt for half a second. "Fine. I'm going in."

"Remember, Mr. Kent, I said only your swimsuit! Nothing else."

I look out at the hole of liquid ocean that the ship created when it cracked through the ice. Behind me, the captain has already gone inside for the bar. He's pointing at me in jest, and in his proximity, Jorie's looking at me with helplessness in her expression. I know what she's thinking: the polo accident, my health . . . our future.

By now she knows me too well.

I step inside and head for my cabin. Standing over my drawer, I'm befuddled at what one puts on in preparation for a swim in the Arctic Ocean. Finally I dig out my swimming trunks, grab my robe and green Wellingtons, and head out the door.

Back at the bar, the vodka is harsh and it catches in the back of my throat. Before I can grimace, I brush past the captain and head out the deck. "Kent's going in!" he yells. As I peel off my robe, the crew gathers in the doorway.

I don't dare stick even a toe in—I jump in full-throttle, shocked almost to death. *It's bloody freezing!* I think, which is positive because it means I haven't had a heart attack. Quickly I build up and transition from treading water into a full free-style stroke toward the boat's stern. For the first few seconds, the water is so cold it literally takes my breath away.

I propel myself forward with every rotation of my arms, and then, somehow, my body adapts to the temperature. I swim fifty yards and then turn around to the boat. The men aren't calling out to taunt me; in fact, they're looking on in silence, clearly watching to make sure I stay alive. "I'm fine!" I call out. Their laughs of relief echo across the water, the steam of their breath rising in the sunlight.

I concentrate on the determination of my own breath, the

260 | Geoffrey Kent

occasional reach in my voice, as I push through the water. It's a perfect liquid body—no slush, no ice—and the sun is shining down closer than I've ever seen it in proximity to earth. *No way would I have died out here*, I tell myself, following the fog of my breath to chase the boat. I've survived near death in my polo career and desperate measures in my business. It would have required more than cold water to take me down.

Finally I reach the ship and climb the ladder as Jorie and the crowd of men gather around to see me back on board. One gives me a towel and urges me into my robe; another hands me my wellies. "I'm going to take a stroll," I tell them, bundling up and tying my bathrobe belt tight.

A few of them look at each other, puzzled. "Geoff—" Jorie starts.

"I'm fine," I assure her. "I just want to have a walk on the ice."

Shrugging, they all turn and trickle back on board. This is my opportunity. I run behind a pressure ridge, where I hide out for a moment until I hear: "Mr. Kent! Mr. Kent? Where are you?"

It's the captain's voice.

"*Geoffreeeey!*" he cries out. "*Geoffrey!* Are you alive out there? Everyone's boarded, Mr. Kent!"

"Oh!" I call out. "Here I am, sorry, I must have got a bit turned around."

"Mr. Kent!" he calls. "Get on board, we've got to move on!"

"Right!" I make my way back up the gangplank and onto the ship. Inside I'm met with blankets, hot tea, and Glühwein, a mulled German wine, in abundance.

And, I'm satisfied: *I'm officially the last person in the twentieth century to stand on the North Pole.*

This makes the entire trip worth telling about.

PRECEDING PAGE: *Incredible ice sculptures in Antarctica.*

Our first day back at sea, the icebreaker powers back up:
Baaaahhhhhrrrrrm
PKOW!
Crunch-crunch-crunch-crunch-crunch.
The smashing and bashing is more intense than before. I know that if there were a serious problem, the captain wouldn't announce it publicly. I head up toward the wheelhouse and run into the first mate on the staircase. "What's going on?" I ask him.

"We've hit multi-ice. It's the thickest on record—no normal icebreaker can even attempt to go through." The scruff on my chin is rough in my hand when I try to conjure some way I can help. Aware of my concern, the first mate says, "Go to your room, Mr. Kent. Right now I have to make sure there's no one on the deck."

Thirty minutes later we seem to be moving smoothly when suddenly I feel:
Baaaahhhhhrrrrrm
CLUNK.
What was that?

In the corridor are shouts and jostling. I slide past crew-members who are racing down toward the engine room and make my way up to the main deck. There, three divers are suiting up in Russian diving costumes—old-fashioned, dome-shaped bell helmets, as if we're living in a Jules Verne novel. "What's going on?" I ask.

"There's a problem with one of the propeller blades," answers one of the crew.

"What on earth are the divers going to do?"

"They're going to try and fix it."

I head for the wheelhouse, where I find the captain staring at a satellite image of an ice chart. With his eyes fixed in front of him, he senses my presence. "Mr. Kent." He sighs. "It's the propeller."

"What does that mean?"

"It means I've lost my steering mechanism, and we have no power. If the divers spend more than a day or two trying to fix it, then we'll run out of food and we'll have to use the desalination system for water." I remember my skeptical half joke with the crewman who showed me around the engine room. Deep down, something was telling me this trip would get twisted somehow. "What's worse," he says, "is the temperature is negative thirty Celsius, and I'm working with zero visibility at the moment."

I join him in front of the chart. "If it's broken, how can we get rescued?"

"We can't!" he says. "There's nowhere to land a plane here, and this is much too far for a helicopter to travel."

My panic is gaining. "What can we do then?"

He turns back to the chart. "We have to find the path we cleared on the way here . . . but in order to locate our original path, we'll have to sail all the way to it."

"Can we make it?"

"It could work . . . but the ice has moved quite far in the last week."

"How long do you think it would take us to reach our original path?"

"Another day or more . . . but even so, that's less time than the divers would need to fix the propeller. It may be the only way, apart from dogs and sleds."

With wide eyes I turn and glance at him. "I'm joking, Mr. Kent!"

I walk to the rail on the bridge and look down to the deck where the divers are suiting up. The captain sends out an order on his walkie-talkie. "Tell them not to get in the water," he says. "Don't let anyone off the boat. We're going back to Russia."

It takes us another two days to locate the path we traveled in on, and then we have to make our way from near Greenland— named "green" by the Viking Erik the Red in 982 AD as a cheeky marketing gimmick, a guide tells me—all the way back over to Russia. We have to miss our tour through the Franz Josef Land, a polar archipelago where the Arctic fox is one of the only existing mammals and the only living plants are grass, moss, lichens and liverworts, and around three dozen species of Arctic flowering plants.

Arctic fox or no Arctic fox, lichens or no, when we dock five days later than the original itinerary had called for, even Murmansk feels almost as good as home.

The North Pole trek is quite a voyage, though frankly, I discover an extreme expedition around the same time that's a slightly more worthwhile trip. The bank calls my chief financial officer to inquire whether we would be interested in taking the *Explorer*, an expedition ship with a storied past for which we've been doing all the marketing and sales. "The German company that owns the ship is in some financial trouble," the bank explains. "They owe you hundreds of thousands for the clients you've sent to them—the ship is yours as collateral, if Mr. Kent wants her."

Does Mr. Kent want her?

I've had a somewhat personal history with the *Explorer*. Known affectionately in the travel industry as the Little Red Ship, the *Explorer* was designed by one of my earliest and biggest competitors, Lars-Eric Lindblad, specifically for expeditions. My mind raced back to a day in the early 1970s when I'd heard that the brand-new *Explorer* was docked in Mombasa, preparing to sail to the Seychelles. I travelled to Mombasa from Nairobi to have a peek.

"Mr. Kent." A young steward approached me as I stepped onto the gangplank. "I'm very sorry, Mr. Kent, but Mr. Lindblad thought you might show up here. He insisted we ask you to exit the boat and not return."

MS Explorer *in Antarctica, which guests fondly called the "Little Red Ship."*

I looked at him, shocked but well aware of my growing rivalry with Lindblad. "I'll exit now," I told the steward, "but tell Mr. Lindblad that one day, I'll own this ship."

According to our bank, that day has come.

The Little Red Ship has never been known as a luxury ship, to say the least, and having been built in 1969, she's nearing thirty years old when we acquire her. For us to take her, we'll have to create a trip so outstanding that clients will be content with her imperfections, and even perhaps find some of them charming. I think to myself that if we can use her while protecting the wildlife and the environment wherever she goes, without leaving a footprint, then it's worth a try.

And this is when we introduce our first-ever itinerary to Antarctica: a journey taken not for a rich vacation's sake, but for a rich education's sake. Species of the world's rarest and largest seabirds and seals live there, and if Abercrombie & Kent can bring in some of the world's most renowned experts on marine life, polar biology, and climate, then we can offer the most leading-edge Antarctica expedition offered by any travel company in the world.

The first few expeditions fill up with reservations, and so we plan back-to-back trips. Clients travel to Argentina or Chile, then take a charter flight to embark from the world's southernmost city, Ushuaia. The Antarctic travel season is short, the area is travelable only between November and February, and the number of ships that are allowed to enter each year is tightly regulated. We book half a dozen trips each season and consistently sell out each one.

At the end of each travel season we reinforce her steel, but despite our loving care, at the start of the twenty-first century the *Explorer* is well ready to retire. We sell her to a smaller company that plans to take her out only a couple of times a year— and then, a few years later, we get word within the industry that she's been sold off yet again. I wish they'd let her rest in peace, but I know the trouble: when she's not hosting passengers to generate profit for someone, she's fiercely expensive to lay up or dry-dock. The *Explorer* is an orphan, in a sense. The only place she's really ever belonged is Antarctica.

On Thanksgiving Day in 2007, I'm with Jeffrey Katzenberg, the CEO of Hollywood's DreamWorks Animation SKG, waiting for a meeting with the Prime Minister of Israel when I look up at the television screen in the waiting room and catch the sight of her: the Little Red Ship, making international news. "Go on in without me," I tell Jeffrey, somewhat alarmed. "I'll join you in a minute." The news ticker reads that the captain of the ship heard a loud bang, and then a passenger reported seeing red paint on a nearby wall of ice. The *Explorer* had hit a glacier, which put a hole in her old, weathered hull. Then she sank.

By now, Jorie and I had determined that our visions for our marriage and for our company were too different for us to stay together. We divorced in the early 2000s, but the *Explorer* wreck stirred my nostalgia. This ship had carved out new oceans; she'd been one of the first ever to sail around the Seychelles; we'd been the first to do the upper Amazon; and she'd even done the Northwest Passage—and in all that time, she'd never gotten world headlines. Now here she is, on her side in Antarctica about to meet a tragic end, and the whole world suddenly knows of her. It's a devastating fate for a boat that provided so much learning and so many memories to so many people: she was made to sail to Antarctica, and today she lies at the bottom of its waters. The good news is that all the people aboard make it off safely.

Not long after this, there comes a new security in my life, as well. One night in the summer of 2007, I'm dining at Chuflay Restaurant in the harbor of Portofino on the Italian Riviera when in walks the most beautiful woman I have ever seen. She's poised and elegant with eyes and cheekbones that remind me of Sophia Loren, and there's an energy about her that has stolen my attention.

When it comes time for me to leave, I approach this beautiful girl surrounded by her friends. "Excuse me," I ask her. "Might I buy you a drink?"

"No, thank you," she nods at the man sitting next to her and says "I'm with him."

"I'm terribly sorry," I tell them both, and wish them a nice evening.

Seven months later, I am in my very sophisticated gym in Belgravia, which has a dining room downstairs where I can take phone calls and have an espresso. During one of these calls, as I am walking past a private booth, I notice a stunning woman and I think to myself that I've seen her before somewhere. I finish my phone call, and then I suddenly realize that she could be the woman from Portofino.

"Excuse me," I approach her. "By any chance were you having dinner at Chuflay Restaurant in Portofino, about seven months ago?"

"Yes," she says, barely meeting my eyes.

"Do you remember me?"

Finally, she makes eye contact. "Yes, a little."

"Are you still with the man you were with that night?"

"No, I've left him, and I just arrived in London two days ago."

This is my lucky day. "May I take you to dinner?"

She gives me another second's glance, and I'm filled with hope. Then, she says, "No."

Deflated, I thank her anyway and get on the treadmill for a long run. I run hard and fast, trying to push her out of my mind.

After a while, I go back downstairs and ask her again. "Dinner with you?" she says. "I'll think about it."

"What's your name?"

"Otavia."

It sounds like the name of a queen, and I have to know more. "Where are you from?"

"Brazil."

And just like that, I'm hooked.

I leave to chair the World Tourism and Travel Council's annual meeting in Dubai, which I am cohosting with the ruler of Dubai, His Highness Sheikh Mohammed bin Rashid Al Maktoum. During the meetings, I text Otavia every day asking her about a date and time for dinner. Finally, after two days, she answers and agrees to let me take her out.

Dinner turns into a second date, and a few dates turn into a trip together, and it's when she agrees to go white-water rafting with me in 2010 in Africa that I realize I cannot live without Otavia—she's the only woman I know who loves adventure as much as I do, and the woman who shows me over time that she is always there for me. We marry in a small ceremony in London, just the two of us present. And take off immediately for a honeymoon in Brazil—where else?

There's new energy in my life, and in the business, as well. Into the twenty-first century, Abercrombie & Kent creates an Antarctic cruise unlike any other, equal parts lavishness and daring voyage: a luxury expedition. Today we sail *Le Boreal*, a ship launched in 2010 that offers everything from state-of-the-art polar technology to an outdoor heated pool and balconies off of every room for immediate views of landscape and wildlife.

In November 2012, when we cruise to Antarctica with a group of clients and one rather high-profile guest, no one is more surprised at how sought-after the ship is than Otavia. "Oh! Sweetheart," I tell her the first morning as we're leaving breakfast in the ship's dining room. "There's something I forgot to tell you about this cruise . . ." I haven't forgotten at all—it's that I haven't dared tell her until she was on board that the supermodel Kate Upton is on our ship.

"What is it, love?" she says.

"They're shooting the cover for the 2013 *Sports Illustrated* swimsuit issue on this cruise. It's the bestselling magazine in the world! Can you believe, Kate Upton, the famous model, is on this ship!"

"You forgot to tell me that *Kate Upton is on this ship*?!" she says.

During the photo shoot, the photographer directs Kate Upton, and Otavia directs me. "Look now—don't look now!" she says with every click of the camera. Not the most harmonious moment in my marriage . . . but it's certainly proof that on land, sea, or ice, nobody does it better!

With Otavia at Port Lockroy, Antarctica.

Chapter 17

The Edge of Space

❖❖❖❖❖

2004

W hen I develop A&K Space around 2004, my team and I have already explored and designed trips on each continent, and Abercrombie & Kent has close to four dozen offices around the world. It's finally time for me to test the ultimate limits—is there any place in the universe too daring for the avid traveller?

Well, I determine, there is no way to know what the final frontier holds for my business without trying it out myself. "Time spent on reconnaissance is seldom wasted" is one of the principles of war and was one of General Frost's favorite slogans from my British Army days. I've employed it throughout my career. The English Electric Lightning was built in the 1950s as Britain's first aircraft able to travel at a rate of Mach 2: approximately 1,520 miles per hour, or twice the speed of sound.

To this day it's the fastest fighter jet in Britain's history; and even having been a guest on the Concorde's last flight in 2003, I've never seen anything like this.

It's four in the morning and I'm inside Thunder City, currently Cape Town's site for ex-military jet flights. Reading the

---

Flying an English Electric Lightning at Thunder City in Cape Town.

release form for the flight, I realize I was right not to have told one person that I was doing this. Any true friend would have called me up and told me not to be an idiot. One line reads:

BEFORE BOARDING, PASSENGER MUST PROVIDE A DE-POSIT OF TWO THOUSAND POUNDS STERLING IN THE EVENT THAT IT IS NECESSARY FOR US TO FLY YOUR BODY BACK TO YOUR COUNTRY OF CITIZENSHIP.

I feel a wave of nausea, not at all helped by the fact that I haven't eaten a single thing in two days to avoid getting sick while in flight. I hurry and mentally review the training I've received over the last week: how to work the oxygen mask, how to activate the mechanism that releases the parachute in the rear of the plane that slows us down when we land, and, of course, how to work the ejection seat. There are two distinct ways of ejecting, they told me: one while you're on the ground, which is completely different from the way you eject while you're in the air. "If you make a mistake, you're dead," said the pilot.

"Listen," I tell him, "these seats were made in the 1950s—has anybody tested them?"

"No, it's difficult to test them," he says. "But we run electronic tests on them all the time. I assure you, it's fine."

A young man comes out and hands me a racing track suit, similar to what a Formula One driver wears: all-black with THUNDER CITY written on it in gold, and a helmet for the real official feel. "You'll just wear your T-shirt and blue jeans underneath," he says. I scan myself, remembering another slogan I turn to often, *Life is not a dress rehearsal*—but no pressure suit? No nothing?

My mind goes instantly to loyal Caroline Wheeler, the only person who knows where I've been for the past week—and the one who will manage everything if by any chance this doesn't go as I hope . . . if, God forbid, they have to ship my body home to London.

My watch reads six o'clock in the morning when the pilot wrangles himself into the cockpit and turns to me with a relaxed grin. "Are you ready, Geoff?" David Stock is handsome, no older than forty-five, and wears a wedding band and a perpetual grin. I'm relieved he is so affable—that will make this slightly less intimidating.

"Am I ready?" I ask him. "Absolutely."

With the jet's canopy up, we taxi across the apron to the start of the runway. The jet sounds like the most incredible race car you've ever heard in your life—it's thundering, it's roaring. Everything's shaking. When I tell this story later, I'll say that it felt like a Ferrari on steroids.

When we reach the takeoff point, David brakes. He turns to me, and in his South African accent he says, "ChristGeoff!" all in one word. "This is your last chance to bail out!"

"No bailing out," I tell him.

"You're sure you want to go on?"

"Yes, I want to go on!" I laugh. "I've been training for this."

"All right," he says. "Then you remember this one instruction: if there's a problem, and I want you to eject, I'm gonna call *One*. I'm gonna call *Two*. And then, there's no *Three*, because I'll be gone and you're the captain of the ship."

"Oh, Christ's sake, let's go."

The canopy closes; I hear it seal tight. Then—

BOOM!

We shoot off, going vertically from zero to forty thousand feet in one minute. At the very top of this climb, he does three loops, and we climb to sixty-five thousand feet and level out. We then accelerate to the full speed of Mach 2.2. David's voice pipes into my ears through the intercom in my oxygen mask. "Would you like to fly it for a while?" he shouts.

"Yes, please!" I take over the controls and fly the jet straight, not particularly interested in doing anything fancy . . . because I can't.

He takes over the controls again.

"You want to see earth?"

"Yes, please!"

BOOM!

Instantly, we're looking down at the purple curvature of the earth.

"You want to see the sky?"

"Yes, please!"

BOOM!

Instantly, I'm gazing up at an endless blue sky.

Then he flies us down, very low at just eight hundred feet over the sea—I can almost feel the jet creating waves beneath us. "ChristGeoff!" David says into the intercom. "This would be a really bad time for me to have a sneeze!"

"I'll say!"

From there we fly around a few minutes more, and within forty-five minutes of takeoff, I pull the lever as David instructs to release the plane's parachutes for landing.

When we get out, my legs are as wobbly as jam. I return the uniform and helmet and get my car back to my hotel. I call Caroline to check in at the London office, and then I can't sit still. *I've got to get some of this adrenaline out of my system.*

I head out and run five miles, thinking, *This has to be one of the most dangerous things I've ever done. I took on 5.5 Gs. How could a normal business guy do that? It would kill him, his heart could stop. I'm a sixty-two-year-old man who runs an average of twenty miles a week, and that was intense even for me.* I'm not sure if most Abercrombie & Kent clients would be up to such a feat, especially because this would be one of our more expensive trips, which would mean that in general, only our oldest clients would be able to experience it.

I call the head scientist and engineer on my A&K Space team;

he had worked on the American Blackbird spy plane. "Listen," I ask him. "I just need to know one thing. If we go into space, what are the chances that we will not have an accident? Can we be one hundred percent sure that won't happen?"

"Let me reword that for you, Geoffrey," he says. "There's a hundred percent chance that you *will* have an accident."

"*What*? There's a one hundred percent chance that we'll have an accident?"

"A one hundred percent chance, Geoffrey. Make no mistake: space is dangerous."

All that night, I lie awake and think about it—and the next morning, there's only one thing to do. I call the head of A&K Space again. "We need to let everybody go," I tell him. "All twenty of them. We cannot pursue this with those odds."

One year later, it became clear that the old English Electric Lightning needed more than electronic testing of its ejection system. David Stock, the pilot who took me to the edge of space, met his own tragic fate. While the plane was at full speed in flight, its main hydraulics collapsed, which meant that David could no longer control the plane. His only hope was to eject— and the ejection system didn't work. David was killed when the plane flip-flopped and plummeted straight down into the ground.

Today it's a relief, not a disappointment, that we had to determine that this was one product we'd never be able to make good on. Starting A&K Space was one of my most audacious enterprises, but a good leader knows when to pull the plug. For me, that was before we could make any mistakes.

Chapter 18

Iguaçu Falls

◇◇◇◇◇

BRAZIL (. . . AND ARGENTINA), 2010

O ne of the prevailing rules that I've learned about travelling with friends is this: come the end of the trip, you'll either like the person a whole lot more or a whole lot less! Travel is *the* best test of compatibility there is—especially when you and your companion are both thrill-seekers.

My staff and I go to great lengths to ensure seamless timing and logistics when I travel with Jeffrey Katzenberg, a revered client and friend, as well as one of the most influential figures in Hollywood. I'll never forget when I accompanied Jeffrey to the Masai Mara in Kenya on one of our early trips together. Our guide spotted a family of warthogs by the side of the road. "Pumba!" he said. "Pumba!" Then he turned to us with excited eyes. "Have you ever seen *The Lion King*?"

Jeffrey smiled. Over the guide's shoulder, I whispered, "This man made *The Lion King*."

So anyone can imagine that when he travels, Jeffrey wants the ultimate on-the-edge adventure *and* scenery that could inspire his next big-budget film. He also needs as exciting an experience packed into as short an itinerary as possible: three-week vacations aren't typically feasible for the Holly-

---

Iguaçu Falls is one of the most impressive sights in the world, with a breathtaking 275 cascades spread across a gulf of nearly two miles.

wood executive who works eighteen-hour days. With this in mind, in 2010 we agree to travel together to the most daring waterfalls in the world: South America's Iguaçu Falls, which divide Argentina and Brazil from each other.

The Iguaçu Falls themselves stretch the length of over a mile and a half as part of the Iguaçu River. The falls follow a dramatic horseshoe-shaped curve such that it is possible to be surrounded on three sides by water that flows vertically with such force that it creates a mist that rises with the illusion that the falls are cascading in slow motion. The water flows at an astonishing rate—over 66,000 cubic feet per second—which is twice the average volume of Victoria Falls's flow. I've never considered myself a spiritual man, but there's no denying that witnessing these falls inspires wonder about who or what might have created something that's simultaneously so beautiful and so intimidating.

At a maximum height of 269 feet and a width of just over 1.7 miles, the Iguaçu Falls are second in the world in height and width to Victoria Falls in Africa—but in my opinion, the falls of the Iguaçu are the most dynamic anywhere. Also, the Iguaçu Falls don't pour down in one constant curtain of water—instead, there are some spots where the water cascades down from one crest, travels along on flat land for a brief moment, and then crashes down a couple hundred feet to a lower level. It's Mother Nature's waterslide.

It's this view that makes the falls most compelling from the Brazilian side. However, reaching this side takes a little savvy, as our flight planners and I discovered on my trip with Jeffrey.

We start our trip in the Atacama Desert in northern Chile, one of the oldest deserts in the world and known to be the most arid—some of its highest mountain peaks don't possess a single glacier. On an airstrip in the desert, we board Jeffrey's Gulfstream V jet—a really cool high performance jet—and settle into our soft leather seats, sitting across from each other with an aisle between us, both working at our own separate burnished wooden tables.

As we buckle in, our guide receives a phone call. Good news, he assures me, our helicopters are confirmed and are already waiting to meet us on the Brazilian side of the Iguaçu River. The first leg of logistics for the day is locked in and ready for execution.

Our takeoff is particularly smooth; Jeffrey has some of the best pilots in the world. Through our windows, we gaze out over the desert, a ghostly kind of a place that's nevertheless worth taking in for its vastness, which is almost spooky, and for what one of our brochures describe as "the occasional signs of life"—the rare glimpse of vibrant desert flowers, a llama, an Atacameno village of tiny red-clay homes.

Jeffrey and I settle in and discuss our itinerary for the day:

After our three-hour flight to Iguaçu, we'll land the jet and climb directly inside a helicopter for an aerial tour of the falls. Then, a speedboat-sized watercraft will take us right up to the falls—a wet and wild experience at the point where the storm of water meets the river. The falls from that point are like a fickle lover, both drawing you in with thrill and pushing you away with force.

From there, the schedule only gets more exciting: we'll descend the rocks on the bank of the river and board an inflatable boat for an afternoon's white-water rafting expedition. Iguaçu's course is rated between a three and a five, depending on how the weather conditions interact with the river and the flow rate of the falls. After the day's tour, again we'll board the jet—this time flying to Argentina for dinner in Buenos Aires.

Jeffrey turns on his iPad, working as usual, and I look out the window, feeling confident that everything is very much in order. The first half of our flight is pure ease. I take out my BlackBerry to get through some e-mails.

Then, suddenly, the polished wood door into the galley

opens. Our guide beckons to me discreetly. "Mr. Kent!" He waves his hand in urgency for me to come.

Come in, I motion. *What's wrong?*

"Mr. Kent!" More gesturing.

Jeffrey turns around in his seat, curious at the commotion. I rise calmly. "Let me go and see what's up." Careful not to give him any reason for alarm, I step quietly into the galley and gently push the wooden door closed behind me. "What is it?"

"Mr. Kent, you'll never believe what's happened."

"What? Is there something wrong with the plane?"

"No," he says. "I've just been with the pilot, I was looking at the flight plan—and there's trouble, Mr. Kent."

"What is it?"

"We're flying to Iguazú."

"Of course we're flying to Iguaçu, that's the plan."

"No, Mr. Kent, we're flying to Iguazú!" I note his emphasis on the last syllable, which sounds to me like the place people go to view wild animals when they don't have time for a safari.

"Igua-*soo*, Igua-*zoo*—I don't follow you, what's the problem?"

"We're about to land in Argentina."

"Argentina!"

"Yes—Mr. Kent, this is the only place in the world that has almost the exact same name for *two* different airports in *two* different countries."

No. This can't happen with Jeffrey Katzenberg. I feel a sweat break across my forehead; I lean myself against the cabinet of the galley and take it all in: the flight planners have sent us to Argentina, while our helicopter, trucks, boats, guides, and security for the day sit waiting for us in *Brazil.* "We have to change the flight plan!"

PRECEDING PAGE: *Torres del Paine National Park in Patagonia is one of the most remote places on Earth and one of the least populated.*

"It's too late to change the flight plan, Mr. Kent. We land in less than thirty minutes. We're already making the descent."

"*Jesus* Christ . . ." I pace for a moment, considering what we can possibly do. This will throw off the whole day—and then it hits me: there's only one solution, and it will work only because we just so happen to have visas to stop in Argentina for dinner. "I'll tell you what," I say to my guide. "Run all the cars immediately from Brazil. Have them meet us in Argentina. Dispatch everyone immediately." I exit the galley and sit down in my seat. "Jeffrey, unfortunately there's been a mistake."

He looks at me calmly.

"We're headed to the wrong airport."

Jeffrey removes his glasses, always very patient. "What do you suggest?"

"We're going to land in Argentina and the cars will meet us there. I'm anticipating just a few minutes' drive from this airport across the river to the Brazilian side of the falls."

"That should work fine."

When we touch down, our handlers unload our bags and we pile fast into the car that's waiting for us on the airstrip. "*Go go go!*" I tell our driver. He takes off and drives like crazy, wheeling out of the airport's parking lot and heading for the bridge from Argentina to Brazil—a few miles that feel like an eternity, with a line of tourist buses idling in front of us. I stare out the window, thinking how our first view of the Iguaçu River is a total panic instead of the peace and perfection that it was supposed to be. Planning a fast-paced custom expedition like this is minute-to-minute, and if we can't recover the time we've just lost, we'll have to cut our helicopter and white-water rafting short—and we still might not make it in time for our grand finale dinner in Argentina tonight.

As we near the Brazilian side of the bridge, there's one final moment for me to hold my breath: customs and immigration.

Our driver stays cool and in control and rolls down his window. The Brazilian customs officer collects our passports and glances over his sunglasses into the back of the car, where Jeffrey and I are sitting. He exchanges words with our driver, who sighs, pins the bridge of his nose between his thumb and forefinger, and then turns in his seat to face me. "They want to check the car," says the driver.

"Check the car? For what?"

"Drugs."

"Drugs!"

"Sir, you're two well-dressed men approaching the Brazilian border inside a nice SUV. He says he has to search the car, or no entry."

This is unbelievable.

In unfazed cooperation, Jeffrey exits the SUV. I climb out on the opposite side. "Go on, get on with it," I tell the official. "We've got a helicopter waiting for us."

He looks me over in disgust, but it's clear he doesn't understand English. His shoulder nudges mine as he leans inside our vehicle, and his colleague begins to go through Jeffrey's things on the other side. I want to bury my face in my hands. The scene is mortifying.

Through our things they rifle, probing into bags, digging around the pockets of our jackets, and examining our electronics. The first officer reaches for my Louis Vuitton briefcase and sets it on the dirt road, and I nearly lunge after him before I recognize the gun that's holstered inside his belt. I shrug and raise my arms in the air, desperate and resigned. "Come on, man!"

"I look," he says, pointing to it.

I crouch to the ground and scramble for my key to unlock it. With a click the briefcase opens, and the officer waves me out of his way. He pulls out two of my phones, turns them over in his hands and studies them. He sets a pile of papers on the

Jeffrey Katzenberg and I in a power boat that went right up to the base of the falls, covering us with spray.

ground, and the pages take off in a gust of wind. *"My God!"* I cry out, bolting after them like a lunatic.

Finally the officer rises, eyes our driver, and lackadaisically steps aside. He nonchalantly gestures for us to get back inside the vehicle and then flags us through.

Our driver peels off. Behind us, the customs officer waves away the cloud of dust that's kicked up in his face.

Our helicopter waits, propeller spinning, and the spinning increases when we climb inside. I turn to Jeffrey and clench my fist in victory. *We're here.*

"Made it!" he hollers to me over the whip of the helicopter blades.

In an instant we're off, ascending fast over the expanse of trees, the river winding through it. Within just three minutes we have a bird's-eye view of the falls, a half-dozen endless baths pouring into the canyon. The land underneath us is loaded with bushes and pines. It forms around the falls in curves and rigid angles, the water shining up at us in greens and blues as it absorbs the hues of the trees and the open sky. Then, *the* moment, just as we move in above the tallest fall, the Devil's Throat: directly over its horseshoe-shaped curve, a rainbow rises in a perfect arc. Our pilot hovers here, and with no words, we all absorb the moment. Jeffrey looks to me, allows the slightest smile, and shakes his head. The image is almost impossible to believe.

The day rolls on according to the original plan. Even with our life preservers on and head-to-toe in rain gear, we still find there's not an inch of us that's dry after the boat ride near the falls. The highlight, however, is the white-water rafting. "The rapids are usually considered level three," our guide explains, "but today with the way the wind is interacting with the falls, we're at a level four. Are you sure you're ready?"

Jeffrey turns to me. We both nod.

Our guide climbs onto the very helm of the inflatable boat, a choice I find so defiant of nature that I can't help but love it. I give Jeffrey a smirk: *Only in Brazil.* Two rowers climb in with us and we push off onto a gentle river . . . only for the first few seconds, then "*Forward!*" our guide yells. The rowers row madly, and we face a foamy wave head-on, bumping and splashing over it, trying to salvage some composure in its aftermath. "*Forward!*" yells our guide again. The rowers' arms go fiercely, and we are both one with nature and against it. "Forward!" he orders again, and we yell as our boat rises with each wave; we laugh like schoolboys when the water calms enough for our heads to recover. The water sways gently toward and away from the riverbank's rocks, and then suddenly we are plunging toward the next set of rapids.

I once told a reporter that the best travel partner is someone who can always go with the flow—but my good friends know that when they travel with me, the flow is the fastest in the world. The trip is such a thrill that a short while later, we plan a return trip for more South America, top to toe. This time we bring along our wives, Marilyn and Otavia, as well as our good friend Mark Burnett, the television executive who created the *Survivor* reality series (and who was a highly trained paratrooper in the British Army), and his lovely wife, Roma Downey. Both Mark and Jeffrey rely on travel to inform their work—Mark and Roma's massively popular series *The Bible* was heavily influenced by their travels, and a while back, Mark asked me, "Okay, Geoff, where's the most impossible place in the world to go where we could do *Survivor*?"

So this is a group that needs my utmost attention to planning. We aim to leave on a Friday and return to Los Angeles the following Sunday, ten days in all—this trip has to be logistically perfect.

Off we go on Jeffrey's jet. The first stop is in Quito, Ecuador, where we take over a wonderful restaurant for dinner. The next day I take them to the Galápagos, where we've booked two nights' stay in the most beautiful home in the islands. Each day, our guide takes us out on a boat and we view the wildlife—blue-footed boobies, seals, giant tortoises—and Mark and I take a snorkeling expedition to see the stingrays. Again, I refuse to let him down . . . but on the boat ride out, I am somewhat nervous: I was once stung by a stingray, though not as critically as the sting that killed the beloved Steve Irwin in 2006.

I was windsurfing in Florida with Prince Michael of Kent and I jumped off my board straight onto a stingray and it wacked me—just like a bullet going in. Blood started pumping out, and I remembered the horror of this injury: for a man, the venom travels right into his male parts. My son Joss hooked my arm around his shoulder and rushed me to the hospital. "What did you use on the way here?" the doctor asked me.

"Ice."

I always told Otavia, who is Brazilian, that the Victoria Falls in Africa has to be the greatest falls in the world. Now I'm not so sure.

"That's one of the worst possible things you could've done," he told me. Apparently on the end of the stinger is a piece of bone, and on the end of the bone is an extremely toxic acid. They used hot water as an antidote to dissolve the venom, and I recovered quickly and lived to surf another day—but on this occasion I stayed very close to the surface snorkeling in the Galápagos with Mark Burnett.

From the islands, we fly straight into Iquitos, Peru, to do the upper Amazon. We charter a boat for two nights, spending our days viewing the wonderful parrots and pink boto dolphins and then we cruise down to the mouth of the main Amazon, where there's a rainforest with ridiculously high canopy walks that we all have to navigate individually. "Go carefully, Geoff!" Jeffrey calls. "It's very slippery."

"Go slowly, darling," I tell Otavia, who's taking the bridge steps in front of me. "This is very hairy." In that very instant, her feet go straight out, and *whap!*

She falls on the slippery slats of the bridge and slides on

her bottom until she is caught by the net that runs alongside the railing, stopping her before she falls three hundred feet into the jungle below. After I make my way down to check that she's okay (thank goodness, she is; she's utterly fearless), we go to scout out the anacondas and baby caiman and capture some photos of them.

We are sitting on our riverboat waiting to be picked up for our return flight to Iquitos. I've worked to secure arrangements with the Peruvian government to let us use a Cessna 208 Caravan, an amphibious air force plane with capacity for a maximum of seven people that can land in the middle of the Amazon River. But today rain is pouring down and the river is hazardously choppy. "Mr. Kent!" the pilot radios. "We can't switch off the engines, it's too dangerous!"

To reach the plane, facing upriver into the current, we board a small launch that pulls up alongside. As the boat and the plane bob up and down, the crew manhandles us one by one onto a pontoon and into the plane. Our wives are hanging in there, but rather nearing the end of their ropes. We're hardly strapped in when the pilot announces, "We've got to go!"

The minute we are all onboard, he revs the engine and gathers speed. I see that the river is full of small logs and jetsam, which he somehow avoids. I hold my breath until he gets up enough speed to lift the plane above the swollen river below.

"Well," I tell Jeffrey. "That was interesting."

"It sure was," he says. "That was one for the books."

Once we're safe, I pull out my itinerary—always in my pocket and loaded with logistics notes. As I review it, the details going forward are nice and tight: In Iquitos, we'll meet Jeffrey Katzenberg's G5 for the flight to Cusco, then catch the train to Machu Picchu for an anthropologist-led private tour of these ancient ruins, built by the Incas around 1450 and then abandoned roughly a hundred years later before being

rediscovered in the early twentieth century by American historian Hiram Bingham. From Machu Picchu, we'll return by train to Cusco and then fly to Lake Titicaca. But, as we are about to take off, my office radios that there are demonstrations in Bolivia and it is too dangerous.

We quickly regroup and file a new flight plan—directly to Patagonia, one of my absolute favorite destinations. The southernmost region of the South American continent, it's one of the least populated places in the world.

Torres del Paine National Park itself has it all: incredible mountains, glaciers, lakes, and the Serrano River (which makes for a thrill of a Zodiac ride), as well as a plethora of untouched ecosystems.

Explora Patagonia Lodge is located in the center of the park on the shores of Lake Pehoe, with breathtaking views of the Paine ridge and the granite towers.

The park can be explored by vehicle, horseback, or boat with trips across Lake Grey to see its namesake glacier. But because our group are all in excellent physical shape, we'll go on foot. The weather is beautiful and on the first day we trek for about six hours to Grey Glacier and witness the amazing sight of it calving into Lake Grey.

Mark and Roma Burnett, the fittest of all of us, get up at 4 a.m. on the last day and trek to the base of Paine Towers, nearly eleven miles over eight hours. They come back tired but triumphant.

On our way to the airport, we all rave about our days in the wilderness. I take it all in, content with another successful South American adventure with fantastic clients and friends.

PRECEEDING PAGE: *We hiked the trails of Torres del Paine National Park and were stunned by the spectacular views of the forest, the beautiful lakes, and pristine glaciers.*

Chapter 19

BOTSWANA

❖❖❖❖❖

2000

In 2014, I am featured in an episode of *In Pursuit of Passion*, a PBS television series that airs in the United States and around the world. The episode focuses on how Abercrombie & Kent started out as a mom-and-pop safari company that took clients into the wilderness, comfortably, delivering a travel experience par excellence, and growing into one of the world's leaders in luxury travel. During filming, I experience a few of my own firsts: I sit directly on the edge of the Victoria Falls and swim in the Devil's Pool, which the UK's *Daily Mail* has nicknamed "the world's ultimate (and most dangerous) infinity pool." Then I fly a microlight aircraft with a small "lawnmower" engine right over the falls, all the way down the gorge. We take a helicopter up with the doors off and do the scariest level-five white-water rafting in the world in the Zambezi River below the falls. When the first huge wave hits me, I fall out . . . and there I am swimming down the falls with the crocodiles. Otavia, my ultimate travel partner, was anchored into the back of the raft—so fitting that she was trying to keep me anchored, as usual, and keeping everything around us in

---

Sharing Jabu with my friend Ted Turner.

balance. She cheers me on when the boat catches up and res-
cues me, and today it's one of the travel memories we laugh
about the most.

During a calm and reflective moment on camera for that
production, I share one of the most significant conclusions
I've come to in the course of my career. Perhaps our neighbor
at our new house in Brazil put it best when Otavia stopped to
greet his dog on the beach. "It's nice to meet you both," he said.
"What do you do?" When I told him, he was shocked. "You
know," he said, "I've traveled on your holidays many times.
Your company is the only place where I spend money and get
richer instead of poorer."

(This has stuck with me just as much as the time decades
ago when a client thanked me because the sound of a roaring
lion outside his tent caused his wife to jump out of her bed
and into his, which was the first time he had slept with her for
twenty-five years!)

In all seriousness, it's true. No matter whom you're hosting
or where you are, the most important effect of travel is that it
does in fact change a person's life and their perspective on the
world. Often this comes at a very crucial time in an individual's personal development . . . and sometimes it even comes at
a critical moment in history.

One journey exemplifies this perhaps better than any other
in my life.

On the morning of September 1, 1997, I wake up to news so
surreal that it jolts me: the night before, on August 31, Princess Diana had been killed in a car crash in Paris. I was in
Florida and saw the news on CNN. It was almost as if I went on
autopilot, dialing Prince Charles. I thought it highly unlikely
that he would answer my call on such a tense day . . . and as the
phone rang, my mind raced.

I thought of his boys, those joyful, kindhearted boys, whom

I'd taken on safari in Kenya with their father in earlier years. I remembered thinking on that trip how as young teenagers, Prince William and Prince Harry visibly shared their father's appreciation for wildlife and curiosity to know nature. They were close brothers growing into fine young men with an understanding of their roles in the world—roles they both took very seriously.

I recall the time in 1992 when I traveled with Prince Charles and Princess Diana on a state visit to India—the very trip where Diana had posed very somberly on a bench for the press outside the Taj Mahal, shortly before they announced that they were about to divorce.

And I think of Prince Charles, my extremely revered friend . . . and in that very moment, he answers the phone.

"Sir," I say. "It's Geoffrey Kent." I search for more words, but only the obvious came out: "I'm so very sorry . . ."

He is deeply saddened about the situation and of course very concerned for his sons.

I say what else was burning in my throat. "If there is anything I can do—really, I mean that—"

"Actually," he said, sounding somewhat relieved for the first time in our conversation, "Harry's half-term at Ludgrove is coming up in October. He was meant to spend it with his mother . . ." Prince Charles went on to explain that he had a state visit planned to South Africa, and by that time, Prince William's half-term at Eton would have concluded. "For Harry, though . . . I think perhaps it would do him good to get away on safari for a few days and meet up with me in South Africa later. What do you think?"

Prince Charles knew his boys had fun when they travelled with me, but now he was saying something more: there wasn't just anyone with whom he'd send Harry off on holiday. In the most traumatic and high-pressure period in their family's

life, he was entrusting the safety and well-being of his son—
probably the most sought-after thirteen-year-old boy in the
world—to me.

Of course I will take Harry somewhere, I tell him. I didn't
want him to worry about a single thing. When we hang up, I
call Caroline. "We need to create an itinerary that starts out at
Kilimanjaro Airport."

"But Geoff, remember when Joan Rivers travelled to the
Serengeti? Even there, the tribesmen recognized her."

"I set that up as a spoof, remember?" In 1994, a Masai tribes-
man stopped Joan Rivers and cried, "Joan Rivers?! What are you
doing on safari?" Joan was a comedienne. I knew she would get
such a kick out of that . . . but for Prince Harry, we would go absolutely airtight and low-profile. "Geoff," Caroline continued.
"The Royal Family love East Africa. Tanzania is one of the first
places the press will suspect that Prince Harry will travel."

"I know," I told her. "That's why I'm taking him to Botswana."

It was in 1968 when I first went down to Botswana to visit
an old friend, John Kingsley-Heath, who was known widely as
a big-game hunter in East Africa, and also here, much farther
south, in Botswana. I'd known John for many years, and he'd
been a helpful resource when I was building our tented safari
business.

On that first journey, it took me about three weeks to drive
from Nairobi down into Maun—at the time a tiny little village with nothing more than an airstrip and a hotel with eight
rooms, Riley's Hotel. Botswana was known to have some of the
best game in the world. However, the purpose for our meeting
was different: John Kingsley-Heath wanted me to bring photographic safaris to Botswana. "Geoff," he said, "you have the
vision to do this."

So I did it. From the very early days of our business, Botswana has always been one of the very best destinations for gameviewing. Because of my knowledge of the country I knew that I could plan an incredible safari where no one would see Prince Harry.

I draft a false itinerary for a holiday in Tanzania and work with our PR agency in London to leak the decoy schedule to the press. The media goes berserk, many of them travelling to Kilimanjaro, camping out with their cameras, waiting for the moment Prince Harry would arrive.

Meanwhile, when we land in Maun (a slightly more bustling tourism hub in 1997 than it had been in 1968), there are only five of us—safe, sound, secluded, and secure: Prince Harry and his schoolmate Charlie Henderson, an armed policeman, and the prince's longtime nanny, Tiggy Legge-Bourke, and me. The only others present were the lions and giraffes.

With a camera and binoculars in hand, Prince Harry is in his glory. For three days we cruise in an open-top Land Rover to view the animals. We canoe and fish in the Okavango Delta—home to thousands of elephants, rare bird species, and plenty of lions and leopards.

But there is something else that really hooks me on Botswana. We meet an American, Doug Groves, who has devoted his career to a trio of orphaned elephants—two females, Thembi and Marula, and Jabu, a male. I feel a tug at my heart when Doug tells me, "Geoffrey, they've got no home. They're just wandering around, and they refuse to leave one another."

It strikes me right then, in the presence of Prince Harry, that life is not a dress rehearsal. There's no better time than now to begin to shape the legacy I'll leave behind. *Somehow, I tell myself, one day soon, I will build these elephants a sanctuary.*

When Prince Harry leaves me, he is all smiles . . . though, I have to admit, maybe that's because he and Charlie Henderson are on their way to see the Spice Girls in Johannesburg.

Sanctuary Baines' Camp was designed to blend into the surrounding environment.

I too am on to my next venture. First, I met with Ian Khama, then Vice President of Botswana (who became President in 2008). Ian had trained at Sandhurst and he flew me in a private army helicopter to scout potential areas where A&K could build a camp. "Gosh, I'd love to do something on Chief's Island," I tell him, referring to the area known as "the predator capital of Africa."

"Alright," Ian said. "I'll arrange for you to bid on the Mombo concession as long as you provide the right design, which is eco-friendly and provides employment with a financial return to the local community."

We discuss a camp that has too much land for one company to run, and it happens to be located in an area that I know has some of the finest gameviewing anywhere in the world. I meet with Prince Charles, who influenced me with his ideas about design and sustainability, described in a 2013 profile in the

Doug Groves with Jabu, Thembi, and Marula.

Telegraph. Journalist Charles Woods describes the impact His Royal Highness, the Prince of Wales has had on society, noting: "[Prince Charles] believes that what people eat, how they grow it or rear it, what they live in, the language they use, the art they produce, how they pray and how they look after one another and care for their health, all relate." I have always viewed him as an others-oriented leader and he taught me that great things can be achieved for the world with the right focus.

I want to understand how we can design a camp and leave no footprint. Prince Charles puts me onto some of the world-class architects he knows. Jorie and I, still together at that time, work closely with his contacts to compile a sizeable book, about two inches thick, full of concepts centered on a commitment to ecotourism. The whole lodge will be built out of canvas, wood, and thick rope and we will source the furniture regionally—all of it completely eco-friendly. We were the first to build a safari camp with a swimming pool years ago in Kenya, and once I secure all the right concessions, we feature pools at our Botswana camps too: the swimming pool is shipped in, two plastic halves that fit together. The design makes it possible for us to move the entire camp and leave nothing behind, apart from the basin in the workshop area for the Land Rovers' oil, which we are conscious to discard appropriately.

Although we bid against many companies, we are awarded the concession to develop Chief's Camp on Chief's Island. We share the concession area with one other camp, each of us limited to twelve rooms apiece. So only a maximum of 48 guests can be in an area of 74,131 acres at any one time. We also secure land in NG32, a 302,457-acre concession next to the Moremi Game Reserve. Here we build Stanley's Camp, and we work with Doug Groves to move Thembi, Marula, and Jabu to this land and provide them with a safe home, where clients can appreciate and help protect them.

A second camp—Baines' Camp—is built on raised platforms that allow guests to look out over the Boro River. We use sustainably grown wood and recycle aluminum cans that we purchase from the surrounding community. My favorite feature is the star beds—beds that can be wheeled out onto your private deck to sleep out under the night sky.

There is also another property I have my eye on: several unsightly A-frame bungalows that overlook the Chobe River. Their design is completely unimaginative, but the property has one of the best views in Botswana, not to mention the wildlife: elephants, hippos, crocodiles, and unbelievable birds. This area, Chobe, has the highest density of elephants in Africa, over seventy thousand, and we will own the most coveted site.

During the building of Chief's Camp, I have one of the most dangerous experiences of my whole career happen. I had flown in late; travelling nonstop from Los Angeles to London to Johannesburg to Maun, I arrive at camp dead tired. I pull out my sleeping pills and put one huge one beside me. *Should I take one and have a lovely sleep?* I think, finally deciding, *No. I'm so tired; I'm going to go to sleep without it.*

I pull the mosquito netting around the bed and fall asleep. Then suddenly, in the middle of the night, I wake up to a horrendous noise: an animal roaring and chewing, no more than twelve feet from my ear. I reach out for my torch and shine the light through the mosquito net, but it reflects the light and blinds me. I switch it off.

Now, it was pitch black, except I could see that the shape of a head had bitten its way through the screen door. At first, I thought it was a lion, but I didn't know what it was. I use the horn that is provided in case guests need to attract attention in an emergency.

But the animal doesn't move. Its head is actually caught in the screen.

I jump out of bed, taking my pillows with me, and throw them at the grunting and snarling head. Then I pick up and hurl a heavy coffee table book. Only when I get up close do I recognize the animal: it is a hyena, one of the deadliest carnivores, which can even take down a hippo in one swift attack.

I have a flashback to the time I travelled with Myles Turner, the famous game warden in the Serengeti. We'd heard two Peace Corps volunteers had camped out one night, and when one of them woke up the next morning he found his friend next to him—dead. His head was completely bitten off, only his neck was left, and the survivor never heard a thing. (The hyena has one of the most powerful bites in the animal kingdom, around one thousand pounds of pressure per square inch.)

I haul off and smash the thing again.

I know one of two things will happen: it will lunge forward and eat me alive, or it will finally make a reluctant exit. Thankfully, the hyena had gotten its head stuck in the screen and had no choice but to edge farther backward and turn around, trolling off into the night.

When the staff arrives to check on me in all the chaos, I learn the animal had been making appearances around camp and something seemed wrong with it; it would have to be destroyed.

It was a wake-up call. I knew how close I'd come to the end: if I had taken that sleeping pill, the hyena would have attacked me and I would have ended up like the Peace Corps volunteer—headless.

Despite that frightening episode, I am committed to making Abercrombie & Kent the best in Botswana. So we replace the screen doors with something much more solid and get back to work. We increase security with guards around all of our camps.

I persuade the owner to sell the A-frame bungalows overlooking the Chobe River to me. The minute the ink on the deed is dry, I call Jeff Squire, the Welsh former pro rugby player and Managing Director of A&K in Southern Africa. He is a get-it-done guy hired to manage our camp development in Botswana and I tell him: "Bulldoze them, Jeff."

Then we start to build the beautiful Chobe Chilwero lodge.

Here we would have our own boat on the Chobe River, where we cruise every afternoon and evening. On these trips, there is a spot that has a rather full-circle kind of significance for me, that links my present to my past: we pass the lodge on the water's edge where Richard Burton married Elizabeth Taylor . . . for the second time.

We hire Gavin Ford, an amazing naturalist and guide, to create a safari circuit—the best of any travel company in Botswana. Where our competitors simply build a camp, we develop the experience first, then build the camp around it.

However, naming the camps remains a continuing struggle. Our competitors lead with their brand name and then

Sunset at Sanctuary Baines' Camp where you can sleep out under the stars and be one with the animals.

call their camps something generic, like the Fairmont Mount Kenya Safari Club. We decide to turn that convention on its head by putting the camp's title first and our brand name second, so the formula is: Chief's Camp, Abercrombie & Kent. We quickly realize, though, that other tour operators aren't keen to promote and sell our camps, since A&K is a direct competitor to many of them.

We need to innovate; to market the camps in a completely different way. These, our first sustainable camps in Botswana, deliver an experience that others don't. I think about my own emotional ties to Botswana—Prince Harry, the three vagabond elephants—and it comes to me. From beast to royalty, we provide a refuge from the storm of everyday life. We decide to call them "Sanctuary Retreats."

The idea behind them is based on creating a holistic experience with true sustainability. We provide guests with "Luxury, naturally." Each Sanctuary Retreat reflects the unique character of its location, and some are developed in partnership with the surrounding community. Our idea is that everything should be sourced locally, providing employment to the people who are so willing to share their lives with our guests and who benefit considerably from the money that tourism brings to their communities. As I write this, there are sixteen Sanctuary Retreats throughout East and Southern Africa, plus river cruisers that take clients deep into the heart of Myanmar, China, and Egypt.

And so, through Abercrombie & Kent's multiple companies, we are committed to a triple bottom line of environmental, economic, and social responsibility.

In 2013, Bill Gates publishes an essay in *Wired* magazine in which he shares how his first safari twenty years earlier with his then soon-to-be-wife, Melinda, shaped the goals of the Gates Foundation. "We went on a safari to see wild animals," Gates wrote, "but ended up getting our first sustained look at extreme poverty." Months before the trip, Gates invited me to Seattle to help him brainstorm a vacation somewhere unlike anywhere he'd ever been.

"Where do you think you would like to go?" I asked him.

"Geoffrey," Bill Gates said, "if you wanted to know anything about software, I'd be the person to ask. I heard that if I have a question about travel, you're the one to ask. What would you suggest?" I designed a safari unlike any that had ever been done before and would be difficult to replicate.

"I know just where I'll send you," I told him, knowing that our staff in Africa will deliver a top-shelf experience. We planned an itinerary flying by amphibious plane all the way from Ethiopia to Tanzania and Kenya, including Kichwa Tembo, our camp in the Masai Mara at the time. Ultimately, that trip helped to spark the Gateses' "catalytic philanthropy" model, which leverages financial investment to yield a bottom line not of profit, but of the greatest benefit to those on the receiving end of a given contribution. The Gates Foundation has driven advancements in developing countries, most prominently in Africa, for widespread disease prevention, agriculture, hygiene, and education. Today, it is the world's largest private foundation that has given millions of dollars in aid to Africa.

When my parents and I went into business in 1962, to most people in the developed world, travel was a treat. Today, it is a way of life as well as a way of changing lives: Travel and tourism is the most important service industry in the world and the biggest provider of jobs and a key economic driver. More than two hundred thirty-five million people worldwide are employed in travel and tourism. This represents over 8 percent of all employment and nearly 9.5 percent of world gross domestic product. The tourism industry significantly boosts employment and contributes to economic recovery and expansion.

Early on, I recognized that for long-term success, the tourism industry needs to operate with sustainability as a major focus. Through industry groups like the World Travel & Tourism Council, of which I am a founding member and served as chairman for six years, we're finding more and more ways to enrich the lives of travellers, our company, and the people in the places we visit.

All of this has certainly enriched my life. In 2010, I marry Otavia. She has as much energy and embraces adventure as much as I do, and very often in the company of close friends, together we're experiencing the very best that the world has to offer. My vision for the next leg of my company's journey reflects this particular stage in my life. Clients today travel with us because they want the ultimate experience. They still want the most exciting and exclusive safari . . . but they also want to go to Coco Chanel's apartment in Paris and have it specially opened for them. They'd like to shop inside Louis Vuitton's boutique at an hour when it's closed to the public. They want Victoria's Secret models at their dinner parties . . . and we make all that happen. As I edit this book in late 2014, I've just returned from one of our Around-the-World by Private Jet journeys, and we've launched a Land Rover Adventure Travel program. As a whole, our super luxury business is on fire: supervillas, superyachts, private jets, partnerships with companies such as Christie's and NetJets. That's where we are today.

In our early days, we found opportunity in places where one couldn't drink the water, and today, in still-developing countries, A&K provides clean wells so that the local people *can* drink the water. We're known as the first to have rebuked the traditional hunting safari in favor of the photographic safari, and we've gone to great effort not to disrupt the wildlife or environment where our clients travel—in fact, one of my most important initiatives is the project on which I'm collaborating with my close friend Ted Turner to save the endangered Bonobo apes. Sharing 98.7 percent of our DNA, Bonobos, along with chimpanzees, are the closest relative to humans. Another important focus is the United Nations' Great Apes Survival Partnership (GRASP), on which I'm working with Professor Jeffrey Sachs, the director of the Earth Institute at Columbia University, and for which I'm on the leadership council of the United Nations Sustainable Development Solutions Network. Having grown up with wild animals as neighbors (sometimes too close for comfort, as one will have read in many of these stories), their well-being is one of my most avid concerns.

We will also continue to partner with local communities, building hospitals and schools, while conserving forest resources, which is a major priority for our company. Kenyans say that the number of trees you plant during a visit is the number of years in which you have to return for another visit. They also say that to dirty your hands in African soil and then to rinse them over the tree you plant is a blessing that your tree will grow stronger and healthier than its neighbors.

At the journey's end, any passionate traveller knows the conflict of wanderlust: the more destinations you see, the more you desire to see. The same is true of my work. From the time I was a boy, my mother always said that I was impossible to satisfy. The more goals I tick off my list, the more I hunger to accomplish. There is always a next destination. There will always be another new frontier to explore and establish. There will also be old favorites, in the case of Prince Harry: he has travelled back to the Okavango Delta many times since that first trip there at age thirteen. The months after losing his mother are a time in his life that most boys might want to forget . . . but that trip truly transported him, and he has returned time and again to relive that feeling of total escape and being cradled in the unexpected, unmatched safety of the wild. I often wonder if Prince Charles hadn't asked me to take Prince Harry back to Africa, would I have gotten that eureka moment to develop Sanctuary there? I credit them with that inspiration.

For my own life, I'm confident that this journey will continue for some time more. In the early days of A&K, I would sit back in my chair at the conference table and ask my employees: "How are we going to win the world?" One destination at a time, we've been the first ones in. We'll continue to do so as long as I'm alive. We're not winding down . . . in fact, we're just winding up.

What we've done with Sanctuary Retreats is an example of one of my chief philosophies: anticipate the future and its sustainability; yesterday's cheers have a short echo.

ACKNOWLEDGMENTS

✧✧✧✧✧

This book would not have been possible without writer Kristine Gasbarre, who read through my diaries and worked to find a way to tell these stories in a uniquely compelling way. We spent time together on an adventure cruise in Japan, a safari in Kenya, and even on the beach in Ibiza while she listened to my countless stories.

Sincerest thanks to my family and longtime friends and associates who made themselves available to provide background information on particular stories or to host visits for our research. And to all those who otherwise contributed to the book's development: Jorie Butler Kent and her daughter, Reute Butler, who summarized the achievements made by Friends of Conservation and Abercrombie & Kent Philanthropy since 1982; Anne Kent Taylor and her schools and staff of preservationists in the Masai Mara; Marett Taylor, Farley Taylor Lansing, Brett Fichte, Norma Cooke, Jean Fawcett, David Stogdale, Roland Minns, David Markham, Tony Church, Gerald Hatherly, Alan Root, Richard Leakey, Fiona Bangua, Peter Ngori, Bernadette Nyambura Githigi, and the staff at A&K Kenya.

Thanks to my longtime personal assistant, Caroline Wheeler, who survived two previous attempts to start this book. She had to carve the time necessary out of my impossible travel schedule (three-hundred-plus days a year). Thanks also to Pamela Lassers, who encouraged me to put these stories down in writing and helped keep the process moving forward.

I also want to express my appreciation to the entire team at HarperCollins, led by Lisa Sharkey, whose inspiration and perseverance made this book a reality, especially Jonathan Burnham, Amy Bendell, Alieza Schvimer, Kathy Schneider, Katherine Beitner, Tom Hopke Jr., Milan Bozic, Joanne O'Neill, Leah Carlson-Stanisic, Robin Bilardello, and Nate Knaebel.

PHOTOGRAPHY CREDITS

ABOUT THE AUTHOR

✧✧✧✧✧

Surrounded by meerkats on the Makgadikgadi Pan, Botswana.

Geoffrey Kent has been inspiring travellers to discover the world in a uniquely stylish manner since founding Abercrombie & Kent in 1962 with his parents. Kent has served as president of the Prince of Wales Foundation in the United States and as chairman of the World Travel and Tourism Council. In April 2012, he was named to the British Travel and Hospitality Industry Hall of Fame for his outstanding contributions to the travel industry, and in December 2014, he received a Lifetime Achievement Award from *Travel Weekly*.